REFLECTIONS ON MISSIONS,
BOARDING SCHOOL AND CHILDHOOD

Foreword by Paul Young, author of *The Shack*

EDITORS
JENNY OSTINI • BERNARD DAINTON
JOHN CHENOWETH • JANET SMITH • BERNICE WATKINS

'The stamp of men and women we need is such as will put Jesus, China, souls first and foremost in everything and at every time – even life itself must be secondary.'

Hudson Taylor
Founder of CIM/OMF

Sent

REFLECTIONS ON MISSIONS, BOARDING SCHOOL AND CHILDHOOD

Foreword by Paul Young, author of *The Shack*

EDITORS
JENNY OSTINI • BERNARD DAINTON
JOHN CHENOWETH • JANET SMITH • BERNICE WATKINS

Sent: Reflections on Mission, Boarding School and Childhood

Compiling Editors: Jenny Ostini, Bernard Dainton, John Chenoweth, Janet Smith, Bernice Watkins

Chefoo Reconsidered Book Committee was formed to publish this anthology of life stories that followed for mission kids Sent away to Chefoo boarding schools from age five, sent so God's work could continue. These 42 anonymous true stories tell of what it meant then, and what it means now.

ISBN: 978-0-6489755-1-9 (Paperback)
ISBN: 978-0-6489755-0-2 (E-book)

Cover design and typesetting by Lankshear Design.

Publisher: John Chenoweth
crbookcommittee@gmail.com

Contents

Foreword by Paul Young

I REMEMBER FLYING into Denver, Colorado, and the drive to Colorado Springs to do an interview with Wess Stafford. The fact that he was six years older than me and about to leave his position as President of one of the largest child sponsorship organizations in the world, Compassion International, and was fluent in eight languages had nothing to do with why I wanted to spend time with him. Wess is a TCK, a Third Culture Kid, a Missionary Kid like me, and only a few years after he experienced abuse in an African missionary boarding school I was trying to find a way to survive a parallel story on the other side of the world, at another missionary boarding school.

We spent six or seven hours together, talking in front of cameras that didn't matter. We laughed, told a lot of stories, and occasionally paused in the holy silence that allows tears to quietly slip from the heart, out the eyes and slide slowly down our faces. We held our hugs long and then he left.

The man who had facilitated the conversation turned to me, "May I ask you one more question?"

I nodded, sitting down in front of the cameras.

"What has it been like for you to spend this day with Wess?"

I burst into a flood of tears, sobbing. When I finally recovered, I turned to him and still with a voice on the edge of breaking said, "Do you know how rare it is for me to meet someone and I don't have to explain myself?"

Who Took Your Voice[1]

You didn't mean to lose it
but when you went to use it
it wasn't there,
and you began to wonder
who took your voice.

There was a story to tell
when you experienced hell
but lips didn't open,
and you began to wonder
who took your voice.

You don't remember giving it away.
It's like it was stolen

but not stolen
because you can speak

but not about that event
or pain
or doubt
or skeletons in your closet.

Maybe that's it?!
You have a voice
but you don't have an ear
to hear
with love
the truth
of what is
and was
and shame
and hurt
and...so

1   "Who Took Your Voice" by David Tensen, used with permission.

...so may it be
that your voice
finds the attuned ear of
a co-suffering other
who'll sing in harmony
the songs of deliverance
you need to sing.

David Tensen is my friend, a poet/therapist/theologian in Australia. I have another friend, an Irish musician named Danny Ellis. His album '800 Voices' is one of my all-time favourites. He was eight when his mum dropped him off at the Irish Catholic boarding school with 799 other 'orphans' between the ages of five and sixteen, with a promise that she would be back for him at Christmas. Everything he owned was packed in his mum's little makeup suitcase, which he kept under his bed and would open in the stillness of the night to try to smell her presence. On Christmas Day, he stood at the gate with his little suitcase, waiting for her in the driving snow. She never came.

There are no words that could express the honour of being invited to write the Foreword for this collection of amazing stories. These stories full of true loss and hope, authentic wonder, gratitude and thoughtful fury. Stories are how we come to understand ourselves and the world we find ourselves in, and for some of us, we are still looking. Four children in the same family would write very different histories, and the one that each would write at eighteen would be markedly unlike the one they would pen at sixty. Since this book contains precious histories, it is a work of fiction. But that doesn't make it any less True. Those who care about examining and defending facts are often deaf to Truth.

My words are those of insider and outsider. "Insider" because like every contributor, I am an adult TCK-er, a Missionary Kid who experienced both the advantages and wonders of growing up in a world larger than my passport culture, and the deep and lasting losses encountered because of choices made by others, choices in which I had no voice. "Outsider" because I didn't attend a Chefoo school and don't have that history on which to build a bridge. But many who read these stories will feel like me, more insider than outsider. Loss comes dressed in many outfits, and while the particulars of our experience may be different, the impacts are sadly familiar. The upside is that we hear in the voices of others, our own.

"God is not served by human hands, as though God needed anything, since God gives to all *people* life and breath and all good things."[2]

This is a remarkable and shattering statement. Think this through with me. God does not need your service, your worship, your agenda, your good intentions, your song, your script, your mission, your novel, your calling, your money, your compassion, your children, your sacrifice.

What does God need?

Nothing!

What does God want?

Relationship! And not because God needs it, God already has it and love shares.

And yet, we human beings can hardly think outside the terms of sacrifice. "Is your all on the altar of sacrifice laid?" That hymn still haunts me. What do they say about good intentions? The road to hell is paved with them.

"But doesn't God need a sacrifice?"

NO!

Molech needs a sacrifice. Baal needs a sacrifice. Penal Substitutionary Atonement needs a sacrifice. Every man-made blood thirsty deity on the planet is an expression of Cain, and each needs a sacrifice. Oh, and the best sacrifice is an innocent child. And what did we do? We created a god in our own image, not in the image and likeness of Jesus the Messiah, but Cain. And our god needs a sacrifice too. And oh, the best sacrifice is an innocent child, required by a god who will find the only truly innocent child, his own son and when that boy is most shattered, will turn his face away from him.

2 Acts 17:25

As God says through the prophets:

"What use to me is frankincense that comes from Sheba,
	or sweet cane from a distant land?
Your burnt offerings are not acceptable,
	nor your sacrifices pleasing to me."[3]

"What to me is the multitude of your sacrifices?"
	says the LORD;
"I have had enough of burnt offerings of rams
	and the fat of well-fed beasts;
I do not delight in the blood of bulls,
	or of lambs, or of goats.
When you come to appear before me,
	who has required of you
this trampling of my courts?
Bring no more your worthless offerings;
	incense is an abomination to me.
New moon and Sabbath and the calling of convocations—
	I cannot endure such iniquity and your solemn assembly.
Your new moons and your appointed feasts
	my soul hates;
they have become a burden to me;
	I am weary of bearing them.
When you spread out your hands,
	I will hide my eyes from you;
even though you make many prayers,
I will not listen;
	your hands are full of blood."[4]

3   Jeremiah 6:20
4   Isaiah 1:11-15

"I hate, I despise your feasts,
    and I take no delight in your solemn assemblies.
Even though you offer me your burnt offerings and grain offerings,
    I will not accept them;
and the peace offerings of your fattened animals,
    I will not look upon them.
Take away from me the noise of your songs;
    to the melody of your harps I will not listen."[5]

The God and Father of our Lord Jesus Christ HATES sacrifice. The story of Abraham and Isaac was not about a test to see if Abraham still made God his number one priority, competing with children for attention. Rather, "I am not a God who will ever require the sacrifice of children...ever. And since you are stuck inside a delusion of self-hatred that requires a sacrifice, that someone must pay, let me reveal to you My nature and character: I will provide MYSELF. Today a goat with its head caught in a crown of thorns, and one day, I will be the lamb you think you need, and by that submission to you, together we will finally and forever end sacrifice.

How scandalous that this God needs nothing!

Did our parents intend to harm us? Did they understand how the turning of their faces away from their children was not an act of God or godliness? Did the Mission comprehend the damage their mandates would affect as they rippled through the tender hearts of children? Was this God's will, the cost of doing Evangelizing? No, No, No, and NO! What seems a 'small price to pay,' to an adult thinking God-thoughts, is undeniably costly to the little ones named 'small price.'

And yet the Redeeming Genius crawled inside all these mixed motives and intentions, both the darkness and the light and blessed with life anything that was still of love's kind and now continues to work within the ripples to redeem everything. Because of the sacrifices made, many did hear about the Love named Jesus. But the ends don't justify the means, ever. There is no justification for a cross

5   Amos 5:21-23

or the sacrifice of children. There is however redemption. This broad spectrum is held inside the pages you now hold.

And so it is, that I also bring my shades of grey, the emerging of true identity still shedding the skin of the false, my inner mix of light and darkness, my longing to be a truth-teller and my fear of being exposed that keeps me isolated and imprisoned, my sometimes faltering faith amidst the surprising sense of your Presence, and ask again, and then again and then again, 'Please kind and loving Faithful One, expose all in me that is not of Love's kind and free me to be fully human and fully alive.

I know that you know.
So, I should probably confess it.
Not because it's a bad thing.
But because it's normal
and necessary to admit
you've disappointed me
and continue to.
Although I don't mind as much
now.

Still, there were many times
I prayed.
Followed the rules.
Gave my two mites.
Did all the things I was told would work
and others certified
with charismatic conviction
to do more
give more
faith more
sacrifice more
lots more.

But still, nothing.
No breakthrough

like I believed
like I prayed for.

I underestimated you.
I wanted to believe
you were containable
constrainable
and reliable
in the 'my way' kind of way.
The magician
hitman
slot machine
deal maker
earth shaker
genie-in-a-bottle
kind of way.

Then I recalled
that on a dark but necessary day
you took yourself
and my kind of way
and the cosmos
to a cross.

Then you went missing for three days.
And my world fell apart.

All my hope exhaled a forsaken surrender,
and my heart broke
and my dreams broke.
My kind of way
kind of died
again.

And there you were
alive and the same
but not really.

A resurrected form of you
that even took familiar friends
by surprise.

And that's what you keep doing.
To this day
you keep failing and disappointing me
in the best kind of ways.

Every time I think I've got you
where I think I need you
you disappoint and disappear
and turn up incognito
on a familiar path
at a regular meal
in an average garden
with a spark in your eye
that demands my attention.
You invite me again
to put my hand in your side
embrace you and kiss you
and get to know you again
in a new kind of way[6].

Wm. Paul Young,
author, *The Shack, Cross Roads, Eve and Lies We Believe About God*

---

6   "Kind of Way", by David Tensen, April 2019, used with permission

Preface
Chefoo revisited

THE RENTAL CAR hesitantly nosed between the mossy stone pillars standing resolutely at the entrance of the property. Nestled in the jungle of the Cameron Highlands of central Malaysia, the sixty year old "Chefoo" boarding school still stood, 1.4 km above the steamy tropical lowlands. It was 2014 and past students from all over the globe were journeying back to Malaysia to reunite. For eighty Chefoo alumni, that gateway stood as a portal back to their childhoods 20–60 years before.

The car continued as the bitumen driveway snaked through cuttings thick with irrepressible growth before, to the right, the view opened out to the clearing that harboured the old primary school. Across a gully lay the Tudor-style main building, the quadrangle, the playgrounds, the gym, the classrooms and the dormitories. The school nestled, seemingly unchanged, in a high, hidden valley of the jungle. The cicadas were still deafening, the birdsong still evident, butterflies flew as randomly as ever; the whisper of running water in the stream through the playgrounds and the dense, impenetrable foliage screening the buildings from a vastly larger outside world felt deeply familiar. Through the open window of the car flowed the cool, intoxicating scent of verdancy and jungle wetness. The visitors felt the years fall from them. They recognised their school... this had surely been a school in paradise.

So why then, at the sight of those gates, did the travellers stop, silent and dry mouthed? Why was there a need to summon courage to enter once more?

As do all who journey on this earth, these individuals had significant events in their lives that had shaped, marked, scarred, hurt and bound them. Before them was a rare opportunity to revisit the landscape of their formative years. A time for reconsideration of a shared past had opened, a time that would expose much hidden hurt and pain – but also open opportunities for healing and resolution.

In the twentieth century, Western culture has become sadly aware of the effects of institutional life on children. In this book you will read our stories, the stories of lives that followed our childhood attendance at mission boarding schools, including Chefoo Malaysia. The tales are sobering reading. As young children, some as young as four years old, we were sent by our parents to distant places for long terms away from their care. We were told that our exile was in the name of God, so the work of evangelisation of Asia could continue, unhampered by us. Our part in the glorious work was to be sent away. The short- and long-term consequences of those separations are recounted in these, our stories.

But firstly, readers will need to understand some of the context.

History

In 1854, at the age of twenty-one, protestant missionary Hudson Taylor left London and sailed to Shanghai. He had felt God call him to tell the 'unsaved millions' of China that salvation was to be found in Jesus. Through his passionate, sacrificial service, Taylor was to go on to be called one of the great missionaries of all time. He formed the "China Inland Mission" (CIM) in 1865 and the Mission grew and thrived. Many Christians from around the Western world left their homes to travel to China and join him.

For those with families education was a problem, so in 1881 the CIM opened an English school for missionary children in Chefoo, a Chinese coastal town in Shandong province. It became a school with a fine reputation. Children would board there – some for years – between family reunions, whilst they completed their primary and secondary education, preparing for further studies at Oxford or Cambridge University.

The Second World War intersected with the Communist Revolution in China, and Mao Zedong swept into power at a time when nearly a thousand post-war missionaries were moving back deep into China's interior. By 1951, the new government had decided that missionaries were an undesirable remnant of cultural imperialism, and the missionaries were told to leave. Three decisions followed that impacted on the writers of our stories.

Firstly, the mission would now work in South East Asia, and eventually be renamed the Overseas Missionary Fellowship (OMF).

Secondly, missionary children would be educated in primary boarding schools, also called "Chefoo Schools", to be staffed by members of the mission. The main Chefoo School was to be located in the idyllic setting already described, 5,000 feet up in the tropical jungle of the Cameron Highlands of Malaya – now part of Malaysia. There were also Chefoo schools in Thailand, Taiwan, the Philippines (German-speaking) and Japan at various times.

Thirdly, to assist in reintegration into society in their passport countries, all children would be sent to "home" boarding schools for their education from around age eleven. Their time of boarding at Chefoo would commence when they were five, turning six, years old.

The Malaysian school opened in 1954 and, after educating several hundred missionary and other children, closed in June 2001. Peak enrolment reached about 100. A survey of graduates from Chefoo, carried out by mail in 1978, indicated that most were achieving well and had not been negatively affected by their unusual early years at school[7].

7   Hogben, 1978

The Chefoo Reconsidered Conferences

However, by 2013, the OMF had become aware of other twentieth century studies showing there was long-term impact on children from early disruption of parental attachment. Coincidentally, at that time Kirsten Leed and some other Chefoo graduates such as David Houliston were starting to reconnect online, and began sharing their life stories. Andrew Lane, in trying to work through his injuries, scars and life difficulties, told his story and concerns to Mission leaders in Singapore.

The OMF responded by sending out a letter, to as many graduates from Chefoo schools as they could find, containing a formal apology to those children and parents who felt damaged by their experience of the Mission's compulsory boarding policy. They followed this up by sponsoring a conference at the old Malaysian school and inviting alumni to attend, to discuss, and to be offered counselling. This was the Chefoo Reconsidered (CR) Conference. About eighty of us, aged between thirty and seventy, took the journey back through those mossy gate posts.

That conference was an extraordinary experience to most who attended. Two counsellors spoke, and led discussions; Ruth Van Reken, co-author of *Third Culture Kids*[8], and Ulrika Ernvik, author of *Third Culture Kids – a gift to care for*[9]. Their input was eye-opening. (William Paul Young, author of *The Shack*[10] was equally valuable when he joined us for the second CR Conference). Each has contributed to this book.

But the power of our time together was felt most strongly in our shared stories. We came together as a group for the first time since leaving Chefoo all those years ago. In daily life, we each tunnel into the stratum of living, following seams of value, sometimes golden, often not. That tunnelling is mostly done alone. Someone may be a metre away in a parallel seam, chasing gold, while another mines stern rock, but neither knows of the other. It takes the courage to come out of

8   Pollock & Van Reken, 2017 3rd edition
9   Ernvik, 2019
10   Young, 2007

those tunnels for the true picture of our journeys to be revealed.

As we shared stories, patterns began to emerge, and we started to see a bigger picture for the first time. It wasn't pretty. The effects and vulnerability of being sent away from family in God's Name, at very young ages, with frequent changes of place, culture, friends, and even family, had etched their marks deeply into the shape of our lives. We had each worked out our way of dealing with those scars. Those dry mouths as we came through the front gates were from remembered pain and heartache. Hearing someone else tell their story made our common childhoods so much more evident. Tears, more tears, laughter, deep conversations – that was a week like no other.

As we parted, we felt a strong desire to maintain contact, forming a private Facebook group which allowed that to happen. Over the six years since, there have been several more Chefoo Reconsidered gatherings – three in Malaysia, one in Philippines, and others in the USA, England, and Australia. There is one to come in Japan. Facebook communications have been critical in continuing the process of review and developing understanding, through our stories. The support and friendship, the feeling of belonging to the Chefoo community as a surrogate family, our 'tribe', of being known without shame in that family, have all made the group of great value to its members.

The writing of this book

There is a very big gap however between having such an experience and writing a book about it. Why this book?

As we shared in the private CR Facebook group, we uncovered so many lifelong effects of our common childhoods that it felt selfish keeping this knowledge to ourselves. The feeling grew within our group that the long-term effects of being a missionary child boarded in the name of God needed to be documented.

Others have written about boarding schools. There are now many good books on Third Culture Kids. We are not aware of other books showing the long-term effects of being sent to boarding schools from young ages, in the name of God.

How could we best do this?

The answer seemed obvious: the strength of our group was the stories we share. We elected to put together a collection of our stories to see if the result also carried similar power. We think it does. Readers will shortly be able to make their own assessments.

An editorial committee was formed to write *Authors' Guidelines* and invite submissions to this collection of stories in the following words:

> This will be a book about missionary children who boarded at Chefoo Schools and in some cases, later spent time away from their parents in their home countries. It is not intended to be a book about our school days and fond memories (though they have a place in our stories) but of how our unique experience of attending boarding school from a young age made us the people we are today. This is not an anti-boarding book, or a pro-boarding book. Our desire is for clear-eyed reflection on, and thoughtfulness about, the people that we were and are. We want to share our stories and the voices of people affected in powerful ways by growing up within a tight-knit Christian environment. We believe that our friendships, our intimate relationships, our values, our faiths, our personalities and identities were all affected by our childhood experiences and we want to share our stories.

We asked potential contributors to reflect on one or more of the following questions:

- How did being a boarder in primary school affect me, then and now?
- As I have aged, have my childhood experiences affected me differently?
- What advice might I give to my younger self?
- What advice might I give to someone thinking about sending their young child to boarding school?
- How were my friendships and other relationships, and identity, affected by Chefoo? What effect has this had on me in later life?

Without further instruction to authors, we collected forty-two contributions in just a few months. We thank each contributor for their willingness to be honest, open and brave in the face of public vulnerability. Their stories represent a significant part of the stories of our group. We also thank the three counsellors who have written for us.

We decided against linking these stories together in an analytic way, or trying to interpret them.

The damage that has been done to many of us by being sent away in the name of God has left lingering suspicions of authority, the System and even truth.

Instead we wanted to go back into the ancient way, the truth of storytelling. Truth-telling around a fire, if you like. In sharing our own lives, in telling our own tales, we leave further analysis to the reader.

Reading this book

As you read this anthology of life stories, some may make you cry and others may make you angry. But keep your brain working, each writer is an individual, each response is different, each writer has been differently affected. Yet you will find common characteristics. Human brains are loaded full of experiences and memories. Although the contributors to this book are different people, we all shared a common childhood, were exposed to the same belief structure, similar stresses and griefs, and much cultural displacement. Perhaps you can try, with us, to understand how godly men and women, sure of their calling and loving their children, still gave them up.

In a world where, sadly, many children continue to experience the loss of parents, dislocation of family and horrible trauma, this anthology makes sobering predictions for their life outcomes in the next half century. Our stories suggest that their early damage may surface as they age, and continue to affect their lives and relationships.

This book comprises stories, thoughts, reflections, songs and poems from forty-five adults. Almost all were OMF missionary children, and nearly all attended one of the Chefoo boarding schools. The stories are grouped broadly thematically. Though many could fit into several categories, our grouping is intended to help clarify the linkages that we saw decades later.

So find some quiet time, sit down around our fire of memories, and read the tales from our past that changed us. May you too see our world with clearer vision, deeper insight, perceive afresh the powerful shaping you received in your own formative years and come to know yourself better.

What happens to kids counts.

Terminology

We need an explanation about two abbreviations commonly used in this book. "TCK" has become a standard abbreviation for "third culture kid". We all as children spent a significant portion of our childhoods in countries, or cultures, outside of our passport countries, and as a result had to create our own unique blend of personal culture – a third culture – if you will. All the contributors to this book are TCKs.

"MK" stands for "missionary kid". All MKs are TCKs, but not all TCKs are MKs, because in today's globalised world, many expatriate adults raise families outside their home country: diplomats, military and business people, migrants and refugees. While many of the issues TCKs face are similar, regardless of their parents' careers, MKs in particular also have to wrestle with issues of faith and how their experience relates to their parents' commitment to serving a "God of love".

We close this introduction with a warning. The writers of these stories mostly found release in the writing. A few, however, found themselves in trouble and needed to seek professional support. Some of these stories may trigger events for readers too. Guard your own heart and seek help early if needed.

Please note:
- This is not a quantitative study.
- Several of our authors have chosen to write anonymously, some for privacy, some to protect parents – while their names are hidden,

their stories are true. We decided not to use author surnames in this book.

- At each CR gathering we remembered those of us who have died, too many in tragic circumstances. In this book, we wish their families peace.

- There are many other stories that could have been told, some of evil; those who survived have not spoken of that here, so neither have we.

This book came together through the contributions of many people across the world. We give thanks to the contributors for sharing their stories, Tim Passmore of The Write Flourish for sensitive editing, Joy Lankshear for the cover design and layout, Ruth Van Reken and Ulrika Ernvik for their contributions, and Paul Young for writing the foreword. We also thank the many financial contributors to the costs of producing the book. You know who you are and how much your support meant to us.

Editorial Committee
John Chenoweth
Bernard Dainton
Jenny Ostini
Janet Smith
Bernice Watkins

Email address: crbookcommittee@gmail.com

Prelude:
Six and Forty-Six
Rachel

IN THE CAMERONS the sheets are cold and damp at night.

This is what we notice the first night at Chefoo when the quiet settles over us, bigger than the jungle. The sound of the sniffling in the dark is a tiny sound. We are little creatures lost in a very large wood.

And it is a very, very long way to the red button by the door.

Later, I do what Lisa tells me and put the bolster against my back, so that it feels like Mom. Somewhere, under the covers, inside my chest I am bleeding. Like a leech wound, there's more blood than I realise until much later.

What does it mean to be six and forty-six at the same time?

Nothing feels simple anymore. We are happy-sad all the time.

The valley is often enchanted. There are Friday treats, brown sugar sandwiches, centipedes that turn into marbles, the sound of taxis speeding towards us in the dark. Sometimes, Auntie Pauline even shares her toast. And there's a whole world in roots and red clay beneath the trees by the drive.

These pleasures pierce us. I write home:

"I am very, very, very, very, happy at school and at play."

The *verys* take up a lot of space, and plus, I almost believe it myself.

The legends sustain us. We repeat them to each other when we can't sleep. For example, Gillian once made it all the way to the golf course in Tanah Rata, her face painted with coffee, before they caught her. That's practically halfway down the hill.

And what would they have done if one of us had made it all the way down the mountain?

But instead we come properly home to Singapore, happy enough to be nauseous, trailing empty grub boxes. We are kings and queens of the summer, we are laughing, we are golden. Fishing for guppies. Eating roti just after sunrise at *Taman Serasi*. We have a secret club that dumps water on the Mission General Director's head. At night, we hear the taxis on Cluny Road, the hum of electricity in the wall behind the bed. The ceiling fan turns slowly, hovering like an old lady, blessing us with a benediction. All manner of things are well.

Mom is there again when we're sick. She hears us call from upstairs, even when we whisper. Dad puts his Limacol on a hankie for us when we have a fever. His hands are warm. Their room is the safest place in the whole world. I stand by the door at night, watching them sleep. I am guarding them like a dragon guards its treasure. The tiles are cool under my feet, and I smell the frangipanis. I am much older than they are. What will happen if Aslan ever tries to take off this dragon skin?

One evening, Paul catches an Atlas moth. It struggles, blind and restless in the net until the powder comes off of its wings. That night, the name tags appear. I watch Mom sew one onto my red towel. I feel every pinprick, as though it goes through my own flesh. I start talking to myself:

"Don't count how many days are left."

"Make sure you smell the baby a lot so that you will remember what she smells like."

"Wake up very early because the days will pass more slowly then."

"Maybe if you lose your shoes, they won't be able to send you."

How did there get to be two of me, one to talk, *and one to listen*? One so big, *and one so tiny* she hardly takes up any space.

They say that love is only as deep as the hole your sorrow digs.

What happens when sorrow digs a hole, and you are too little to climb out?

When the hole is deep, and you are at the bottom, and all you can see are the vast branches of that ageless forest, waving against the sky?

Starting to Rethink our Past

For some of us, processing the complexities of our childhoods was a task deferred as too hard. For some of our writers, seeing their own children reach age five to six was the call to understand and deal with their pasts.

In the eyes of their child a parent can see themselves. The long-buried questions arise. How could my parents have sent me away like this?

Rosann

As my oldest child turned six, I had to face the emotions that churned inside me. I wrote this letter to process my feelings and tell my story to my son.

March 10, 2017

To my dear son,

Today is your sixth birthday and I am so proud to be your mama! As your birthday has been drawing nearer, I have been excited to celebrate you, but I've also noticed a lot of fear and sadness inside of me. These conflicting emotions confused me. Finally, I realised my body was remembering my own sixth birthday and what happened shortly afterwards.

Forty years ago, when I turned six, I said goodbye to my parents, boarded an airplane, and flew to another country to attend boarding school. This shattered me! I lost my strong, daily, loving connection to my parents. I lost my safety. I lost my security. Who would sing songs to me in the dark, as I tried to fall asleep? Who would brush my tangled hair after I had a shower? Who would stand up for me when the neighbour kids teased me? I didn't know how to handle life's problems. (Nor should I have, since I was still a little child.)

Leading up to my sixth birthday, I had a lot of mixed feelings. I was excited about going to boarding school because my big brother and parents talked about it. I was sad, because I had some idea that my life, as I knew it, was going to end. No more trips to the colourful market on a crowded bus with my mother. No more cuddling with my little sister at naptime. No more excited storytelling on my dad's lap.

It took weeks of preparation to get ready for school. My mom lovingly sewed me dresses, bought me clothes and shoes. We had the "required" list of items we had to bring, plus all our clothes, sheets, towels and jackets needed a name tag sewn into them with my name. Can you imagine how easily things can be confused in a boarding school of ninety kids? Leading up to my departure, my mom and dad tried to prepare me by showering me with their love. But, in reality, a parent can never prepare a child for the devastation that was about to happen.

I went from being a cherished, loved child with two siblings and a happy home, to being a number among ninety students, and a "name tag" on an article of clothing in a big school. Even as I write this, I have tears in my eyes and my heart feels like lead.

You may wonder why my parents sent me to boarding school. Well, at that time, it was standard for missionaries to send their children to boarding school. Home-schooling was not yet a real option. All the kids in my parent's mission, Overseas Missionary Fellowship (OMF), were sent to Chefoo School in Malaysia. Missionaries were expected to put serving God first, and their kids second. We now know, of course, that this is wrong. God never asks us to put our family second to ministry. Loving God means caring for our families in ways that honour them.

There were many positive aspects to boarding school – I made deep, deep friends and learned so much about getting along with different people. The jungle surrounding the school was wild and full of adventures. The teachers and dorm aunties worked hard to make the school a fun place – and it was in many ways. We had games and laughter at every recess, Saturday morning outings to waterfalls, swimming pools and the local shops. We had cookouts in the jungle and after-school clubs to learn crafts and skills, like jungle survival. These relationships and activities helped me during the day and I rarely thought about my parents or Indonesia. But at night, and every Sunday afternoon, when it was quiet and still, the deep sadness and dread would set in. I had to face another day, another week, alone.

Crying silently under my bedcovers at night, I wondered what was wrong with me to get sent away to school.

Many years later I entered adulthood feeling split in a thousand pieces – outwardly functional but starting to fall apart. Would I ever recover that little, happy, cherished five-year-old? Over time the most beautiful thing happened – God took my shattered self and slowly rebuilt me. I faced the deep sadness inside me, and I cried many of the tears I had stuffed down as a child. I looked honestly at what happened to me and how it affected me. I talked to my parents, sometimes with words of rage, and I was disarmed by their humility and lack of defensiveness. I chose to accept myself and believe that I was deeply loved. This helped me figure out how to be in relationship with others from this place of "belovedness" and not from a place of anxiety or shame. And I made the choice to forgive my parents, forgive God, forgive my school and the teachers and staff, and forgive my parents' mission. If I hadn't made the choice to forgive, I would still be in bondage. I would still be weighed down by bitterness, hatred and fear. I lived with all of that for a while and it was yucky. Because God helped me to choose to face my injustices, forgive others, and forgive myself for my responses to them, I am now free. And that's the best thing in the world.

So dear son, you too, will have injustices done to you in this life. You won't ever be sent away to boarding school, but other things will happen to you because this world is messy and imperfect. You, too, have the same God by your side who wants to pour his love into those sad, hard places. You have the same God who will help you forgive, if you ask him. You have the same God who will take your ashes and make them something beautiful. His deep, deep love can bring peace and wholeness.

I love you, and I can't wait to keep being your "everyday" mommy for the next 12+ years. And your forever mommy, for the rest of your life.

Your mama

* * *

Rosann went to Chefoo from 1977–83 and graduated from Faith Academy in the Philippines for High School. She then moved to Seattle,

USA to attend the University of Washington. She is married with two boys and works as a teacher. Rosann's Mom lives with her and her family, and her siblings live close by. They love being close together after so many years apart as children.

Anonymous

I WAS BORN IN SAIBURI Christian Hospital in South Thailand on August 19, 1983. Hours after my birth, as my mum was captivated by her firstborn daughter, a fellow missionary arrived to visit and the first words out of her mouth were, "Oh, how lovely, an August baby! She'll have her birthday at Chefoo School." From birth I was destined for boarding school in the remote rainforest of Cameron Highlands, Malaysia.

Only as an adult and young mum have I been able to face the deep grief and consequences of being sent away and raised in a boarding school far away from the nurture of a loving family. When my first child turned five I found that many of these feelings and memories returned, as I saw myself at that age, and was overcome with the shock of how my parents could have sent me away at such a young age. Though my parents never explicitly talked about me going away to Chefoo until it was an imminent reality, I was well aware that this was going to happen as I watched my friends' older siblings leave for Chefoo. What a strange notion for a young child, to grow up with the understanding that after your fifth birthday you will be sent away on an airplane to live in another country, far away from mummy and daddy. I vaguely remember feelings of confusion, fear, excitement, anxiety, grief, and being plagued by night terrors as I awaited this fateful day.

After much preparation, shopping, special outings, dinners, early birthday celebrations and the frantic sewing of name tags onto every item of clothing I owned, the big day arrived. I was a little five-year-old girl at the Hatyai airport trying hard to be brave in my brand-new pink dress. A flight attendant led me to the plane with all of the other kids. I could see mummy, daddy, and the other parents standing behind a glass wall. They were waving and crying. This was the only time I did not cry while saying goodbye to them, as I did not realise what was happening to me, and that it would be four long months before I saw them again.

Not long into the flight, I opened a small jewellery music box that I had coveted in one of the few shops in our small town, as a "going-away gift". What mixed messages those gifts sent to us as kids, one of the few things we had to hold on to as a sign of our parents' love. Drinks were served on the plane. I asked for a cup of orange juice and shortly after spilled it all over my new pink dress. I did what any five-year-old would do and cried for my mummy to come help me, and clean me up. But she wasn't there, and that empty feeling began to take form, of being helpless, and the belief that I couldn't trust those in authority to care for my needs.

At my daughter's sixth birthday party, memories and emotions from my own sixth birthday party began to return to my conscious memory. It was only a few weeks after I first arrived at Chefoo that I celebrated my sixth birthday. Mummy and daddy had sent and wrapped lovely gifts that I had asked for and wrote cards telling me how much they loved me. But I felt numb and lost. I had spent the first three weeks at Chefoo crying myself to sleep every night, desperate for the comfort of my parents. All I wanted for my birthday was to be home, to be safe in their arms again. That was all I wished for when I blew out the candles on my beautiful baby-doll cake. My dorm aunty had tried so hard to make it a special day for me, but she was not the maternal type and her attempt at comfort only made me more distraught. As I watched my own daughter surrounded by her loving family and friends, utterly delighted with all the treats, gifts and activities at her party, I realised that this is what every six-year-old's birthday should be like. But I was left with the empty, lonely feeling once again, and the belief that I didn't deserve to be celebrated.

Another particular memory that was triggered when my first

daughter turned five, was a disturbing night terror I experienced during my first term at Chefoo. I woke up screaming after dreaming that evil witches had kidnapped me and taken me away from my mummy and daddy. The frightful witches told me that I would never see my parents again and that it was all my fault. I screamed out for comfort and finally a dorm aunty came to get me. She took me in her room and tried to console me, but I was inconsolable. I was just a little girl who needed her mum's comfort. The dorm aunty finally became fed up with my screams and used a wooden paddle to spank me hard on the bum. My screaming turned into a whimper and immediately, in my heart, I began to believe that no one could help me and that I couldn't trust people to care for me. I felt so alone and ashamed.

After my first year at Chefoo, my parents took a six-month furlough in New Zealand. My mum wanted my brother and I to experience life in New Zealand and thought it would be a great idea for me to go to a public school[11] for one term of Primary Level 2. I was a young, naive seven-year-old, but they thought that since I'd already attended Chefoo for a year, I would have no problem adjusting to a low-income Kiwi primary school. I remember feeling very overwhelmed, out of place, confused and alone.

A particularly strong memory of this time has come back to me. I would wait after class each afternoon outside the school gate for mummy or daddy to come pick me up in the car. We had only lived there for a couple months and had stayed in more than one house, so I was very unaware of my surroundings or of how to get around. One afternoon, I waited and waited for mummy or daddy to come get me. After what seemed like hours, they never came. So I began to walk in what I guessed was the right direction. I walked, running and stumbling along, trying not to panic while the tears ran down my face. I was so worried about what had happened to my parents and why they couldn't come get me. I was afraid that they might never find me, but they did, walking aimlessly on the road. My parents very apologetically confessed that they had fallen asleep while putting my younger brother

---

11   In New Zealand a public school is a state school, funded by the government and free for students.

down for a nap. However, that excuse brought little comfort to the little girl who had already been abandoned at Chefoo. This experience was one of many that just confirmed the belief that I wasn't important, couldn't trust others to care for me or be there when I needed them.

It's funny and often distressing how memories, fond and awful, are triggered and recalled randomly and abruptly. In recent years, I went with my family and friends to cheer on close friends' sons at a track-and-field event at an International school. As we watched the kids race, I became plagued with deep emotions of anxiety, grief and loneliness. I felt a desperate need to cheer on every single child competing, and couldn't hold back the tears as I watched them run. Once again, the painful memories began to return.

Every term at Chefoo, we had a sports day. It was supposed to be fun, an epic event that every child relished. It was torture for me. I was not blessed with exceptional athletic skills, and I came last in almost every event. But this was not the painful part of these sports day memories. It was the fact that in every race and event, there was no parent present to cheer me on. The teachers and dorm parents cheered everyone on, they didn't have any favourites. The child in me longed to be somebody's favourite – to have my mum and dad present, cheering me on, shouting my name and expressing their praise and pride in me. Instead I was left with the emptiness and loneliness again. I believed I wasn't seen, and that I wasn't worthy of being praised and applauded.

Now as a parent of four beautiful children, I have dealt with spills, bedwetting, diarrhoea, vomiting, and every other normal child accident. Each of these events has triggered feelings of abandonment, through having had to face these things on my own at Chefoo. One night, on one of the first nights back at Chefoo, I woke up in a new bed, in a new dorm building, desperate to go pee. It was pitch black and I couldn't see a thing. I had no idea where to go. I knew better than to cry out for help as I would wake up the entire dorm and likely get punished. So, after desperately fumbling around, I lost control of my bladder and peed all over the floor. I tried to mop it up with my pyjamas, but I was so tired that I ended up just leaving it and going back to bed. In the morning, the dorm aunty came in and asked about the big puddle in the middle of the floor. I was too ashamed to admit that it was my urine and denied having anything to do with it. There were countless other times where I remembered cleaning up my own messes, even when I felt terribly sick with a stomach bug. I was ashamed of myself, believing that I was alone and not worthy of being cared for.

When my son turned six, I began to recall memories of my brother at the same age when he first went to Chefoo. I was only eight or nine years old when I held his hand on the plane. As was common for all of us on the journey up the hill from Kuala Lumpur to the Cameron Highlands, he threw up in the taxi on the winding road. As I helped clean him up, and comforted him when he cried for our mum, I quickly realised I couldn't worry about my own needs anymore. I needed to help my little brother. When we arrived at the school after dark, we were quickly ushered off to our own dorms and didn't see each other again until breakfast the next morning. I remember feeling sick that night, with worry about how my sensitive brother would survive living in a dorm full of rowdy boys. The next morning I watched with horror across the dining hall, as he sat with his dorm at the long tables, and looked like he was close to vomiting as he forced down his most abhorred food – bananas. We couldn't leave the table until we ate every morsel of food on our plates. How I longed to go and rescue him and eat it for him, but I wasn't permitted to leave my seat, let alone go over and talk to my brother. Time and time again, I knew that my brother was struggling with life at Chefoo, and it pained me that I couldn't do much for him. We were in different dorms and different classes and our interaction was limited to short periods on the playground and at church on Sunday. I remember once, when he was sick, they called me to the Sick Bay to comfort him. I did my best, but nothing seemed to help. I wasn't our mummy, the one he really needed.

Feeling at a loss to care for my own brother's needs, I looked after the younger girls in my own dorm out of necessity. One young Korean girl had never slept on her own in her entire life. She would cry every single night for hours, and the dorm aunty, fed up from comforting her would yell at her. I took pity on this girl and after the lights had gone out and our dorm aunty had left, I would go and get her and bring her into my narrow single bed to sleep with me. She didn't cry after that, and before the morning I would make sure she was back in her own bed so that the dorm aunty wouldn't find out. Another young dorm mate often wet the bed. I couldn't bear it when she was regularly humiliated by our dorm aunty, so another dorm mate and I would wake early each morning to change her sheets and pyjamas. There were many other times when I would help fellow dorm mates clean up soiled underwear and clothes, as we were too ashamed and scared to ask for help.

Many years of boarding school later, I attended Faith Academy in Manila, Philippines, and lived in the OMF boarding home. These were also very difficult years of separation from parents, and I remember failing as an older sister to support my younger brother. One night there was a terrible typhoon in Manila. The wind howled all night and outside debris, including sharp sheets of corrugated iron, were hazardously flying around. My brother came rushing into my room in the middle of the night, terrified. I was scared myself and had no comfort to offer him. Instead, I made fun of him and told him to go back to bed. Around the same time, I remember that he was being bullied and manipulated by his room-mate. I should have protected and defended him, yet I often partnered with his room-mate in teasing him. That left me with a sick feeling of guilt and responsibility for my brother's struggles.

Again I looked after the needs of the younger middle-school girls who were often my room-mates. Several of them got their periods for the first time in the dorm and thought they were dying. They were too embarrassed and afraid to tell the dorm parents, so I would come to the rescue, explain what was going on, and teach them how to use pads and tampons. To this day, I carry deep resentment and sadness toward their mothers, who were not there and did not prepare them for this important part of coming of age. Thankfully, my own mum had prepared me well, so that I was able to help others. But these responsibilities left me carrying weight and guilt that I was too young to handle.

Another difficult memory that recently returned was of my high school graduation from Faith Academy. I honestly hadn't thought about it in many years, until I attended a close friend's son's high school graduation. At one part during the ceremony, there was a time for honouring parents and all that they'd done to bring these graduates to graduation day. Several students gave moving speeches of heartfelt gratitude to their parents for all they'd given them. While moved that the students honoured their parents in this way, I was also very disturbed by memories of my own graduation. My parents came from Thailand for the event, but I felt very distant from them, almost like we hardly knew each other. They certainly didn't know this boarding world I had been raised and educated in. I didn't know how to interact with them in this setting, let alone honour them. On top of that, I was very hung-over, from having drunk too much the night before. A party with friends that I was about to say goodbye to, and would likely never see again. I was anxious and stressed about how I was going to walk straight down the stage to receive my diploma. The shame, guilt, loneliness and despair were overwhelming as I remembered this day. I had survived ten years in religious boarding school alone. All I could offer my parents was my grief and regret that I had not spent more time with them.

The years of separation and countless goodbyes had led me to believe that God's work was far more important than raising me. I blamed God and twisted religious teaching that would encourage parents to sacrifice their kids for the sake of their ministry. I felt robbed of many years of life that I could have spent in Thailand with my parents. How could I possibly believe in – let alone worship – a God who had allowed so much pain?

Through a long process and some significant experiences, I have come to know that God is not the angry, distant, only-concerned-about-sin, and often disappointed God I had been taught about. God has shown me that children are a gift, given to parents to love, cherish, and enjoy. Family is actually at the centre of God's heart. He is a loving father who would never dream of putting His work before His kids' needs. In fact, his number one work is meeting the needs of his children. This is why his most preferred title is "Father", because children are always his priority. I have come to know and trust this God, and it has only been in allowing myself to receive his love that I have found the healing and comfort I so desperately needed and longed for.

God has shown me that it was never his will for us to be sent away to Chefoo, or Faith Academy. That has been hard to accept, because for a while I wanted to blame God. I now know that he isn't afraid of our blame – he is big enough to handle it and rather invites us to blame him, if that would help us. But knowing that God wasn't the one who demanded or required us to go to boarding school has left me confused with my anger. It helps when we know who the bad guy is and who to be angry with. But that always tended to lock me in my pain. Keeping the effigy burning, whether that be the OMF missionary system, God, or my parents, has only kept the anger alive in me. So, as I've faced these memories and the pain they carry, I have cried out for answers and comfort. I have cried out to God in anger and agony, "Where were you then? How could all of that have happened in your name?" Every time – in each of these painful memories – he has appeared as a safe and beautiful being, to help rewrite the emotions these memories carry. It was like he was taking me by the hand and saying gently, "I want to show you something."

The first time I left mum and dad, I see God take my hand and walk with me onto that plane. He sits beside me, holding me, and wipes away the stains when I spill my juice. He wipes away my tears and comforts me. I feel so safe with him. He tells me, "Don't worry, I'm with your mum and dad too, wiping away their tears." His words give me so much peace. I am not alone.

At my sixth birthday party, he walks in the door with big, wide-open daddy arms. He picks me up and throws me in the air. He holds me in his lap and tells me again how special and important I am. We laugh and giggle together and it becomes a happy, joyous memory. I am a joy to celebrate.

I see myself back in my bed in the dorm where I was plagued by night terrors. Now there are huge angels beside each bed post, and

Jesus is beside me, holding me and wiping away my tears. I feel so much peace and relief. That memory no longer plagues me, because I know now that I am loved and easy to comfort.

When I remember the trauma of being forgotten at school in New Zealand, I see angels all around me, carrying my bag and skipping with me. We laugh together and I no longer feel alone or abandoned. I forgive my parents for letting me down, and I'm learning to trust them and others again. I am important.

On sports day, and in many other competitive events throughout my life, I see Jesus cheering me on, loudly calling out my name. Whenever he wants me to know how he feels about me, he reminds me of returning to the Hatyai airport in South Thailand, where I would walk out of the arrivals door and see my mum and dad holding a huge sign, "Welcome Home! We love you!" My dad would jump up and down shouting my name, full of pride, so delighted to see me. He would then lift me up and give me the biggest bear hug. I hear Jesus say, "This is how I feel about you every minute of every day." I am celebrated, worthy, and loved.

In the memories and shame of bed wetting, he shows me that he is there again cleaning me up and wiping my tears. He does the same for my brother and frees me to forgive myself for not being the sister I couldn't be. My brother's struggles are not my fault. I am free from shame and guilt.

At my high school graduation, I see him handing out our diplomas. With my head hung low, he calls my name and comes running towards me. He lifts my head and chin, holds me in his arms, and declares, "My beloved daughter, I couldn't be more proud of you today." He removes my cloak of shame and gives me a royal gown and a sceptre. He tells me that I am his princess, powerful and free, worthy of love and honour. He helps me to forgive my parents. I am learning to receive their love. I am loved and worthy of being loved.

The healing I have received has also enabled me to find healing and reconciliation in my relationship with my parents. Surprisingly, they have been incredibly humble and supportive on this journey. They have owned their mistakes, apologised and sought forgiveness. I've been able to see that in spite of the missionary system that led to these choices, they have always loved me. I realise now, as a parent myself, that their parent hearts were aching for me as much as my child heart was longing for them. We each still struggle with the shadow pains from those never-had memories when we should have been together. As I have acknowledged the real pain and hurt, and chosen to forgive them, I have been able to receive their love and affection. Puncture wounds leave holes, and our hearts have their fair share of leaky spots. These heart holes have been very slow to heal – I'm discovering new levels even as I write this – and though a lot of repressed grief now runs quite freely in our family, we have found much healing by just being leaky together.

I recently realised that, other than short birthday cards, I have never written a letter to any of my kids. I had received and cherished many dozens of letters from my parents as a child. So, I was tempted to feel bad until I reminded myself that I've never had the need to write letters to my kids, because I've never been apart from them for much longer than a few days. While my own kids have been a tremendous gift on my journey of healing, many of these painful memories I have mentioned were triggered through raising them. I still get triggered at times, and I am trying not to project my own childhood issues onto their experience. The fact is, though, my kids are getting a much different childhood than I had. And I'm so thankful I get to be with them through it.

* * *

Anonymous writer
Attended Chefoo Malaysia from 1989–95
Attended the OMF Dorm at Faith Academy Philippines 1997–2001

Sophia

I'M A MEMBER OF A CLUB. It's not one that I asked to join, and its membership is pretty exclusive. I used to be quite proud that I was a member of this club, that it meant I was resilient and strong and didn't fucking need anyone or anything. (Though of course, I never used to use language like that.) My family used words and phrases to describe my membership of this club that I now recognise as the language of abuse of power: "You were so excited about it," "You wanted to do this," "You couldn't wait to be a big girl," and now what I know is the worst, "You chose this". This is the language of complicity, of taking a wrongness and making you believe it to be right and, even worse, making you actively reinforce it in words and deeds. This complicity, being part of a club, the rules of which dominated my life for nearly forty years.

This was boarding school and I was five years old. This was boarding school in another country from my parents. This was four months at school, two months with my parents, then four months at school – repeated until I was sixteen. This is how I became the person that I am, not bitter but angry in my bones in a way I have only come to recognise in my middle age. Anger sits deep in my skeleton, part of my marrow, regenerating with each cycle of blood. Rage sits below the surface boiling up at inconvenient intervals:

...when I look at my children as they each in turn reached and passed the age at which I left home, and they were so small and so much a part of me that I could not imagine cutting them away from our entanglement in each other.

...lying in bed beside my children, listening first to their stories of friendships gained and listening then to their breathing as they slid into sleep.

...when I listen to their ordinary stories of ordinary days at school and get mad at them for losing another school hat. (Do you know what it meant to lose things at school? How much they cost and the disappointment of your parents that you couldn't look after things they had sacrificed for? Or worse, when dorm parents wrote letters home reporting misdeeds, and you got that aerogramme weeks later, and you couldn't really remember what you had done wrong.) Old anxieties run strongly at times like these.

...when my mother says things like, "Why can't she tie her own shoelaces? You could when you were five." And I want to say, I had to because there was no-one else to do it and we got in trouble if we fell over untied shoelaces. But I don't because we don't say impolite things like that in my family.

...when your teenagers finish high school and move away from home to pursue their dreams, and your parents *tsk tsk* about you "letting" them go off on their own and you want to scream at these rosy faced old people, "At least I waited until they can vote and drink and look after themselves!"

...visiting my parents and feeling complicit again as I take part in family rituals so as not to hurt them.

...never being able to speak about boarding school beyond happy stories of childhood.

...when your parents tell you that they don't want to go to a nursing home or retirement village because they hate institutions.

I was complicit. I talked about the fun times and the good friends. I packed my bags, managed my passport, sent letters that did not speak of such things as gulping for air through tears in airplane bathrooms, choking on sobs as I brushed my teeth those first nights away, turning around in my bed under the blankets so that I could not see the monsters that roamed in the intense dormitory darkness below the level of the top bunks that tall me was always allocated. I stood up in churches, often wearing cultural dress, and spoke about how wonderful it was to receive a good education while my parents were serving God and, my worst shame, as a young teenager I took part in a panel organised by a church on why boarding school was "a good thing". I behaved myself in public so that I would not be a stumbling block, preventing people from coming to God, or worse, bringing shame upon my parents.

As the years passed the anger took over more and more. I vowed never to make my children feel ashamed of their behaviour. either on my behalf, or on God's. I tried to help them to become strong, thoughtful, critical thinkers for themselves even if it meant childhood battles of will. I became less able to play the missionary kid role expected of me. Two incidents stand out. My mother gave me a book to read about the experiences of missionary mothers that completely left out the children's experiences, children who are, in fact, central to the whole concept. The second was a well-intentioned church elder in Malaysia thanking Chefoo children for giving our parents to God's work. Both of these completely misunderstood the lack of agency of the children involved. We had no choice; our input was neither given nor sought – justifying it on the basis of lives saved seems like theological rationalisation. I read the book and returned it to my mother. I stood up in church and walked out while the elder was still speaking. I had never done something so alien, or so empowering before. I felt the shame of complicity begin to retreat.

I was given a book of Adrienne Rich's poetry for Christmas from someone who knows me perhaps even better than I do. Almost every time I dip into it, I come across words that shoot into my soul. Last night I read her poem *Letter from the Land of Sinners* and realised that this is the place I have come to, a different country with different rules and norms and expectations from where I was raised, and also a place where "our gates are falling down/And need not be replaced." In another poem, she writes of anger and tenderness as her selves and I see myself in that. My experiences have left me angry and they have left my soul so tender that it can be easily bruised. I guard it very carefully and let few within the gates. Coming back to meet with friends of my childhood, and friends whom I have never met but who know me because of our shared experiences, has meant that I do not need to gate my land so diligently and can perhaps allow a few visitors. It also means I can guard those I love a little less fiercely and let them make their own mistakes.

I really like this metaphor of another land with its implication that I have arrived somewhere by choice, made decisions, chosen my place. It also allows me the illusion of autonomy, that I can live in a land and allow visitors, that I can hold my anger and tenderness in balance to guide and guard my life. I told my father in a fit of bravado years ago that I was choosing to live without guilt. He responded, "How will you know when you are doing the wrong thing?" In this new land I will have to work that out for myself. I am framing it for myself as a new adventure, exploring this land and working out its boundaries and rules. Wish me travelling mercies.

* * *

"Sophia" attended Chefoo Malaysia in the 70s.

Anonymous

ALL MY LIFE I HAVE tried to pretend I was something I'm not. I pretended I was normal, that my life had been normal. A lot of the time people have believed me. I have become quite good at omitting certain aspects of my childhood, or at least downplaying them. Over the years I have avoided anything to do with my past, many of the people I once knew, as well as any Third Culture Kid or Missionary Kid meet-ups. I told myself I didn't need any of that, I wasn't like those people. I was strong enough to be my own person, not defined by my parents' choices, and certainly not affected in a negative way. If anything, my boarding school years had made me more resilient and more independent – and surely that was a good thing? All those wasted years, opportunities lost to discover who I really am, and what I want from life. Could it be too late now?

My daughter is about to start school and I suddenly find myself remembering. And as I remember, I rediscover the pain, long buried, which I believed had dissipated by now. I am suddenly forced to confront my past and deal with it. And I am realising just how much is wrong with me, and that I am well into my thirties and hardly beginning to understand myself, or the actual impact of the trauma I experienced as a child. I hope I still have the chance to figure it all out.

As I was growing up, I was barely aware that the way I was being raised wasn't normal. In fact, it is only fairly recently that I have truly realised just how utterly strange my childhood actually was. Now, as an adult, I look at the people around me, people who, for the most part, have no idea how I was brought up. And even if they knew, they probably would not be able to truly comprehend it. I envy their sense of belonging, their confidence in who they are. I now understand that I am broken and that what was done to me was not right.

As a parent myself, the idea of doing to my children what my parents did to me is not only horrifying, it is impossible. I am not sure what is worse, the fact that they chose to do what they did, or the fact that they have washed their hands of all responsibility, claiming they "had no choice" in the matter. In reality, however, it all comes down to one thing: that God and their work always took precedence and that I, their child, was less important.

My experience of boarding school is not synonymous with the "typical" Chefoo experience. I was sent to an OMF hostel, something I feel is best described as a strange form of foster care, whereby you live with your birth family in the school holidays but may otherwise only contact them through the medium of a weekly letter and a phone call on birthdays. The size of the hostel fluctuated in the years I was there, ranging from around eight to fifteen children aged between six and sixteen. The school itself was a secular private school filled, for the main part, with privileged kids, the children of diplomats, business people and the like. Those of us who came from "the hostel" were known as the uncool, religious kids who never had any money, who dressed oddly, who were never allowed to do any of the things everyone else did. We were outsiders, never part of the inner circle, oftentimes bullied by other kids, or at least that was my experience.

In that sense I think I sometimes envied those who went to Chefoo because at least they had each other, that community, that bond (I am not sure if this is true, but it was certainly my feeling at the time). It is, without doubt, a bond which appears to have formed in the long-term with former Chefusians of all ages, connecting and helping each other through difficult issues resulting from their shared childhood trauma. This is not something I have experienced at all with the few people I am still in touch with from my hostel. Most of them appear to view that time in their lives as largely positive, to the point that I have wrestled with my own negative outlook, feeling that perhaps I am exaggerating everything, making things up, or just being overly dramatic about it all.

It was therefore comforting to be included in the Chefoo community. At the same time, however, I must admit that I still have a nagging feeling about not truly belonging to the group. I continue to feel like a bit of an intruder, like perhaps my experience is not as valid. Yes, of course there will be a great many similarities to the experience of those who were sent to one of the traditional Chefoo schools: the sense of abandonment, the weight of the expectations placed on me, the fractured relationship with my parents, the shame and guilt, and feelings of low self-worth. However, this does not make me a "real" Chefusian.

It does not help that the alternative stories of those who were sent to hostels seem to be generally ignored within the wider OMF narrative. Somehow our experience has been deemed less important, perhaps because there were fewer of us. I know that general apologies have been made to those children who were forced to go to boarding school, as well as their families, but the main emphasis has always been on those going to Chefoo, not the fringe groups.

This is one of the reasons I have decided to write this, to ensure that at least one alternative story is told within this book, especially with the rise of smaller hostels within the OMF in recent years. Perhaps someone will read this and realise that sending their children to a hostel is no better than a real boarding school and reconsider. I realise that a lot of the OMF children being sent away these days are much older than we were back then, but children are still vulnerable and in need of parental protection and love, even when they are much older. And even when the children agree to the decision it is not always fair, since they might feel that this is what is expected of them, and may not wish to disappoint their parents. However, more on this later.

I was six years old when I got on a plane on my own for the first time. I remember feeling scared, confused and heartbroken. In the coming year I would see my family three times: during the Christmas, Easter and summer holidays. This is a terrifying prospect at any age, I think. Many young people who leave home for the first time in their lives to go to university will experience some of those feelings, as they leave behind everything they have ever known. But at the age of eighteen, one has had time to learn to be independent, at least to some degree. One is an adult, at least in name, and has had years to make mistakes and learn about life and oneself within the safety of the family home. Leaving home at the tender age of six is a different story altogether. You are forced to grow up quite suddenly, at least in some ways, and long before it is healthy to do so. All those experiences, all the firsts, all the little hurts and joys that you are supposed to undergo in a safe environment, with people who love you and are there for you, looking out for you and protecting you – you suddenly realise that there is no one there and that you will have to go through them alone. And because you know that no one is there for you, no one you can trust, you learn to bury the pain, the vulnerable part of you, and become tough, at least to the outside world. It is not something a young child should have to do – and yet it becomes necessary in such a situation.

The responsible adults in my hostel were generally not much help. I will not go into detail on the neglect and abuse, as that is not what this book is about. What I will say is that there was a general expectation that we be independently responsible for ourselves with minimal intervention. For me, this meant that I was often reprimanded at school for not having the correct materials and that I was frequently excluded, or even bullied, by the other children with nowhere to go for comfort or support. It also meant that I learned that there was no one there for me and that the only person I could rely on was myself. If I was homesick or upset, I had to deal with it myself. I would lose myself in books, imagining myself to be one of the characters in them. I would escape the confines of the hostel, where there was never any peace or privacy, and wander around on my own, pretending I was a different person living a completely different life. I would frequently imagine running away in great detail, including what I would take with me and which route I would take. I would cry into my pillow at night, hoping that nobody would hear.

Suffice to say that there was a lack of warmth and love. This, combined with the perceived abandonment of my parents, changed who I was. I went from being a confident, happy and rather outgoing child to a painfully shy, even reclusive, and depressed individual. On the one hand I became incredibly independent and self-sufficient, having learnt at such a young age to take care of myself and that no one would be there for me. On the other hand I remained incredibly vulnerable, feeling worthless and that nobody cared enough about me to want to look after me properly. I was desperate to please those around me, to be loved, yet did not know how. So I presented a thick skin to the outside world and pretended to everyone, including myself, that I was fine.

It would be impossible to write this without alluding to the religious facet. My parents doing "God's work" meant there was a constant expectation on me to behave in a way that would reflect well on them and – even more importantly – to follow in their footsteps when it came to "following Jesus". I was raised on a steady diet of prayer, hymns and Bible stories and the idea that I might ever stray from the faith was impossible to my parents, I think. I do not think I ever questioned any of it as a child. I accepted what I was told as the truth and did my best to never disappoint anyone, particularly my parents. I always felt the weight of expectation on me and was aware that my failure might make them fail – or even be disgraced entirely. This is a huge burden of responsibility to place on a young child and the cost was high. I spent an incredibly long time wrestling with a huge amount of guilt and feelings of low self-worth, believing my own value to be dependent on how good a Christian I was. I did what I was told, I never complained about being sent away, I never told my parents just how bad things were. This has continued into my adult life, the idea that I must protect my parents' feelings and image at all costs. Which is the sole reason I have been hesitant to write this at all and why I am doing so anonymously.

This all-encompassing, almost cult-like version of Christianity was continued in the hostel. It was very definitely pushed on us, leaving us with little room for our own opinions or decisions on the matter. Everything we did was classed as either godly or sinful and evaluated as such. Looking back, it is difficult not to take offense at the huge amount of hypocrisy displayed by all of the adults in my life. The continuous and very persistent verbal message was that we should follow Jesus and live in a godly manner at all times. Yet this expectation did not seem to truly pertain to them. Yes, they obviously all gave up a great deal to "follow God's call", working ridiculous hours for very little money. But when it came to protecting and looking after the children in their care, this no longer seemed to apply. For my parents, saving strangers' souls was more important than their own child. While those supposedly taking their place in caring for me ranged from neglectful, to abusive (with only one exception that I can think of in all the years I was there). How could any of them reconcile the two? And how do my parents feel now about spending decades trying to save other people's souls, only to lose that of their own child?

As I grew older and became a teenager, then a young adult, a lot of the feelings that were more difficult to identify as a child really came to the fore. I struggled with severe depression and attempted suicide more than once. I did not consider it as clearly then, but I suppose I believed I would not truly be missed. After all, my parents did not care enough to find a way to live with me when I was a child, so I could clearly not be that important to them.

It was also incredibly difficult to make lasting friendships. Moving around so much meant that I was frequently the "new kid", and in turn, that I was attempting to enter well established social groups. Add to this how painfully shy I had become, and the fact that I did not believe I had anything of value to give or add to any group, and things were doomed to fail.

The few friendships I did manage to form did not, in general, last very long either. I spent every waking moment after seeing my friends worrying about every detail of what had taken place, about whether I had said or done the wrong thing, or perhaps not said or done something I should have. Always convinced that my friends would eventually decide I was no longer worth their while, I suppose I inadvertently brought about the end of a number of these friendships myself. This became even more extreme when I became a young adult and had the autonomy to make my own life decisions. Each time things became difficult, each time I began to feel excluded, or unloved or simply worried that I was an annoyance to those around me, I would move to a new place. This happened fairly frequently.

It is crucial to mention that religion also continued to have an enormous impact on my emotional state at this point. I noted earlier that the adults around me seemed to associate my value with how good a Christian I was. This became a particularly immense issue in my teenage and young adult years, as a part of me always struggled to believe everything I had been taught. The supernatural side of things always seemed a bit far-fetched and God seemed very far away. Yet I was simultaneously terrified from years of being told I would go to hell and be punished for my sins if my faith were not great enough, or if I did not try hard enough to be a good Christian. The outcome was that I see-sawed between giving in to my agnosticism (though I hid this from everyone around me, especially my parents) and desperately trying to be a good Christian. In the moments when I was trying my utmost to be good and not disappoint, my sense of self-worth declined even further. The fact that I was not good enough, was not praying hard enough, or reading the Bible enough, was perpetually on my mind. People spoke of God as a loving father but how could I even relate to this when my relationship with my own parents was so damaged? In addition to this, there was a notable focus on our sinful nature and how we must ascribe any good that we do manage to accomplish to God. In essence, it was like they were saying, "You are a bad and worthless person but if you are lucky and try very, very hard, God will forgive and save you."

Deliberately cutting those strings and leaving the faith, quite publicly I should add, was a definite step towards emotional healing. I do not think I will ever be completely free from my religious past, but leaving it behind me has brought a great deal of relief. And it was the first step to confronting my past, even though I did not realise this at the time.

The next step only came much later. I now have children of my own and can see what was done to me through the eyes of a parent. Having my children in my life and watching them grow up, I find what my own parents did completely inconceivable. It has drawn out feelings of anger and resentment which I did not realise were buried inside me. As a child I did not really think of my parents' choices as being their own. The missionary life and everything connected with it was so normalised that I did not even question any of it. I suppose I believed my parents' claims to have been called by God and thought I had to comply, in order to ensure that I did not cause them to fail. As a teenager I was aware that I was fairly troubled, but then I grew up in an international environment where so many kids were so utterly messed up that I did not really stand out at all. As a young adult, I was convinced that the past had no negative impact on me whatsoever and that I was – or at least could become – normal. For so many years I defended my parents' choices, both to myself and others. It was only becoming a parent that made me realise that what they did was in fact indefensible. And this is something that remains as yet unresolved. It is not something I feel I can discuss with my parents and every time the issue has been broached there is a sense of it being whitewashed. They certainly do not wish to take responsibility for their own actions, for whatever reason. This has of course affected our relationship, however subtly. I continue to relate to them, for their benefit (as I have explained above), as well as for that of my children. However, it is becoming increasingly difficult.

I must admit that I am not sure what it would take for me to forgive my parents truly. Would taking responsibility for what they chose to do, and a heartfelt apology be sufficient? I'm not sure. My parents continue to work towards the same goals they did back then, they continue to believe in the same things that have been so toxic to my own mental health. Perhaps I want them to admit that their entire way of life was wrong, that they should have chosen between doing the work they did and having a child. Perhaps I want them to be more accepting of the life choices I have made, including leaving the faith they tried to force on me. Perhaps I want them to acknowledge the impact their choices have truly had, how I have had to deal with years of mental health issues and am still far from healing. Yet for this to happen, I know I would have to take the first step and explain, really explain, how I feel. And this is not something I am ready to do right now, perhaps ever. I am not completely sure I even want to forgive them at this point, let alone speak to them about anything this intimate.

I have gone for so many years showing them only my tough side and I do not remember a time when we ever connected on a deeper level. It is certainly not something I ever learned from them. When I was a child, my parents never shared anything intimate with me, their hopes or worries, how they felt about things. It was always hidden away, maybe they thought it was too complex for a child to understand. But how do you suddenly start sharing these kinds of things later if you have not made a start early on? So nothing changed as I grew up and I cannot see it ever doing so.

On a positive note, however, I have begun to work through some of my past and identify some of my vulnerabilities, as well as some of the reasons behind them. Emotional instability, depression, low self-confidence and a sense of minimal self-worth are still ever-present (though the joy of being around my children has certainly helped to reduce this), but I can now acknowledge these emotions and understand where they come from. The dichotomy between self-reliance and vulnerability is also still with me. I suppose I can come across as fairly aloof, unapproachable, sarcastic and judgmental. To some extent this is most definitely a coping mechanism to ensure that my insecurities and self-doubt are not visible to all, as well as to ensure that I do not get hurt again.

I also still find it rather difficult to talk to people, being unable to free myself from the constant feeling that my contributions are less valuable, that everything I say (or don't say) is inappropriate, and that the people around me are merely tolerating me because they do not wish to be rude but that they wish they were not stuck with me. This has largely prevented me from forming close friendships.

At the same time, I suppose that a part of me is in fact a bit reserved and judgmental, perhaps because I learned quite early on not to rely on anyone but myself. As a result, it is often a great effort to be patient and empathise with other people, especially those who do not cope well with minor problems. After all, I dealt with things far worse than many of them will ever have to go through when I was still very young, and I am fine. So why are they unable to deal with their own problems? It is not that I can't empathise at all, but it is possible that my parameters as to what constitutes a good enough reason to complain about one's life are somewhat unfair.

Recently, I have realised that the people I tend to get along with best and have the most respect for are those who have experienced some form of childhood trauma themselves, even if that trauma is very different from my own. And it is generally these people with whom I have (finally) begun to talk about my past and share certain parts of my journey. It is strangely comforting to make myself vulnerable like this, to speak about more painful issues, rather than perpetually pretending to be strong to everyone around me. How odd, considering how hard I have tried my entire life to hide my vulnerabilities and appear tough – and how much I believed in my own strength and resilience. Furthermore, connecting with people in this way has helped me to open up a bit, in general, and try to speak about some of this with other people around me. Not usually in great detail, as most people cannot fully comprehend it and either look at me blankly or are frightened by the magnitude of what happened to me at such a young age. But it is at least a start.

I also think that realizing and admitting that what I went through as a child was traumatic, and especially speaking about it, is yet another step towards healing. Writing this has also had quite an impact. It has been incredibly difficult and painful, and there have been times when it has brought me to tears. Yet at the same time, I strongly believe that it has enabled me to learn more about myself and why I act and react the way I do.

With regard to my children, I think it is safe to say that my childhood feelings of powerlessness and insignificance have, to some extent, had a positive outcome. I now, very deliberately, make all major decisions based on my children, not myself. I never would have thought that I would live as I do now: stuck in one place, in a small town where very little ever changes. And so I struggle against my own nature every single day. I struggle against the desire to move constantly, to start afresh. I struggle against the desire to see the world and live in random places across the globe. I struggle against my desire to live in a place where I am surrounded by globally aware people whose background and experiences are more similar to mine. But I do not want to make the same choices, the same mistakes my parents made, which they still do not seem to truly recognise as such. I want to ensure that my children have stable, happy lives and are always surrounded by close friends and family. And so I do my best with what I have and try to be content.

Whatever the case, my children will always come first, and it is incredibly important to me that they know this. I never want them to be in any doubt about the fact that they are loved and valued, I tell them so on a regular basis and try to show them in as many ways as I can. Whatever happens, whatever they do, they are my children and I love them more than anything in the world, and this will never change. No, I am not perfect and yes, I often make mistakes, both of which have unfortunately led to even more guilt on my part. I begin to worry that I am no different from my parents and that my children will end up being just as broken as I am. Perhaps they can somehow sense the damage in me and are internalising it. Perhaps they will grow up to resent me in the same way that I resent my parents. But in the end, when it comes down to it, I know that I am present and strive to provide them with all they need for their emotional well-being. I will never leave them. And as they grow up, they will be able to do so in a loving home with someone who cares about them and will keep them as safe as is physically possible. They will have the chance to make mistakes in a safe environment, learn to become independent and mature in their own time. I truly hope that all of my good intentions and my being there for them are enough for them to grow up to be happy, confident adults.

May the damage end here.

Interlude 1:
Half-Term Cinema
Jemimah

IT WAS HALF-TIME BREAK in the middle of our half-term movie – *Winnie the Pooh*! In the middle girls' dorm, we were singing the *Winnie the Pooh* song while we waited in the queue for the loo.

"Winnie the Pooh, Winnie the Pooh, tubby little chubby all stuffed with fluff,"

"No, it's tubby little cubby," I called out, a stickler for getting the words right.

Meanwhile over in the little girls' dorm, my sister Abigail was fidgeting in the queue and fiddling with the bathroom door while she waited. Without warning, Beth burst out of the bathroom yelling, "I'm done!"

Suddenly Abigail was screaming and jumping up and down with her finger in the air. Blood was dripping onto her jumper and along the floor. Annette ran to get Aunty Miriam.

"I like the bit where he eats all Rabbit's honey". I was chatting to Claire when I realised that she wasn't answering anymore from the other side of the toilet door and I was the last one left.

I flew out of the dorm and down the stairs, negotiating steps and drains to race through the area where we queue up for the dining hall and was just careening around the corner towards the assembly hall when I saw Abigail in Miss L's arms holding a fist up in the air and screaming for all she was worth.

"What's happened now?", I thought and kept on going. I don't think I even slowed down.

As I emerged from the dark hall at the end of the cartoon movie, I started to hear snippets of news.

"It was hanging off by a thread"!

She had to get three stitches.

2

Abandonment & Separation

How does a young child - say at age five - deal with being sent away to school? What are the long-term effects of prolonged separation from parents and family at such a tender age? Many of our stories explore this question. Here are some strong answers.

Brian

WHERE TO BEGIN?

I guess I could start with the sudden and unexpected death of my wife.

Or maybe I should go back to that first night at Chefoo School and that five-year-old boy crying into his pillow – back in the days when I still knew how to cry.

But in order to really appreciate just how screwed up it all became then I guess I have to start with the recent funeral of my mother, just a few short weeks before her ninetieth birthday.

Almost a year to the day after Dot died.

I was sat at the front of the church with my two motherless sons, listening to a selection of random strangers offering up eulogies and anecdotes about some old lady that I evidently didn't know, and I began to feel like maybe I was at the wrong funeral.

Like I had somehow turned up at the wrong church.

As if I had gate-crashed the funeral of some other grieving son's mother.

And when the minister stood up and started talking about this wonderful caring woman, this saintly "Mother Theresa" – who dedicated her life to the people of South East Asia and went out of her way to care for the needs of others, the elderly, the infirm, the homeless, the disadvantaged; who sacrificed so much for her faith – I began to feel decidedly uncomfortable.

You see, for years I had convinced myself that this woman was not my mother at all.

Sure, I had fond memories of her reading stories to us on the veranda back in Thailand, in the heat of the afternoon, in that place I once thought of as home.

I remembered a time as a child when I felt safe and secure and, above all else, loved.

But things had changed beyond all recognition and circumstances demanded that I forget the past and look instead to an uncertain future.

And so, I created this pleasant fiction wherein I had been adopted at birth by some well-intentioned missionary couple with absolutely no understanding of the needs of small children, oblivious to the pain and suffering, the abandonment and exile, that would ultimately follow. People with no comprehension of the far-reaching consequences of their actions, of offering up their sacrificial lambs in the name of faith.

So, I created this alternative reality out of a desperate need for self-preservation.

To avoid contemplating the only other, truly terrifying alternative: that they just didn't love me enough!

I learned very quickly during those early years, that everything in this life is transitory.

Nothing lasts forever.

That no sooner do you form an attachment to a person, or a place, or an idea, than it will be taken away, replaced, forgotten.

And my coping strategy, the way in which I learned to avoid feeling the pain of that separation, that loss, was to completely detach myself. To become void of emotion. I will endeavour to explain, and I hope that you will understand because this IS how I am – this is exactly what I have become. *Comfortably numb.*

Home was just a name.

It was a place that you found yourself in for an unspecified amount of time, knowing that as soon as you began to feel comfortable in that place, or developed a sense of familiarity, of security, of belonging, then you would be uprooted and relocated – sent away to a new "home".

To start all over.

Home was just an idea, a dream, a vague sense of belonging somewhere.

No more real a concept than Narnia or Wonderland or perhaps even Heaven.

Like stories from a book, read to a small boy in the heat of summer in the relative cool of the veranda, under the cover of bougainvillea, in a place that felt like home.

Try explaining snow to a five-year-old Thai child – one who doesn't even understand that he's not Thai.

A child with absolutely no experience of cold and even less comprehension of his true national identity, his ethnicity, his roots.

And then try to explain to him that he is to be sent away to some frozen wasteland, some strange ice-covered world. A land that he cannot even begin to comprehend because all that he has ever known has been baking heat and burning sun, sheltering right there beneath the bougainvillea, listening to stories from the Bible.

Or send him away on a long train journey into the unknown, in the company of other equally bewildered, confused, terrified children to some distant foreign land in the middle of a jungle so far from home. A land where the cicadas scream in the blackness of night, and tigers prowl beneath the canopy, as he drowns his tears in his pillow for fear of being heard; praying to a God that doesn't care, that doesn't answer, that isn't there.

And try to explain to him that this will be his new home for a time, with this his new family. Out here, in the company of strangers. Where he must follow this course without question, without protest, without remorse, because it must be.

That child is destined to become forever a nomad. Homeless, stateless. An alien. An outsider. Someone unable to identify exactly where is home.

Home was Manorom.

The town of my birth (1961).

Where, for a brief time, I had a family and security and love.

Deep in the heartland of central Thailand – a land of paddy fields and
dykes, where it was baking hot for nine months of the year and then it
rained relentlessly, for weeks on end, and the flood waters rose to what
seemed like biblical proportions as the nearby river broke its banks
and the dykes struggled to contain the deluge.

Home was Chefoo School.
That garden of Eden (1966–71).
A magical place, paradise on earth, but so far away from "home" for
such small children!
Set within a clearing in the lush dense jungles of peninsular Malaysia
– surrounded on all sides by tropical rainforest, flowering orchids,
beautiful butterflies, birds of paradise. And when the clouds rolled in
over the mountain the whole place was shrouded by a thin white mist,
enveloped in a cool refreshing cloak of fine water vapour that we called
"the white witch".

Home was King Edward's.
A boarding school in Surrey, England (1972–79).
My place of exile on the other side of this uncaring world.
And I never felt less "at home" than in that cold alien world –
incarcerated within those red brick walls, with its labyrinth of dark
soulless corridors and whispering grey stone courtyards. Like the
doubting castle of Bunyan's Pilgrim, where pain and suffering and
despair prevailed.

Home was Donnington.
My orphanage (1972–74).
The place we escaped to in the school holidays, a large country house
in Berkshire.
That place where I finally learned to forget. Where I began to live
again in the company of a similarly disenfranchised generation of
discarded, abandoned, rejected children – separated from our families
by thousands of miles and the slow creeping progression of time;
families we would only see for a few short weeks every summer, whose

memories gradually faded like the black and white photographs on our bedside tables.

Home was Guildford.
The new "family home" in England (1974–80).
A place where, when my parents finally returned for me, we would try once again to play at happy families. As though we could make believe that none of it had ever happened, that what had been done could just be undone. As if we could start over and make believe that it had all been some strange dream – a family that I had long since learned to forget and for which I now felt nothing.

Home was Farnham.
The scene of my self-destruction (1981–85).
Art school. Where the prodigal son left home and pursued a modern-day debauchery on a scale that would put the biblical narrative to shame. But on returning home he found his father dead – the story doesn't go that way in the Bible – and thus reconciliation was (tragically) never an option.

Home became London.
And the wanderer finally found a place to call home (1986–present).
Where, despite everything that had gone before, regardless of his past, his struggles, his secrets, his anger, his resentment, his lies, his mistakes; someone recognised the very best of what had been engendered by this process – and she made it all OK. And they created a family on the understanding that there would be no more sacrifices.

And then she died.
Without warning.
Totally unexpectedly.

He came home one night and found her dead in the bathroom.

And his reaction was so cold, so void of emotion, so "numb", that the police held him as a suspect for three hours while they waited for the coroner to arrive and deliver a verdict of "death by natural causes".

So, I return to where I began.
My mother's funeral.
Where I realised that my desensitization was complete.

I HAVE BECOME COMFORTABLY NUMB!

The experiment was a great success, the process really does work.
Take a child, send him away, tell him not to overreact but to keep a stiff upper lip, take everything in his stride, swallow his pain, hide his sadness, don't let on when he's feeling down – because there is a greater cause, a cause for which the sacrifice is ultimately justified.

And I wish I could cry into my pillow.
I wish I could just cry.
Because my wife passed away and all I can feel is numb!

Bronwen

I AM SIX AND I am going to Chefoo in Japan for the first time. My brother is already there, and I know many of the children with whom I will share a dormitory and classroom. Going to school involves travelling by ferry for four hours from the top of the main island of Japan to the most northerly island. We gather with other OMF Japan "missionary kids'" (MKs) to hug our parents goodbye, and as we hang over the railings on the deck, waving intermittently, the ferry plays *Auld Lang Syne* and we watch our parents recede – oh, so slowly – into the distance. We keep looking until they are dots on the horizon, then turn our backs on them to explore the ship and enjoy the adventure.

I am nine and am at the Singapore railway station to get the night train to Chefoo in the Camerons. The heat and humidity are still intense although it is late evening. The "Singapore party" is a relatively small group compared to the "Thai party" who would already be on their way from Bangkok. (I was always slightly jealous of the Thai party – which had a festive aura about it – partly because of the sheer number of kids, and partly because, without actually having witnessed the pains of parting on Bangkok station as a child, I imagined that the word "party" retained it's celebratory and festive meaning.)

Once on the train, we bag our bunks and stow our luggage and then spend time on the platform with parents and younger siblings – half hoping that the time for the train to leave would never come, but wanting the final parting to be over. Tummy aches and headaches brew as we all kill time. Final squeezes, assurances of how much we are loved, that they will write, that the term will not be long – Oh, the fake cheery voices! – and we board the train to wave from our bunks. Younger siblings run alongside the train as it starts to move – stretching out the final glimpses until they run out of platform. On board, we all dive for the customary gifts stowed in our luggage – a small compensation and distraction as we pull away from home. Soon lights are glinting in the water as we cross the long causeway between Singapore and Malaysia – which signal time to turn, exhausted, to our bunks and settle down to be rocked to sleep by the train's rhythm.

We wake to cooler mornings and mile after mile of rubber plantations. Indian workers are seen amongst the geometrically planted rows of trees that reveal a sequence of angled avenues as the train passes. In dappled light they scar the trees with a diagonal cut to release more latex and change the cups to catch the liquid rubber when they are full.

A picnic breakfast prepared by our parents is our last "home food" for many months, and part of the ritual of transition between home and school. This is consumed sitting on our bunks and gazing at the passing landscape – often a moment of quiet bleakness, as the reality of being away from home for the long-term ahead sinks in.

I am fourteen years old and on holiday with my family in the Camerons. We are staying at "The Bungalow" – a place of comfort and solace, and much more associated in my mind with family times than with being away from home at Chefoo, only a couple of miles down the road. The autumn term is just starting, and I am caught between the familiarity of the place where I was a student for three years, from the age of 8–11, and the strangeness of the place I have outgrown. The kids are SO small. I am virtually a grown up in their eyes.

Then I witness a scene I will never forget. Two parents are saying goodbye to their small son at the back of the busy school hall. A couple of staff are trying to distract him into some activities with other children so his parents can leave. He is having none of it. He is clinging to his mother as though his life depends on her. She is comforting him, and he continues to hold tight. He knows what's coming and it's not what he wants, so he clasps, he clings, he will not let go. And for some reason, the staff decide to embark on a tug of war. They try to pull the boy away from his mother. He starts to scream and cry out. His mother is torn between holding him tight and never letting go and knowing that she is here to do exactly that: to let him go. So does she side with her son, or with the other adults who are trying to help this awful moment to be in the past? I am not the only observer of this scene. The room is full of children who have said goodbye to their parents in the previous 48 hours. Yet I am unaware of anyone else around me – a fourteen-year-old horrified at such a graphic manifestation of what I have experienced myself so many times, and unable to turn away from the scene in front of me.

He was a small child, and the adults were stronger, so they won. And the parents' last view of their son was an outraged, kicking, screaming and sobbing child being dragged away by well-meaning staff.

In only a fortnight's time, I too will undergo being separated from my family when I board a plane to return to boarding school in England. And I will avoid the physical clinging, kicking and screaming by crying private tears into my pillow every night for a week before the moment of saying goodbye. And no-one will ever know.

I am fifteen years old. It is nearing the end of the summer holiday and I have been visiting my family in Singapore. My youngest brother Glyn is due to start school at Chefoo for the first time at the age of five. He will have his sixth birthday at school in September. We are incorporating dropping him off at school in the Camerons into our holiday itinerary, and five of us will go on to have a holiday on the beach on Pangkor Island after we have left him. We have cine camera footage of the few days that we all spent at Chefoo before leaving for Pangkor. We play on the swings with him. We put his teddies on his little bed. My mother takes his hand and skips with him to the dormitory to join the other kids for bath time, and she waves for the camera – a show of breezy casualness and cheeriness which is recorded and replayed many times in the years ahead at family slide and cine viewings.

What is not on record is the silence in the car as the five of us drive away from Chefoo having said goodbye to him. We have no words that will comfort each other, and it seems that we are united in private grief

– each alone with our unexpressed feelings. I am both the one doing the leaving, and sensing echoes of the one who has been left many times in the past. We stare in silence at the jungle we drive through, with every turn of the road down the hill taking us further from the little boy who is part of us. We are weighed down with aching but dare not articulate that ache for fear that we would release something overwhelming. The accepted routine on parting is to be tight-lipped and deal with it on our own, so we fall in line and do what is expected, as we wheel towards our time on the beach without him.

I am thirty-one. I am married and have a mortgage and a career. My parents have moved to Canada for the last chapter in their working lives, and are working at the University of British Columbia, lecturing in theology and mission studies. We have enjoyed several holidays with them, taking advantage of the great outdoors and travelling up country and learning to ski. After a brief trip home to the UK, it is time for Mum to return to Canada. I work only ten minutes from Heathrow, so it is natural that I would take her to the airport. I wave her off at Terminal 3, quite the picture of a young woman in charge of her life. By the time I reach work, I am in shreds. Waves of old but unrecognised loss sweep over me, and I am 6 years old all over again. I am due to have an appraisal that afternoon and know that is not going to happen. I take the back entrance and dive into a friend's office, a sodden, sobbing, heap of misery. She sends me home and covers for me with my manager.

I am thirty-three and in the process of getting divorced. We are both keen to "divorce well" and our decision to part is mutual, so we see a counsellor for several years in order to achieve this. However, this "leaving" prompts deep memories of leavings from many years before. My sense of abandonment is vast and totally disproportionate to the situation. Waves and waves of old but unexpressed anger, loss and hurt are finally allowed to surface, causing my soon to be ex-husband to be bewildered at the force of feelings being released. But these are the feelings of a child, not the thirty-three-year-old woman. There starts a journey of acknowledging and grieving for all the losses of those early years, which goes on still today.

I am thirty-five, and my two- and three-year old niece and nephew are coming to stay for the weekend for the first time. I collect them from the appointed meeting place at a motorway service station – two energised and glowing children have transferred to the back of my red sports car with their little backpacks filled with crisps and drinks and other goodies. They are beside themselves with excitement at the prospect of going to stay with Aunty Bronwen. My brother John and his wife Karen are full of wide smiles as they say their goodbyes: "Be good," they lean down to call to the back seat. I am suddenly incapacitated at the wheel, choked with old sadness and with tears on my cheeks – deeply uncomfortable at finding myself the adult who is removing children from their parents. My sister-in-law points out the happy children in the back, the smiling, waving parents who can't wait to get off for some child-free time – and that if I am crumpling, the discomfort and distress is all mine.

At any age, the opening sequence of the film *Love Actually* triggers in me what a junkie I am for watching people reuniting at airports. Small children running under the barriers to throw themselves at a returning parent, or grandparents they have not seen for months or years. Couples flinging their arms round each other in a long embrace to seal their commitment to have and to hold. Seeing these re-meetings holds more poignancy for me than partings – perhaps because the long-wished-for anticipation of such reconnections in my past was always far more powerful than the actual reunions themselves. I am left choked and vulnerable at the demonstrations of joy and closeness that these moments between humans reveal. Should I ever feel emotionally blocked, the best medicine is a visit to Terminal 3 arrivals at Heathrow.

I am fifty-something. I have just got off a flight and am standing by the carousel to collect my suitcase. I hear a child is starting to wail and look round to see a three- or four-year old child lying on the floor in a state of deep distress. He is pounding the floor with his fists and screaming, "I want my mummy. I want my mummy." His legs are flailing behind him. A man stands by, looking helpless and telling him gently to be quiet. Whether the mother has just gone to the toilet or has been left in another country is not clear. The pain expressed by the child takes him over: his whole body is involved in demonstrating his rage. It is all I can do not to scoop the boy into my arms to comfort him and tell him it will all be alright. And I find myself wondering where it goes – and at what cost – that full-body expression of abandonment.

* * *

In the 60s, Bronwen attended Chefoo School in Japan for one year, then had three years at Chefoo in Malaysia, when her parents moved to Singapore. Teenage years were spent at boarding school in England (co-ed King Edward's School) and OMF hostel Donnington Hurst. Bronwen is now living in London and is in close contact with her wider family who are scattered across the south of England. She is married to Colin and has three stepchildren, and two step grandchildren.

Richard K.

THE YOUNG PASTOR looked at us and said, "Tell me about the family you grew up in." Here we were, two seventy-somethings with over seventy-five years of marriage between us to our first spouses, grandparents of nine, and multiple advanced professional degrees between the two of us, receiving "mandatory" premarital counselling from a pastor younger than our children. Sherri went first, discussing her growing up in Midwestern America, the child of a judge and a homemaker mother, in a family of six children. No abuse, no neglect, good solid middle-class values, and a generally happy childhood straight out of *Ozzie and Harriet* or *Father Knows Best*.

Then the pastor turned to me and I suddenly realised that I had never been asked that question at any time in my life and had never really thought about it. Of course, I had thought and recounted other aspects of my story countless times in my seventy-five years, but I had never been asked directly to describe my family and my childhood within the family. I blurted out that I didn't actually grow up in a family, even though I had two parents, a brother and a sister. I wasn't raised in backwoods isolation, as portrayed by Jodi Foster in the film *Nell*; or as a feral child by a wolf, as documented by a few anthropologists; nor was I an orphan – my parents lived into their seventies and eighties; I was a missionary child.

"You don't choose your family," is a popular saying, but obvious on its merits. This isn't to say that my own family situation was a disaster or that I regret all aspects of my growing up. My parents were brilliant people: my father was the leading Tibetan linguistic scholar in the Western world and my mother earned a Master's degree in literature in the 1920s, at a time when few women had the opportunity to even go to college. I didn't recognise it while growing up, but this brilliance of mind hid a deeply troubling aspect to both of their personalities, namely that they decided that service to God came ahead of their responsibilities as parents towards their children.

This religious "faith" did not manifest itself in physical abuse, nor in traditional forms of abuse or neglect, but rather in what I now see as almost total abandonment of parental responsibilities: to form and maintain a family, to raise children. The dawning of my understanding of this began when I was four years old and my brother, aged six, was left by my parents in Shanghai, China with a non-English speaking German family, so that he could start at the China Inland Mission school. We had just returned to China on the first American ship to enter the country at the end of World War II. My parents were determined to get back to the Tibetan city of Kangding, in what is now Szechuan province in China, from where we had had to flee the Japanese when I was one-and-a-half years old. Abandoning a child was a small price to pay for them to bring Jesus to the Tibetans.

During the war, our trip home to the United States in 1942 took eight months, with a flight over the Himalayas to India; a train across India; by ship to Cape Town, South Africa; across the South Atlantic to Buenos Aires, on an Axis ship to avoid being torpedoed by the Germans; a bus across the Andes to Chile, where my father learned Spanish in two months; a ship through the Panama Canal to Cuba, finally landing in New Orleans and taking a train to Minneapolis, where a Minneapolis paper records a photograph of my mother, weighing 85 lb from having cared for two boys under the age of three on that harrowing journey. The story of that and other trips throughout my lifetime will be told at another time. We now return to my painful memories of a strange upbringing outside a traditional family.

Two years after my parents left my brother in Shanghai at the Chefoo school there it was my turn, and I was sent to the same school 2000 miles away from my parents to begin a 3½ year separation, first at

Shanghai and then at Kuling. While such an action is unthinkable to the modern mind, particularly American, for centuries the British have had a tradition of boarding schools, to which the upper classes sent their children. British colonial rulers would send their children back to Britain, while parents sipped gin and tonics in far off India. However, even though I was sent to a British style boarding school in China, my parents were neither colonial rulers nor upper class. Instead, they were part of a very large contingent of devout Christian missionaries from the US, Britain and Europe who answered what they believed to be the call of God to bring Jesus and Christianity to China. In their fervour to "spread the Gospel" they somehow forgot, or never knew, the impact of their decision on children who might be caught up in their religious quest.

On return to the US, in my childlike naivety, I thought that perhaps now I would have a chance at a "normal" family, but God once again intervened, and with the closure of China to missionaries, my parents left me at a "mission home" in Illinois as they returned to mission work in South East Asia. Every 3–4 years, they would once again enter my life during their busy furloughs, only to once again find reason to abandon my brother and me for the sake of "China's millions". Thus it has been impossible for me to describe my role in a family in which I was never really a part.

Each Sunday throughout my childhood and adolescence, separated from my parents, I would write a letter telling of my experiences that week, and usually closing with the words "I am fine", all the time knowing that something was deeply wrong about being abandoned at the age of six. It may sound hard to believe to the contemporary secular mind, but I seldom questioned that what they were doing was for God or that the destruction of our family was normal behaviour. The choice they had made between serving God, on the one hand, and separating from, or abandoning, their children on the other seemed to me, at the time, to somehow place them and us on a higher plane. That my parents were serving a "greater good" didn't really cross my mind, although the heartache of separation and regular abandonment have had lifelong effects. It is hard to compete with God.

In hindsight, and after a lifetime of introspection and observation of what such an action did to me and hundreds of other children abandoned throughout the world in the cause of a religious crusade, I have had to conclude that I had personally experienced some of the horrors that can too often result when blind faith and bureaucratic cruelty substitute for common sense and human reason.

That's not the end of the story. In 2016, much to my amazement, many decades after my being sent away to school at the age of six, the Overseas Missionary Fellowship (the successor to the CIM which had decreed that children should be raised in boarding schools) contacted those of us so affected with a letter apologising for the staggering pain they had caused not only us but our parents, and admitting that in the name of God horrible things had been done. My brother, sister and I managed to survive and even thrive by most standards, but numerous friends with whom I grew up in China have spent a lifetime fighting the demons of mental illness, depression, and addiction. Many exhibit the classic symptoms of PTSD, a result of horrific decisions being made by sacrificing one's children on the altar of saving the souls of strangers.

Thus, it came to be when asked at age seventy-five to describe the family in which I was raised, for the first time in my life I answered, I don't know. I wasn't raised in a family.

* * *

Richard (Chefoo, Shanghai and Kuling 1947–53) spent his adolescence at the Wheaton CIM/OMF home. He graduated from Wheaton College (BA in History), Michigan State University (PhD in International Education), taught and researched at university for fifty years. He has worked as an international educational consultant (missions, Fulbright, World Bank, USAID, UNICEF) throughout his career in higher education.

J.D.C.

IF I WERE TO GRAPH my relationship with CIM/OMF as a child and young person, it would be a jagged bar graph: up and down over fifteen years. The left side of the graph would be marked "supportive and compassionate" at the top and "uncaring and harsh" at the bottom. These would be the descriptive terms of the people who assumed responsibility for me while my parents were busy evangelising, starting churches, and translating the Bible into the language spoken by the Yao/Mien people in north Thailand. Across the bottom of the graph would be the years 1952 to 1967. Those were the years I was in school in Bangkok and in the highlands of Malaya (as it was then called) and then living on a thirty-acre farmstead owned by the Mission near Ivyland, Pennsylvania.

I won't name the people at the bottom of the graph, but I encountered them as soon as I was sent to boarding school in Bangkok, when I first arrived in Thailand in November 1952. I had grown up in the loving home of my mother's sister in southwest Iowa. I lived with her because my mother had died when I was an infant, and my father wanted to return to China as a missionary as soon as he could after my mother died, so he handed me off to my aunt and uncle, along with my older brother and sister. When my father remarried in 1951, he reclaimed his children – sort of. He took us from our aunt, who had provided the only home we could remember, and placed the older two (aged ten and eight) in a mission house in Wheaton, Illinois, and took me with him and his new wife to Thailand, where he sent me to boarding school in Bangkok. Later, he explained to me that he had managed his children's lives this way because he wanted us to have a strong connection with the OMF.

The house parents in Bangkok were Dickensian ogres, harsh disciplinarians whose attitude to children ranged from impatient tolerance to open dislike. At age seven I had long ceased wetting the bed at night, but almost as soon as I moved to Bangkok, I started wetting it again. The male ogre responded by waking me before he himself went to bed and insisting that I relieve myself. He stood watching me, scolding me in impatient whispers and slapping me in the face with a wet washcloth to let me know that I needed to wake up and do what he told me. Invariably I was unable to produce anything under those circumstances, and invariably I wet the bed again, provoking fury and displeasure on his part next morning and shame and resentment on mine. I entertained fantasies that ought never to be induced in a child – imagining ways I could torture and kill him. When the school moved to Malaya, the ogres told me I should inform the new house parents, Henry and Mary G., that I was a bed wetter. Accordingly, I conveyed this information to Mary the first evening, when she tucked me in. "You'll be fine, deary", she said. I never wet the bed again.

Henry and Mary are somewhere near the middle between the top and bottom of my imagined bar graph. Henry had grown up in the original Chefoo School in China, and he tried to revive it in Malaya. As soon as the wake-up bell sounded, we boys had to rush to a large bathtub full of cold water and jump into it. We jumped out again as quickly as we could, of course, chattering our teeth and shivering as we dried ourselves off. Henry caned me once, along with two other nine-year-old boys, because he thought we had been trying to see the female servants in their shower. We hadn't, but the more we protested our innocence, the more convinced he became of our guilt. We had been in the vicinity, and that was enough. Mary G. was a trained physician, probably with more awareness of child development than Henry had. She was not harsh, and I think her way of being may have modified his. Still, I remember being puzzled as to why they left their only child in a boarding school in England while they presided over a boarding school for other people's children in Malaya.

In 1956, when I turned eleven years of age, I was repatriated, and the following year the Mission assigned me to a new house for missionaries' children in Philadelphia, because the house in Wheaton had run out of space. Again, the Mission showed its trademark ignorance about young people by appointing an elderly missionary accountant and his wife, whose children had long since grown up, to preside over twelve of us who lived in the mission office building in Germantown. Fortunately, the location was temporary: within a few months, the Mission bought Ivyland, thirty acres in the countryside north of Philadelphia, including a three-story mansion, part of which dated to the seventeenth century, and an enormous barn. The only drawback was that the elderly caretakers came with us. During the first winter, the female house parent once ordered us boys to supply fuel for the large brick fireplace in the kitchen. No firewood had been purchased and stacked, so we were obliged to seek out twigs and branches that had fallen from the many trees on the estate. We decided to play a joke on her. We found a huge fallen branch that took several of us to lift and carry. We knocked on the kitchen door, and when the woman opened it, we called out, "Here's your firewood!" She burst into tears and fled upstairs.

For me, the bar graph tipped up again in 1958, when Ken and Maybeth Gr. accepted the Mission's invitation to serve as house parents in Ivyland. They had been missionaries in China but were unable to return there because Ken had contracted amoebic dysentery. The disease remained latent in a temperate climate, but doctors warned Ken that it would flare up fatally if he returned to the tropics. The Gr's had had more than their share of sorrow. While fleeing the invading Japanese army in China in 1942, their oldest child had died, and they had had to bury her hastily beside the road. Later, scratching out a living on a small farm near Toronto, their youngest son had died at age two of an incurable congenital disease. Despite this, they brought with them not only three adolescent children but cheerfulness, kindness, and genuine care for all the children in their home.

Ken had grown up on a ranch in western Alberta, so he knew a lot about horses and farming. He advertised for horses to board, on the understanding that any of the Mission kids could ride the boarded horses if they wanted to. I learned to halter a horse and to ride bareback, which Ken insisted we should do before we tried to ride with a saddle. I learned to swim and paddle a canoe on the property's three-acre pond, I learned to ice skate and play hockey, and I learned to drive a tractor. Ken bought a small John Deere tractor, which he used to cut two acres of hay in the meadow and to rake it into windrows. The first couple of years, we brought the hay in loose, with a machine that drove over the windrows, picked up the hay, and fed it onto a hay wagon, where we arranged it in a good-sized stack with pitchforks. The tractor pulled the wagon into the barn, and we drove specially designed hay forks into the haystack. These forks were attached to a long rope, which the tractor, now disengaged from the wagon, pulled to lift the load of hay, move it over the hay mow, and dump it. There it provided not only fodder for horses but also hours of endless delight for young adolescents, who played tag on the rafters and often jumped into the hay mow to escape close pursuit. Luckily, no one fell on the wrong side – the side without hay.

Ken used the tractor to plough an open space on the property, where he planted a large vegetable garden. He subscribed to *Organic Gardening and Farming*, and he put its principles into effect. In a couple of years, his garden supplied most of the vegetables for 12–15 hungry adolescents – tomatoes, green beans, beets, carrots, sweet corn, and more. Ken also remodelled a space in the barn for eighty laying hens, who supplied all the eggs for the large family, with many left over. Ken sold eggs to neighbours and kept an account book of expenses and income from this small business, whose proceeds helped defray the cost of other food. The state police helped, too. When a deer was struck on the highway, they phoned to ask if we could use it, and Ken always said we could. He hung up the carcass to bleed in the estate's multi-stall garage, and he skinned and butchered it, packaging and labelling the venison, and freezing the packages in a walk-in freezer that he added to the back of the house. We had venison roast virtually every week for Sunday dinner. Its origin as roadkill did not diminish its nourishing appeal.

Maybeth worked every bit as hard as her husband. She planned menus, bought cartloads of groceries every week, watched over stores in the enormous basement pantry, cooked all the meals, and presided over household chores assigned to everyone. A sheet of paper hung on a bulletin board in the hallway, listing various tasks on one axis, together with the days of the week on another. Where task and day met, a person's name was inscribed, so everyone could see which task was theirs on a particular day. The paper was enclosed in a plastic folder to keep it from becoming worn to illegibility by fingers that constantly ran across it. Maybeth also made jam. I have an indelible mental picture of her, with her glasses on the end of her nose, because they had fogged up from the steam rising out of a huge pot of simmering strawberries that she was preparing to put into sterilised jam jars. The basement pantry held several shelves of these paraffin-topped jars, gradually emptying over the winter until another strawberry harvest came around. I once brought a New York friend home with me from college. "Oh my God!" he exclaimed, when urged to help himself from a heaping bowl of freshly-picked strawberries, "I'd be a Christian too, if I could eat like this!" Most important, Maybeth did the principal emotional parenting – at least she did for me. "Moody" and "adolescent" are synonyms, and I always found in Maybeth a ready listener for my vivid hopes and urgent fears.

That place was my home for ten years – throughout my secondary schooling and four years of college. While the amenities were wonderful, what made it home was the welcome and support provided by Ken and Maybeth. The whole mob of us attended a local Baptist church, until the pastor there preached a sermon called "John Calvin Versus the Word of God." The preacher was a glib Armenian, and Ken was a Presbyterian Calvinist. I can still see him during that sermon, in a rare (for him) adolescent pose: leaning forward, staring at the floor, with his elbows on his knees and his head in his hands. Soon afterwards, he found a church that was more compatible with his theology. Of course, we all followed him there, though it took longer to get to. He was, after all, *in loco parentis*, and we were not equipped to second guess his judgment, because none of us understood the theological issues at stake.

Even from the vantage point of several decades after my sojourn with the OMF, I am not sure what to make of it. Everything depended on the particular people who were charged with my care at any given time, so it was chancy at best. Of course, I had opportunities for travel and cultural enrichment as a child that few children enjoy, but without loving care and support the best opportunities in the world mean very little to those who are presented with them. One effect on me as an adult is that I determined to offer my children better care than I had been shown as a child of the Mission. I found a loving partner who felt the same way I did, and I think we succeeded. But I know that we enjoyed whatever success we had in spite of the OMF, not because of it.

* * *

J.D.C. joined the Overseas Missionary Fellowship at age 7, attending the small school in Bangkok and moving to the Cameron Highlands in 1954 – a blessed relief! He lived for ten years in Ivyland (1957–67) and remained in close contact with Ken & Maybeth for many years after they retired.

Anne

GROWING UP IN a tight-knit Christian community as a missionary kid initially felt safe, like I was in a protective environment. However, all that changed when I was sent to Chefoo School, Malaysia as an innocent seven-year-old. What I ignorantly thought had begun as an adventure, turned into a journey of abandonment, depression, mental illness, and dysfunction that would profoundly and irreversibly affect me deep into adulthood.

I had severe separation anxiety when I started going to Chefoo School. I could not adjust to the fact that my parents had practically dumped me in a place where I barely knew anyone, and that initiated a profound lack of trust for years to come. Intertwined with that distrust was a sense of deeply etched loneliness that followed me into my adult years. As a result of being effectively abandoned, I began not wanting to be alone at all. Even now, at the age of thirty-five, I cannot bear the thought of staying in my apartment alone. I must be constantly engaged in activities and meeting with people so that I do not feel that same sense of abandonment I had at Chefoo. And I desperately need my parents, who are now seventy-three and eighty-one years old. Usually when our parents reach that age, we are the ones helping them. Those roles have been reversed. I depend on my parents heavily, because they were not there for me at a time when I needed them most, and I am now trying to make up for lost time. I realise that I must move on, and be a strong, independent adult, but there is still a young child in me who needs my mom and dad.

In some ways, I reflect the image of an adult who is a capable, successful, autonomous person who can proudly manage her own life without my parents' intervention or assistance. Yet there is an inextricable link that binds us together, making me yearn for their presence and help because of what they were not able to provide for me at a vulnerable time in my life.

The Christian aspect of missionary life and living at Chefoo was difficult as well. I never questioned my parents' faith, although I was never interested in God as much as they were. Subconsciously I must have felt that God was distant because he allowed me to be placed in a location so far away from my parents, and my heart bitterly resented that. Therefore, I never permitted God to be close to me; I just followed the motions of the Christian belief system because I felt that was expected of me. Yet I strongly felt that a God who permitted his own beloved child to suffer in an environment far from home must be a harsh and contradictory God.

My faith was deeply affected as a result of the boarding school experience. It was not until I was a teenager in Chiangmai, Thailand, that I became willing to give my testimony and become baptised, but I don't think I truly knew what I was doing. I was simply bowing to peer pressure and attempting to meet the expectations of my parents. I had an amazing spiritual experience with God a year or two later, but my Christian walk has been bumpy because I could not reconcile a God who allowed me to suffer in silence at a boarding school far from my parents, with a loving, compassionate God. In fact, it was not until my adult years that I matured in my faith and started believing that maybe, just maybe, God loved me. Those three and a half years at boarding school, and my parents' decision to send me there, certainly indicated to me that he did not. My heart strongly resisted being in a relationship with a God who did not prevent my parents from participating in such an awful deed. Yet part of me struggled against that resistance because I had been taught, since I was young, that I needed to be in church, worship God, and respect my elders – that is what a good Christian was supposed to do. As a teenager, my resistance turned into rebellion, and I began hanging out with people who were of questionable influence, at least according to my parents. Spending time with these friends did not result in drug use, joyriding, self-harm, or anything of that nature, but my parents suspected these people had had a negative impact on me. My father insists to this day that he had to crack down on me because of my rebellious behaviour, but I think the truth is that I rebelled because he was so strict with me. And I simply did not want to follow the straight-and-narrow like he and my mom did. I wanted a little flexibility, along with the freedom to explore life more than he allowed me to.

I felt numb and sorrowful much of the time that I was in boarding school. In fact, I truly believe that my depression began while I was at Chefoo. I knew I experienced a deep internalisation of my feelings while I was in one of the upper levels at Chefoo; I believe it to have been fourth or fifth grade. I could not function very well, and I withdrew from people. That depression later resurfaced in ninth grade, when I was living in Chiangmai, Thailand, once again reunited with my parents. At that point, little was known about mental health and what treatments were effective, the medication that was prescribed for me was ineffective, and I continued being depressed off and on throughout high school.

My parents made another questionable decision in sending me to college before I was prepared for it, and even at the beginning of that first semester, I had severe depression and was not connected with an educated therapist, or psychiatrist, who could offer the help that I needed. My "depression" was later diagnosed as bipolar disorder, when I was twenty-three years old and living in Los Angeles, California. Although there are numerous theories about why I developed bipolar, a very wise and knowledgeable psychiatrist once said to me she believed it to be partially a genetic predisposition, and partially a product of nurture. Therefore, I think that my childhood experiences could very well have contributed to my bipolar disorder. Although my mental-health disorder is in full remission now, there is still a deep-rooted anger, which emerges at unlikely times from unpredictable triggers, and this anger is likely due to my unresolved issues concerning having been placed in boarding school. There is a medication I am taking for this anger component, but it only controls it at an 80% effectiveness. I must control the remainder of the angry feelings through wise choices. It is still a difficult road, and a permanent condition that I will have to deal with for the remainder of my life, but it is manageable, and I am still able to enjoy a very productive, humorous, and sociable life.

I have burned many bridges of friendship throughout my life because I get easily hurt and take things the wrong way much of the time. I believe this is due to not having been able to confide my hurts to my parents while I was a child. If I had had a healthy childhood, I think I would have been able to have healthier adult relationships, but because I had no one to turn to when I was young, I was not taught how to handle disappointment, pain, and disagreements between friends. I was also not taught how to navigate social cues, guard my heart, and respond appropriately to others, which severely impacted my ability to respond wisely to issues that I had with friends while growing up. I think that my parents simply assumed that I was taught these things at Chefoo; it was like they expected the dorm aunts and teachers to parent me, when their roles were simply supervising and teaching, respectively.

As a result of not being taught how to be a friend, I stumbled blindly in that area and got to the point where I handled friendships in a dysfunctional manner. I pushed people away when I didn't know how to handle confrontation and disappointment, and I rejected people, who would have been a positive influence on my life, because I was simply shell-shocked when it came to knowing how to navigate those waters. My parents did not try to help me, even when I was a teenager and living with them. They were also older parents who did not know how to guide a teenager through the difficulties of that world. Consequently, I did not have a functional social life. I was a total misfit who, once again, desperately needed her parents' guidance but did not receive it.

My identity as a whole was greatly affected by my time at Chefoo. I strongly believe that the separation anxiety led to the depression, and later bipolar disorder, which became the pendulum around which my entire life functioned. Indubitably, I would not have had this burden to carry if I had not been abandoned as a child. For a time before I was officially diagnosed (and this took years), I greatly resented the parental presence. I gave birth to my first child when I was twenty-three, after which I experienced severe postpartum depression. This led me to adopt him out and move to California, believing my parents were the source of my problems. I blamed them for everything, regardless of whether it was related to them or not, because I was so angry about their ill-informed decision to send me to boarding school. I suffered a toxic psychotic breakdown due to a lack of support and mental-health intervention while I was in California, and I was sent back to New York State to live with my parents. But I absolutely did not want to be around them, so I wandered around like a vagabond, sleeping on people's couches and beds from night to night.

I met someone who, upon learning of my story, bought me a one-way plane ticket back to California, where I landed in another two hospitals before being stabilised. I firmly believe that my abandonment at Chefoo is the cause of my bipolar disorder, the shock to my system disconnected something in my brain, which led to a series of diagnoses including: Bipolar Disorder, Schizoaffective Disorder (diagnosed by one therapist), Post Traumatic Stress Disorder, and Borderline Personality Disorder. My mental health simply could not handle the trauma that I had to endure, so it developed coping mechanisms that would allow me to survive amidst the horrors that were being done to my brain.

Chefoo almost ruined me. I have had numerous setbacks, including four hospitalizations, a series of panic attacks that I have to battle with each day, and constant anger directed at my parents, or at random strangers. I also could not hold down a job between 2010 and 2016. I can function now, yes, but that anger has not dissipated, nor have my diagnoses altered at all. I have to see a therapist every two weeks, just to deal with daily life problems that I cannot manage on my own, and a lot of the time I am an emotional mess. I am dealing with all of these issues, in addition to attempting to raise a ten-year-old by myself, who can be more than a handful. It is overwhelming most of the time, and I have chronic anxiety as well.

I have held down a job as a cashier for three years, but some days my illness makes me want to throw in the towel, pull the covers over my head, and never show up to work again. However, my son keeps me going, and so does the love and support of my friends and parents. If it were not for them, I would have quit a long time ago. Despite my difficulties with this illness, I am pressing on, hoping to use my recently acquired paralegal degree, and Notary Public status, to attain a different job where I can use skills that are more suited to my abilities and education. Usually, I triumph, saying with conviction that I got out of bed today, went to work, dealt with my problems, and parented effectively. So the effects of having been at Chefoo have not completely vanquished me. But I still greatly feel the impact of Chefoo, a negative one that presses at the back of my mind and never goes away.

Having mused about all of this, I have to conclude that young children should never be sent to boarding school. Some have turned out just fine but the risk is too great to take. Numerous children, including myself, have been psychologically harmed by the feelings of abandonment associated with being left in a boarding school setting. The confusion, hurt, separation anxiety, and psychological shock evidenced from many kids' experiences at boarding school should make parents think twice about sending them there. Children need to be raised primarily at home in their early years, so that their parents can teach them how to navigate through the emotional responses of life, and so that they can receive the love they so desperately need at that vulnerable age. That love cannot come from a teacher, dorm aunt, or any other staff member. It must be given by the parent, and that cannot be adequately done if that parent is hundreds of miles away.

I was never in a situation where I had to consider sending my own son away to boarding school, but I know I want to be the person that he gets his love, guidance, and teaching from. I keep him very close to me, I'm extremely protective of him and overly concerned that I provide everything that he needs. It seems that our parents were primarily concerned with offering heathen people what they needed, (I still feel that others came before my sister and I in my parents' eyes), rather than making parenting a huge priority. I firmly believe that prospective missionaries should responsibly exercise planned parenthood and postpone their career on the mission field to be nurturing caregivers. Then, when their children are older and can better withstand the changing of the tides, they can follow their dreams, or God's calling, as some call it. I wish our parents had considered our needs before their own, because as a parent, that is what a person is called to do. I think it is a load of crock for them to claim that God's calling on their lives supersedes their calling as parents. Because they acted in this way, I have trouble accepting missions in my life when they appear in my church, or my community, in the form of a Missions Conference. I cringe when I have to listen to the work missionaries are doing around the world because it reawakens the emotions associated with my being in boarding school.

I believe I am a stronger person now than I was ten years ago, but that does not change the fact that I have compounded emotional issues as a result of the boarding school experience that first scarred me twenty-eight years ago. I feel that I would have a more settled and beautiful life now had I not experienced that abandonment from my parents. I will live with the daily impacts of bipolar disorder, and borderline personality disorder, for the remainder of my life because of the one life-altering decision my parents made all those years ago. I still struggle with forgiving my parents because they do not acknowledge that they chose to make this decision; to them, it was inevitable, something Overseas Missionary Fellowship made them do. Yet I hope that my struggle, that I live with every day, will someday help someone else with similar emotional difficulties, or life circumstances, and that my struggle will not have been in vain.

* * *

Anne attended Chefoo School between January 1992 and June 1995, when she had her fifth-grade graduation.

Interlude 2:
Alone

Steve

There was a place
A green and cool and lovely place
A place where children told of high times
and laughter
and fun
and together
A place far from the new heat
far from the raw smells
and embrace of strange sounds
and prickles of sweat

These were promises given by adults and children who had been there
before

A place where fun in the clouds, lessons in books far from foreign
tongues,
a place of together
and good
and cool mountain freshness

But what was not mentioned was the Alone

The trip was long,
the scream of train wheels in the night,
the sliding back and forth on leather seats
with scowling taxi drivers
around corners into the clouds,
racing from the slightly known
and embrace of family
to the unknown slopes of where God has decided we must go

And amidst the rush and smiles and promises there was also
Alone

The new parents,
women with no children yet somehow many
Who embraced
yet also held at arm's length those who felt the lack of
mothers
fathers
family
Who claimed that good children did not cry
Good children were loved by God for being
Alone

And so the days of fun
and laughter
and secret sighs began
The digging in dirt
erecting sticks and ferns into jungle forts
Running through mists with battle cries
Chasing wings of bluest blue
and greenest green
through the forests in the clouds
Days of laughter and delight
And yet nights of nothing but
Alone
The time passed,

soon it was time to return home,
to travel back down into the heat
and the humid stench of tropical bodies
and smells of foods unknown
Back to arms of
parents
siblings
who claimed love and care
who showered hugs and tears
But there was still
Alone
Hovering over the hugs
with threats of soon
With remembrances of loss and crying silently
or not so silently
in the night
There was still
Alone

3

Damage Done

Long term separation from parents leaves children vulnerable to trauma. A child can cope with trauma if they have a safe person with them. These stories tell of events that hurt and left scars.

Kerry

AS THE DAYS TURN colder in the fall, I light the old wood stove in my living room and my daughter watches. Almost every time I remember other fires; fires I lit in the past. I feel the room change like it did when I was a boy of ten, tending the evening fire for my parents at a missionary bungalow. I remember the smell of the kerosene I used to start the fires and the shine of the copper mantel over the bungalow fireplace. I remember the gaze of eyes from the past, the eyes of missionaries who sat before my fires. And more than anyone, the fire reminds me of a missionary named Minka H.

Every day, missionaries came up from the heat of the lowlands, from far lands, ascending out of Tapah to wind up thirty-six miles of road into the Cameron Highlands, a lush, green, and cool mountain region on peninsular Malaysia. While I hunted butterflies on the quiet, jungled banks of the bungalow I could hear the buzz of a Mercedes 190 diesel taxi engine, lugging up inclines and around sharp curves, then revving with the upshift, a steady rhythm, rhyming sometimes with the din of cicadas. Now, if I close my eyes, I see the insides of the taxis – spotlessly clean, filled with the smell of leather, diesel, and hair tonic. Little Buddhist lanterns dangle from the rear-view mirror while the driver hums softly to the muted clamour of a Chinese opera on the radio. Sometimes, if you caught the ride from Kuala Lumpur, the driver was a Sikh, wild-eyed and dark-bearded with a cream or pink silk turban. I used to watch to see if it was true – if Sikhs carried knives in their turbans. Eventually the taxis came through the gate, up the drive and I heard the soft crunch of gravel and the chuckle of the diesel motor as it slowed to an idle in front of the bungalow's entrance porch. Then, if my butterfly net hung still, unstirred by the wind of a chase, I leaned against its handle and watched them get out of the taxis: tired, careworn, on the verge of nervous breakdowns, broken down, close to divorce, depressed. Wrung out by a life they had chosen.

That's how I first remember seeing Minka. Minka struggled from the taxi seat, a missionary from Southeast Asia, come for vacation, or "holiday" as the British ones were apt to say, in the Cameron Highlands. Come to stay at the Bungalow where my parents were host and hostess. The bungalow was a Chinese millionaire's mansion, donated long ago to the mission. It faced west, looking out over a valley. A stone breezeway connected a short tower to the main building. Peep holes in the tower let the Chinese avoid the police when mahjongg and all other gambling was illegal. My job, my chore that let me meet missionaries like Minka, was to take care of the fires at the bungalow, to split the wood, manage the woodshed, lay the evening fire, and replenish an old green bottle with the kerosene used to start the fire. And I polished the enormous mantle that hung over the fireplace. As a boy I thought it was huge, a long piece of pure copper, moulded and ball-peened for texture. I rubbed it with Brasso, cleansing it until it shone white-orange.

In the evenings, before the missionaries came in from dinner, I went to the fireplace, pulled the cork out of the bottle, and poured out some of the kerosene on the fire I had laid, covering it with fluid like a peace offering. When the kerosene ran through the wood and paper and started dripping on the grate, I struck a match and lit it, stepping back for the initial explosion of flame and black smoke. Standing before the growing fire, I felt eyes in the room looking at my back and turned to see the missionaries sitting, dazed from my mother's dinner cuisine. Some were tatting[12], while others were knitting or crocheting. Men were usually reading or trying to tune in the BBC, sometimes

12 Tatting is a technique for handcrafting a particularly durable lace from a series of knots and loops. It was hugely popular at the time amongst the ladies. Auntie Ina even gave lessons.

talking quietly or ardently. Others stared in silence at the gathering flames beside me, sitting there only to treasure moments of peace and warmth, remembering homes and relatives who were not the same homes and relatives they had left. Some would question my judgment as I doled out the kerosene on a sometimes-sluggish fire,

"Are you sure you know what you're doing, young man?"

The crocheting had stopped for one woman, and she peered at me over her glasses. I left the room that time and told my father, but he knew what I was doing, that I was responsible, and the questioning words had no lasting effect.

Other missionaries talked to me, brought me into their life like I was one of them, as though I were their age. Minka was one of these, one who told me stories, showed pictures, asked me about the house butterfly collections, or pulled practical jokes on me. One woman taught me how to play the ukulele, another showed me how to tat. Others just loved to talk. Today, I cannot remember Minka's words, I cannot remember her voice and I can barely see her face. She was from the Netherlands and I remember that she came and sat before my fires, resting from her work with another woman in South Thailand. When you see someone's eyes and you talk to them, when you hear their stories and they listen to you, a bond is established, memory grows and stays, burning warm. I cannot remember Minka – but I can.

I can because she died a violent death and she sat before my fires. I had heard about death, seen it on the newspaper page, talked about it. But it was not a part of my memory until Minka. Minka worked, with another woman, in South Thailand, riding the jungle trails on old Honda trail bikes. Years of service increased the burden of her heart to help the tribes of South Thailand. I had walked jungle trails similar to the ones she rode, flat rotting ways through dark canopies, spongy to the step for all the roots and decay that lay above the clay soil. When I heard the news that she had been taken hostage by terrorists I could see what had happened. The sputtering of a trailbike, pushed to its limits up a hill, then snapping and crackling from back pressure as it rolled down another, and then... brakes because a group of men stood on the trail. Some wore black clothes, traditional clothes.

Others wore modern pants. Doubtless, all were armed and one, or all, wore sunglasses. And doubtless, they greeted the women with a smile, the Asian greeting that can symbolise embarrassment, pride, humour, and whatever else its wearer chooses it to mean. Perhaps their faces could not be seen at all. What third world anarchy they had in their hearts I do not know. Perhaps the power and ability to take a life consumed their minds; they knew that others, small factions like themselves, had differing views and were just as eager to shoot out their minds. Was it the political flavour of the week? Had they upset a local drug lord? The women may even have known the men; familiarity provokes ideas and stimulates plans. Western women meant western money if extortion were successful. They held the women hostage. Tied them up. My young mind thought of no other terrors that might have been inflicted but my mind now knows, and my spirit groans, to think too long. Policy. What policy meant was no money for the terrorists. No money, no negotiation. Two lives for the lives of the many others, whom others would follow if demands were met. They shot the women in the back on a jungle trail. Was it a short burst, or the full-automatic squeeze, the angered unloading of magazines at a system that would not provide?

I can't remember where I heard the news. I do know that the colour of life was more golden, purer yet harsher. I know that I had to catch butterflies, that I had to be near my parents, that I had to climb jungle trails with my friends while I still knew them. Life had an end. The evening fires continued beyond the news of Minka's death. I held that responsibility until I was twelve and my family left Malaysia for America and Washington state. I split the kindling, replenished the kerosene, and laid the fires. I paid more attention to their warmth and sometimes I tried to make them as warm as possible, so warm that the mantel was too hot to touch. The missionaries' eyes continued to watch the fires, holding the warmth, adding a pleasant memory to the painful, soothing away the creases of a life of sacrifice.

* * *

Kerry's family arrived in Asia in 1964 when he was four. He was at Chefoo from 1965 until 1972, with a year for furlough stateside in 1968. He is an English major run amok – after working over 25 years in high tech and IT, as a technical writer, UNIX system administrator, Enterprise Resource planning system Database Administrator, staff manager and finally as an executive, he called it quits and now works as a writer, travel coordinator and general factotum for whoever will hire him.

From the beginning through to today, Kerry's question is "Does it have to be this way?" Kerry lives in Vancouver, Washington, with his wonderful wife Marla, where they daily live to hatch new adventures and take as many pictures as possible.

Anonymous

By the time I turned eight my parents' missionary career, and therefore my Chefoo school days, were already over and my whole family was living together for the first time back in our "home" country. I remember one night when my mother was tucking me into bed, and I started crying, "I want to go back to Chefoo ...*(sob)*... the teachers love you there." My unhappiness at grade school (where I evidently didn't feel cared for by my teacher) wasn't the biggest challenge I faced during the next few years that my family lived together full-time. While I had many fun times with my family, some of my experiences, as the youngest sibling, left me deeply traumatised and have had long-term effects. I would like to write about why I think boarding school contributed to some of the destructive dynamics between us, and therefore to my trauma.

My sister (quite a few years older than I) was sent to board at Chefoo a few months before I was born. She once told me that she came home from her first term of four months away, saw this little baby girl (me) and thought, "So *that's* why I was sent to boarding school." Being the perceived, or possibly true, reason for her being sent away from the family wasn't a great start to my relationship with my sister. In my early childhood she was a big, grown-up person whom I saw for a few days at Chefoo when we visited each term and who joined us twice a year for two months' holiday.

My brother and I, being closer in age and the only children left at home, were hardly ever apart. We visited the neighbours' pigs together, ran away from vicious black dogs, climbed trees in the backyard, imitated the noisy frogs under our bedroom window, and watched our gardener chase chickens with his machete (for dinner!) When I was five my beloved brother suddenly disappeared from my life, for it was now his turn to be schooled, and he too had been sent to Chefoo. I pushed my bed next to his empty one, in the room we had shared, to try and feel close to him as I went to sleep.

By the time I went to Chefoo the following year, it was a familiar place to me, but I don't have any clear memories of my brother there, and my sister had already left for further schooling in another country. My brother and I would have sat at the same table for Sunday lunch (the only meal for which the seating wasn't arranged by dorms but by family groups). I have a photo of us sitting on the step outside one of the classrooms, on either side of our "letter writer" Miss T., to whom we dictated letters to mom and dad, since in Levels 1 and 2 we were considered too young to write fluently.

When the Mission asked my parents to leave Asia to do a different job, mom and dad collected my brother and me from Chefoo, and my sister from her boarding school, and flew "home". Thus started our real family life. Some of my abiding memories of these years, with us all living together, are of my sister letting me sit on her lap, and of her playing really fun games with my brother and me. I cherish these memories. My sister, by this time, seemed to me like a grown-up, though she was only a teenager, and she was immensely powerful in my eyes. Another memory of these years is of being called a "cry-baby". Although my sister was often very kind and loving she did not seem to cope with any tears on my part. In fact sometimes she was the cause of those tears: pulling my hair, pinching me or doing other things that made me feel hurt or afraid in some way. When I went crying to my mother my sister would say, "Don't be so stupid, it wasn't *that* bad." (Maybe I was a really annoying little sister and she had reached her threshold of tolerance with me.) Mom and dad often left my brother and me in my sister's care, especially as she got older. On days when the mercury was over 100, they would let us skip school and go to the local swimming pool where we would play the whole hot day. Sometimes in the middle of playing, my sister would hold my head under the water, not long enough to actually drown me but long enough for me to feel like I was going to. I didn't tell my parents. I knew my sister would say she was just playing, it wasn't that bad, and that I was a weakling. Perhaps from her perspective these things were true.

My brother and I were once again sharing a bedroom and played happily together much of the time, as we had done before our Chefoo days. But now, post-Chefoo, he started to hit or kick my arm or leg when he got frustrated or annoyed with me. Like my sister he would call me a cry-baby when I went to mom or dad upset about being hurt by him. When I started developing breasts, he started hitting my breasts instead; he knew that *really* hurt. One day when I was walking down the hallway, I heard him call out to me from our parents' bedroom. I went in. I still looked up to him, and always went along with his games, until they weren't fun anymore. On this particular day, the moment his game stopped being fun was when I realised that he was trying to have sex with me. I had no construct in my mind for this. What I knew about sex was that mommies and daddies did it to make babies. I couldn't understand – why was my brother trying to make a baby with me?

In the following years, my brother and I were each other's only companions, with my sister now in college. Like most children who have been sexually abused I tried to act as if nothing had happened. I also knew that I was stuck in the same family with him, so I had to make the best of it. We never had a normal brother/sister relationship again, although I don't know if any adults noticed. I had stopped telling mom and dad about most of the things that made me feel hurt; I think I sensed it wouldn't help. Also, I could see that mom and dad were stressed about many issues to do with coming "home" from Asia, some of which lasted years.

Once, when we were teenagers, mom and dad were away for the weekend, so my brother and I were in our house alone. We started to argue over what to watch on TV. When I decided (for once) to be more assertive in what I wanted instead of just giving in to him he reached out and slapped my face hard. It was a bitterly cold night, but

I went outside to walk in the snow by myself to try to process what had just happened.

Around this time he stopped hitting my breasts, but he regularly made comments about my appearance and my bodily functions. He often looked at me and spoke to me with what I felt was disgust. He would say things like, "You're fat. I don't want a fat sister." I experienced my brother as emotionally abusive and demeaning towards me into our adult years, until I decided to stop seeing him.

I know that my mother deeply regretted sending us all to boarding school. Maybe she sensed the destructive impact on all of our family relationships, even though she died before I could tell her about the worst incidents I had experienced from my siblings. Part of the culture of Chefoo– from the staff, – was not to cry, so when my sister called me a cry-baby, perhaps she was copying what she had been told (implicitly or explicitly) at Chefoo. Perhaps she couldn't tolerate how it made her feel, seeing me crying and going to mom for comfort, because when she was my age she *couldn't* go to mom for comfort but had to be tough. A child who is inadequately comforted can end up despising weakness in others. I think, from her perspective, I was far too sensitive and cried too much; I think it was true that I cried the most out of the children in our family.

I wonder about the impact on both of us of me being the "reason" she was sent away. Maybe my sister's behaviour towards me made her feel powerful in a life which had left her feeling powerless. Maybe my feeling of being bullied was partly because the powerlessness I experienced in boarding school had made me less resilient, even to normal rough and tumble. Thus perhaps Chefoo helped to create both a "bully" and a "victim".

I recently read some research which stated that adolescent boys who sexually abused their younger sisters are much more likely to have experienced early separation from a primary caregiver, and/or bullying or other trauma. In addition, I've heard through the Chefoo network that some boys were sexually abused by local people before they even got to boarding school, which led to sexualised behaviour in boys' dorms at Chefoo. I wonder if these contributed to my brother's sexual abuse of me. I know that mine isn't the only Chefoo family in which an older brother sexually abused his sister.

The effect of Chefoo on me, directly and indirectly, left me with a deep shame about feeling sad or hurt. After my mother died, I wrote in my journal "It's my fault that this hurts me so much." Even now, when I feel distressed it is almost always followed by feeling afraid and/or ashamed. Unfortunately, I still feel it is not safe for me to show distress in my family. Fortunately, I have friends who think it is fine to cry and be upset. I long for a closer relationship with my siblings.

I don't know for sure if things would have been different if we hadn't been to boarding school; I think there were some underlying unhealthy family dynamics and attitudes present. But I suspect that the separations, which interrupted family bonding, the trauma for all of us of going to boarding school so young, and the culture of not being allowed to express sadness and distress all contributed.

* * *

Some details have been changed to protect the author.

Bruce

Otago Daily Times, Saturday 6 October 2018, Life & Style Magazine.
Included by permission of the Editor, Otago Daily Times

I VIVIDLY RECALL the moment I thought I had gone mad.

Minutes before, I had phoned the Dunedin Central Police station to alert them to an email threatening violence against the Prime Minister. Now, I was sitting at my newspaper office desk waiting for the police to arrive, wondering whether I had made it all up. Panic, which had become a constant and cruel companion, hugged me tight. Cold sweat soaked my armpits. My head spun. I gripped the underside of the workstation, fighting to extract one objective thought from a terrified fog-filled brain. Maybe this illogical, gnawing fear, which I was desperate to keep secret, was a sign I was losing my mind. Maybe I had already stepped over the edge. Maybe the email did not exist at all. Maybe the police were on their way to cart me off. That was all 10 years ago, this month.

That year, 2008, was a colossus. Sir Edmund Hillary died. China hosted the 24th summer Olympics Games. The Global Financial Crunch hit, and the Great Recession began. Helen Clark was toppled by John Key. I was a few months back into a reporting job at *The Star* community paper in Dunedin. After a three-year diversion that ended messily, I had scampered back to journalism, tail between my legs. The fear had built in waves during the previous 18 months.

The first couple of instalments, months apart, were a curiosity to me as someone who enjoyed the pace and pressure of news media, was an experienced public speaker, an idealist, a risk taker, a husband and busy father of four fabulous kids. Yes, there had always been some inner tension, some underlying dis-ease. But that was ankle deep, whereas this was threatening to submerge me. By October, as each successive wave mounted with shorter intervals, fear of the fear took hold. It is this panic that the panic will overwhelm and expose you, that is the deep demon of anxiety disorders.

The years 2008 to 2010 were a living hell. Days were spent fighting panic at every conversation, every ring of the phone, every effort to find an angle and construct a story. Nights were worse. I often woke about 3am, adrift in a sea of unfathomable dread. I never wanted to kill myself, but the idea of no longer existing seemed sweet relief.

It was horrific – yet unremarkable. Anxiety and depression are a plague on Western society, especially New Zealand. It is only getting worse, becoming decidedly common. About 17% of New Zealanders have been diagnosed with depression, anxiety, bipolar disorder or a bitter cocktail of the above, at some point in their lives. During the next 12 months, 228,000 Kiwis are predicted to experience a major depressive disorder. Globally, the World Health Organisation believes mental illness will become the second leading cause of disability within two years. Garden variety, moderate-to-acute anxiety and depression. Myriad indistinguishable panicked snails sliming their tortured way across a seemingly endless salt pan.

Ten years ago, Sir John Kirwan was still blazing the honesty trail, getting Kiwis to talk about it. As anxiety flared in my brain, I got the opportunity to interview him, by phone, in Japan, where he was coaching that country's national rugby team. The conversation was to be wide ranging, allowing my desperate, secret question to be asked, "Does the anxiety go away and never return?"

"That's not the point," he replied. The point was that there was always a positive step one could take to get to a better place. With hindsight, he was right. At the time however, it left me comfortless, still nursing my awful hidden reality.

It is pleasing, and important, that we now hear more voices owning their experience of mental illness. What we do not hear so much about, is the process of recovery. The long, difficult, but decidedly do-able road back to our old selves and, hopefully, eventually, to somewhere even better. For me, the secret of my mental ill-health was the first prison that had to go. For what seemed like an eternity, I had been locked in a state of anxiety about my anxiety, ever fearful that the next moment would be overwhelming, without an understanding of what was happening but unable to access that information for fear that telling anyone would only confirm I was indeed an inadequate failure. I wish I had sought help at the first flushes of panic. But I can dig in like nobody's business. I endured two years before the torment forced my hand.

"You're not going mad. And I can tell you, you will get better." A soothing ointment, a lifeline, from a wise, kind counsellor, a woman in her 70s with decades of experience, after she had heard me out. Reaching out was the beginning. But there was so much ground to recover. Once, I had enjoyed asking difficult, probing questions. Now, each time I lifted the telephone receiver, intense anxiety flooded me. In the past, I had scaled scaffolding to the top of the Dunedin Railway Station Clocktower. Now, walking down a flight of stairs made my head swim. At home, once passionate, witty and adventurous, I was reduced to an automaton. (Those closest to me paid a price. That is my one true remaining regret.) The worst part of each week was the Thursday morning planning meetings at a local café. I was a competent capable journalist, but performance and social anxiety reduced me to stony faced, clipped phrases as I clung to the underside of the table, fighting the urge to bolt from the building.

At the bottom of it all, of course, there lay baggage. Childhood insecurity, followed by almost two decades of theoretical belief that I was loved, that I was okay, was belied by strenuous efforts to get significance and approval from others; and then a series of events that washed away the wobbly pillars of my house. All that was left was a largely theoretical foundation. We all need an immovable bedrock. For some, it is themselves. For others, their reasoning, the Universe, Elvis... Mine became God, in practice, not just theory. Some would say that should be enough, everything. Reality is, while I now truly knew for the first time that it was okay, would be okay, no matter what, a fear process had established itself in my brain. For several years, my brain had been building an extensive back catalogue of experiences it interpreted as fearful. A mind loop was set up. The amygdala, the almond-sized primal brain detected a threat. A flood of adrenalin and cortisol was released, creating a hyper-attentive state. The neo-cortex scanned memories for explanations of this arousal. If what was going on – a phone ringing, having a conversation, driving across a bridge – had been labelled "fearful" by a past experience, then fear was offered to my conscious brain as the appropriate emotion. Deep ruts were created that ran directly from any stimuli (past, present and future) to a fear response. By simple, tragic repetition, I had trained my brain to be scared of virtually everything.

And it had layers. Boy, did it have layers. Imagine reaching for the phone. Try panicking about how the person will respond; the possibility they will be angry or tearful. Add a sudden consternation that you might freeze and be unable to explain yourself. Run a system scan to assess how panicked you are. Panic about that. Also try to gauge how anyone within earshot might be reacting to your phone manner and catastrophise your possible involuntary reaction to their undoubted scorn. Do all the above at the same time. I concluded I would have to be content with years of rewiring.

Shaun Robinson, chief executive of the Mental Health Foundation, says New Zealand has a smorgasbord of treatment options for mental health and addiction issues. He cites therapeutic, peer support, kaupapa Maori, physical exercise, psycho-educational and community support approaches. He says during the 2016–17 year, 1.5 million individual treatment sessions were provided. I sought skills wherever I could find them. Cognitive Behavioural Therapy, Mindfulness, Acceptance Commitment Therapy... For five or six years I was a serial therapy monogamist, diligently squeezing one approach dry and then moving on to the next.

Giving my terrified mind timeout was an important tool. There is a toilet cubicle on the second floor of the ODT building in Dunedin that has a simple but beautiful, early 20th-century geared locking mechanism. For a couple of years, three or four times a day, I would slide it shut, slump against the wall and, with my eyes shut, imagine my body floating in a tropical island lagoon. Then two or three minutes later, I would go back down the hall and carry on with whatever article I was working on.

For years, I carried scraps of paper in my pockets; affirmations I would pull out and read on my way to interviews or whenever there was a quiet moment. Many of these affirmations had started as moments of night-time terror. I learnt not just to lie there in a pool of cold sweat but to go sit in the lounge under a small pool of lamp light and, with pen and paper, identify and own the fear. Then I'd write down what logic told me about that feared scenario. Next came advice to myself about how to think about the situation. Lastly, I summarised it in a few concise affirmations, tore it off the sheet and carried it around for several weeks until I felt it getting through, creating a new pathway in my mind.

There were a couple of tricks that I haven't seen in any texts on anxiety. Like, yelling. I wanted a faster way to get reality through to my subconscious. So I tried yelling, as loud as I could, a bunch of statements about what I believed to be true about myself and my life. And it worked. I remember returning to the office and having a whole glorious afternoon almost free of mind-fog. It did not work so well the next time, but I knew it was helping.

So, I started yelling, every morning, while driving to work. I tried not to yell while following or driving towards other traffic. But it wasn't always possible. If, a few years back, you were thrown by the sight of someone apparently, inaudibly (I hope) and unaccountably yelling at you from their car, I apologise to all of you. It really was doing me some good.

Another place I yelled was at the beach. Once a month, on a beautiful, isolated stretch of sand between Brighton and Taieri Mouth, I let it all hang out. Whatever wanted to come to the surface was allowed to, then examined and dealt with. A lot of abuse, and forgiveness, was meted out on that stomping ground. The time spent alone with nature, observing its rhythms and truths, taught some valuable life lessons. Lessons I turned into a possibly unforgivable piece of performance poetry.

The other magic trick was massage. When your fear is stored as tension in your body, and awareness of that only adds to your worry, a good 25 minute, $30 deep-tissue massage at the local mall can seem as beneficial as a 50 minute, $175 session with a highly qualified psychologist. There's a PhD in that, right there. I still get neck and shoulder massages once a month.

For some, what's needed to improve mental health is more fundamental than a good counsellor and a soundproof car. Robinson agrees New Zealand needs increased access to free or heavily subsidised therapies and supports, "so that help is accessible and affordable for all". But he also emphasises that the country needs a high level Mental Health Action Plan that will reduce the "social drivers" of poor mental health. I didn't take medication. I would like to have. But every time I got close, I pulled back, knowing the pain was keeping pushing me forward and that psychotherapy, if applied consistently, promised lasting results.

In 2012, in this limping fashion, I was named joint news feature writer at the *Otago Daily Times*. Since then, I've twice been a finalist in national media competitions. This year, the *OTD's* weekend magazine [*in which this article was originally published – Ed's note*] was named the best newspaper inserted magazine in the country. I add these boasts simply to underscore the point that mental distress does not mean you're only good for the scrap heap. It is important to realise the recovery process is not smooth, or as Robinson puts it, "not linear".

"There can be set-backs and triumphs along the way," he says. "What's important is that people have good support from *whanau*, friends and health professionals."

Two steps forwards, one back. In the middle of this crazy little rhumba, however, it often seems the order is reversed. The new job felt like a huge step forward. A year later, however, my 20-plus-year marriage had stalled and died. It was a greater tragedy than the disruption that had triggered the original attacks. But I now had an expanding anxiety toolkit. It did not sink me. In fact, I grew. As they remind themselves at AA meetings (presumably plagiarizing the advice on packets of laxatives), the reality is always that "this too shall pass". Deliberately retaking the ground I had ceded to anxiety was crucial. Joining Toastmasters; taking up Tai Chi; returning to church; swimming and cycling; initiating a regular curry, beer and pool night with an eclectic bunch of old and new mates – they were all calculated ways of giving fear the middle finger.

One autumn, when I had not talked to a counsellor for at least a year, the anxiety suddenly surged. Two sessions with a psychologist and a book on mindfulness later, I was back on path. Learning to live in the present – the ordinary, mundane moment – rather than living in an ever-looming catastrophe inside your head, is a wonderful skill. Almost a year later, it happened again. Back to the psychologist, a new set of tools to begin applying and away I went again. Each new stage felt like being on a circus trapeze. In order to lay hold of the new freedom proffered, it was necessary to let go of something that was giving security right now. In doing so, there were always those scary moments when I was holding neither, in freefall.

For instance, learning not to worry about being worried. Growing up, being able to imagine what might go wrong and prepare myself for it, was a coping mechanism. As an adult in the grip of anxiety, capturing those anxious thoughts and replacing them with truer, more positive ones, had been an important, almost fulltime job. Being confronted with the idea that paying close attention to the anxiety was counterproductive seemed almost sacrilege. Telling a worrier it is important (and therefore requiring worry) that they don't worry is a serious discombobulator. Dismissing the anxiety with "Oh, just that again. That's nothing to worry about" was a significant leap of faith.

The third autumn, before my old seasonal affective friend could revisit, I met someone new. Love is the opposite of fear. It gives energy, directs the focus outwards and encourages all sorts of healthy risk-taking. My world expanded. I felt better than I had in years. We've been married 18 months.

It's Wednesday afternoon. I'm sitting at my desk, typing these concluding paragraphs. Around me are good journalists, good people, busy at their work. A decade after the first panic attacks, I'd say by most measures I'm 80% to 90% back. I have wrested my body and mind from fear. I have skills to manage the residual low-level anxiety. I still want to make headway – some situations in the newsroom continue to unduly concern me and I'd like to ride a rollercoaster again. But I am once again able to freely, gloriously, lose myself in the journalistic process of thinking, investigating, writing. Last month, a friend and I spent 90 minutes with the Highlanders rugby team leadership group, outlining findings and strategies from a book we co-authored – something that would have been unthinkable for me three years ago.

By other, perhaps more important measures, it's probably 150%. The boy that never felt at peace can now sit still, inside and out, genuinely enjoying a sunset. The drive to be acknowledged, to have my value constantly validated, has been replaced by a freedom that increasingly doesn't give a toss and so is more able to more truly give, care and love. Without the mental distress, I doubt I could have got there. I'm grateful.

What about you? How are you going? If you are secretly anxious, depressed, manic or addicted, talk to someone. Get good help. There is hope.

If you are on the recovery journey, good on you. Keep going. Life can be good. If you've never experienced any of this, thanks for reading. Be thankful. Be kind.

This performance poem was written during the second half of the dark years, as the dawn was returning.

The truth is fucking awesome, my God reigns.
The eyes to see it bliss, He truly reigns.

On a southern beach I stand,
toe-toe, flax, volcanic rock, white sand.
On-shore southerly spraying spume,
keeping it real.

Dark horizon slips over the edge,
into infinity.

Eighteen months have passed,
upon this stomping ground.
First, large deep figure eights,
as I flung my anger, my cries of fear and pain,
upon the wind and waves.

And here I was confronted by what is;
the beauty in the storm,
the rock that is not moved,
the ever-looming waves always spent, foam at my feet.

The seasons have reshaped this beach,
and reshaped it again;
nature is too honest to remain unchanged.
And it has changed me too;
sucked pus from my soul,
lightened my load,
set my feet free to roam.

The truth is fucking awesome, my God reigns.
The eyes to see it bliss, He truly reigns.

Bruce is a father, husband and journalist, living in Dunedin, New Zealand. He went to Chefoo School as a seven-year-old in the mid-70s. Being raised in upriver Malaysian Borneo was wonderful. Chefoo was a fabulous, traumatizing experience. Our family returned to New Zealand when I was ten. For two years, I cried every morning on the way to school without understanding why. For decades, I rationalised my boarding school experience as a praise-worthy example of counting the cost and making a sacrifice for Christ. But mid-life, facing failure on multiple fronts, confronted by the reality of a life largely built on insecurity and approval-seeking, I also owned the damage Chefoo had done. I was undone. It has taken a decade to (largely) climb out of that hole[13]. My faith in Jesus is intact. My security is finally in Him. Much of the baggage of cultural Christianity has been dropped. My experience of, and capacity for, grace is, I think, much wider and deeper. Our Abba is the master of turning shit into shiny stuff, if we'll give it to Him. Chefoo was fantastic. It also did great harm. I can now hold both of those realities at the same time. And who would I be if I hadn't been to Chefoo? As so many of you know, it's an important part of our unique identity. And I wouldn't want to not be me.

13 You can read about it here: www.odt.co.nz/lifestyle/magazine/road-recovery.

L.J.

I WAS LUCKY ENOUGH to attend sixth grade or "Level Six" at Chefoo School in Malaysia, where missionary children were educated in a rainforest in the Cameron Highlands. For me, a non-missionary kid, being accepted was a brew of exultation, fear, and relief wrapped up in a charming requirements list that included unfamiliar things like dressing gowns and handkerchiefs, all needing to have name labels individually affixed. It also included a Bible, and I received my first very own light purple New International Version just before school was to start. My younger siblings and I had been living in southern Thailand for a couple of years, attending local Thai schools and being home schooled by my mother in our American curriculum.

My father is a language consultant who was hired locally in Thailand by an American oil company. His contract was renegotiated annually. In the early years, the uncertainty of how long the position would last – not to mention my increasingly vehement resistance to home schooling – made Chefoo an ideal solution to the problem of my education.

My expectations were romantic and informed by novels like *The Little Princess*, by Frances Hodgson Burnett. The reality was also romantic, but in its own way. I loved the weather, my new school dresses, and my first view of the older girls' dorm decorated in a bee and honeycomb theme. I had a small (unlockable) locker with my name written on an adorable honey bee name tag; I was introduced to the concept of "play clothes", I had my own upper bunk assigned which gave me privacy, and I was instructed by an astonished classmate on how to make a bed with hospital corners.

Unfortunately, I wet that bed on my second or third night at school during a nightmare that I was drowning. In the ensuing mortification (I was eleven), with the bed stood out on the balcony for airing, my dorm-mates successfully comforted me with their difficulties when they had arrived, mostly in Level One at age six, or even five. These included their own tales of incontinence, emotional and otherwise. The girls seemed sheltered, but at the same time much more mature and self-sufficient than I was, and I scrambled to learn the new rules of my world.

Those lessons in my first semester at Chefoo have carried through my whole life. I went from feeling conspicuous and vulnerable, in my Thai schools, to a friendly place where I was new and odd, but I never felt unsafe. I went from a school system and culture that valued girls' submissiveness, manners, looks and deference to a place that put emphasis on Christian priorities like kindness and honesty. The girls were expected to participate in sports, while I had been teased and bullied at Thai school when I played soccer with the boys. We were rewarded when rules were followed, rather than punished when we didn't know them. I was rapped on the knuckles with a bamboo stick in Thai school before I even understood enough Thai to know what I had done wrong. (I had failed to put my chair upside down on the desk before leaving for the day.) At Chefoo, helping kitchen staff dry the dishes after Sunday brunch led to caramel and hard candy "sweeties". To this day, I lay out the dish towels as they showed me before drying my silverware. The only male attention I got was from boys my own age. My ignorance about things like religion and creationism were embarrassing but not shameful. I wasn't the tallest person in my class. My blond hair wasn't special, there were kids who were fairer, and certainly nobody touched it without my permission. I was allowed to just be myself. I didn't start with a lot of friends, although everyone was friendly. I really was weird to the clique-free but insular missionary children. My admission that my father smoked a pipe led to a flurry of gossip in the Chefoo grapevine. I didn't know any Bible verses by heart, and my idolatry was a seven-day wonder when it was discovered I had been raised Catholic and had prayed many a rosary to Mary and even – gasp – saints. I came home after my first semester significantly happier than I had been when I left, and my family and I counted it a success.

When my siblings came back with me to Chefoo the following semester, my brother seemed to have no trouble at all dropping straight into Chefoo life. My sister was six and coming in half-way through Level One left her homesick and confused. The first night, her kind dorm auntie brought her across the school to kiss me goodnight, apparently because she had misunderstood that, in going away to school with me, she thought we would still be in a room together. She was baffled and tearful, and it made me cry as well. Like my brother, it only took a little time for her to be happy and thrive at Chefoo. She attended Chefoo Malaysia until she graduated.

That semester, I broke my elbow doing a flip off a swing, and got a lot closer to my previously terrifying dorm aunty. It was in the second half of Level Six that I found my footing and made friends. This was helped by the huge array of activities that Chefoo staff organised. Most memorable for me were the campus-wide games of Capture the Flag played in the rain and mud, and over the creek; fireball soccer games, played at night on the field, with kerosene soaked rags assembled into a ball with chicken wire and then set on fire; building forts in the jungle, and forts with sheets in our dorms; the incredible school-wide sound of the *Hallelujah Chorus* played triumphantly on Easter morning; and even the mundane chores like the weekly polishing of shoes, bleaching of hair brushes, and letters home. To this day, I seek out activities to feel part of a wider group, including my book club of close friends that has been active for almost ten years. My personality did very well with the structure, and I have tried to recreate that outward accountability in my life since. This has had varying success, as I am far better at meeting external expectations like deadlines than solely inner expectations, like a resolution to meditate more. I do credit much of this self-awareness to Chefoo.

Graduating and having to leave was a serious wrench. I was

concerned about leaving my siblings, especially my little sister. My classmates were going on to missionary schools that would not be available for me. My parents did their best to find a school that would be a good fit for me, and I assumed my school in India would have a similar adjustment period to Chefoo. Of course, it was an entirely different experience. At twelve, coming from Chefoo's highly structured environment, I was ill-equipped to ask for help when I needed it, and again I was dropping into a school where most people had known each other since first grade. I was sick, over and over, from the drinking fountain water, contracting amoebic dysentery and giardia despite repeated courses of antibiotics, and lost twenty pounds I really could not afford to lose. I threw myself into schoolwork and excelled. I was involved with the girls' soccer team until I kept missing practice for being sick. I passed out after a cross-country run. At one point, I fainted on the stairs coming out of the infirmary. I was desperately miserable, but I knew there was nowhere else I could be. I completely stopped writing letters home. I was so depressed and suicidal I started seeing a counsellor at the school, which did help. Toward the end of the semester I started to feel more comfortable, became closer friends with my room-mates, and could even contemplate my return next semester with a little more equanimity.

There was unrest in New Delhi that year, and concerns rose about how we would all catch our flights home after finals. We would miss the scheduled flight from the Delhi airport if we could not make the trip from our campus in the foothills of the Himalayas into the city. When the riots led to checkpoints into the city, we evacuated school right before final exams on school buses in the middle of the night. At the checkpoints, soldiers got on with flashlights and guns, clearly uncertain what to do with all of us, but we were allowed through and stayed at a hotel until our flights out. At the hotel, it was mostly boring, to a backdrop of occasional gunfire from the other side of the city. I wrote a lot in my journal during that week, knowing the experience should be life-changing without being sure how.

When I finally returned home to my parents in Thailand, they were astonished that I was expecting to return to India. Someone from the Overseas Missionary Fellowship had made it possible to accept me into their hostel for Chiang Mai International School. I could not believe my unhappiness had actually led to a change of schools, and I was ashamed that I had, through inertia if not malice, punished them by not writing. I started to understand that although I was still a child, I was not powerless, and that if I was that unhappy I should have told them, so they could have decided what to do about it. It had not occurred to me I could switch schools at all.

That feeling of helplessness was partly from ignorance of my options, but mainly true powerlessness. I will always identify, in my absurdly privileged way, with the immigrant experience. I was separated from my family for my education and the hope of a good future, afraid, and at the mercy of choices by people and institutions I could not control. Even in Thailand living with my family, I knew how it felt to be dropped into a foreign culture and be expected to learn a language by immersion. I know what it is to be displaced, and I learned the value of self-advocacy. I also learned to ask for help when I need it.

I did a lot of healing at CMIS for the rest of seventh and all of eighth grade. I never did become good at correspondence, although I have improved at the emotional wrench that is saying goodbye. Even now, friendship maintenance is made easier by proximity, and my true friends are happy to pick up where we left off even if we only see each other once a year. My nuclear family is the same and, as years pass, we fall naturally into comforting family patterns.

For high school I returned to school in the United States for the first time in five years. I got a scholarship to an all-girls, Catholic boarding school in California, called Catalina, that many of the women in my family have attended. One of my cousins taught there as a nun in the early days of the school. It was a good way to be eased into the culture shock of returning to the United States after nearly five years of no television, minimal popular culture, and a lot of personal upheaval. I was admitted as an international student, technically, and received a good deal of tuition assistance. I got more interested in Catholicism, as the school had a humanitarian, love-centred message to which I could relate from Chefoo and my childhood.

At sixteen, I was sexually assaulted during a weekend away from school. One of the nuns took me to Planned Parenthood, when I returned the following day, for the "morning-after pill", which I hadn't heard of, and the school ensured I had access to therapy. I cannot and have not been able to adequately express my gratitude for what I see as their truly Christian determination to put my well-being first. I will donate annually to that high school, and to Planned Parenthood, until the day I die. Of course, first I had to call my parents from the office to tell them what had happened, and during that awful call I told my parents to stay in Thailand. I could not imagine how anything they could do would help, and I could not bear the burden of their pain on top of my own. I eased back into my routine at school. I still feel strongly that was the right choice, although I wonder if, without that early separation, I would have been desperate for the comfort and reassurance of my mother instead. Still, perhaps not.

Later that year, I started dating a "Missionary Kid" (MK) I had known at Chefoo who lived in northern California. In typical teenager fashion, I believed I could not really care for someone who hadn't shared that third-culture-kid experience with me. I told him of the assault early on, but when it made things uncomfortable, told him I had exaggerated its severity. I don't understand why I was so ashamed of it, even knowing how common that reaction is. We were together well into my freshman year of college, and I thought we would probably marry and travel the world. When he broke up with me, I was at Berkeley, and I really felt like the world was ending. In reality, that breakup freed me and changed the trajectory of my life.

I had always felt like a misfit, overly empathetic with total strangers, and moved too easily to tears. I was always perceived as a person I never felt myself to be, but I knew everyone felt like that. I majored in psychology (and Southeast Asian Studies, since I loved my Thai language classes) and let go of a lot of old expectations. I stopped affiliating exclusively with the skateboarding culture that I'd found with my boyfriend and started making friends across cliques of all kinds.

I had a wonderful time at Berkeley. I attended a Wiccan ceremony, went to dance at goth clubs in San Francisco that were eighteen and up, went to underground raves and experimented with drugs. I moved into the LGBTQ co-op where I met and dated a girl, in between other boyfriends. I went to Taiko drum performances and chess tournaments, took all kinds of dance classes, and did work-study while doing personal care for other students who were wheelchair bound. I dated a guy in a fraternity and went to a few Greek events. I tried out a *Dungeons and Dragons* role-playing game. I attended Catholic services at the Newman Centre when I wasn't hung-over or cramming for a test. I studied abroad for a semester in Turkey, and during the 9/11 attacks, had to fight to turn the dorm TV station from the soccer game to the news coverage. I went to punk shows and joined in the mosh pits, and crowd-surfed at metal concerts. I protested at demonstrations. I had my heart broken by a different boyfriend. Strangely, the experience of early boarding school meant I never really rebelled against my parents. To their carefully moderated dismay, I told them all about all my adventures, even those that must have worried them sick, while they remained in Thailand. I still treasure those years of experimentation and freedom, and marvel at the fearlessness I felt during that time. I know I am lucky that none of my choices have negatively impacted my life.

I graduated on time and took a year to figure out what I wanted to do with my life. I already knew I did not want to have children. I donated my eggs to a lovely couple near San Francisco that year, and I keep in touch with them, and love to see their pictures of my biological children. I was an aide in a kindergarten class for children with disabilities in the mornings, and in the afternoons and evenings I worked as an Activities Coordinator at a locked psychiatric facility. I felt that Chefusian, or perhaps Catholic, conviction that being as lucky and blessed as I was, I was meant to help people who needed it. I took the LSAT[14] and did well, and sort of backed into the decision to go to law school. In college, I had already worked part-time at a law firm, for an older cousin who did public benefits law, and I had found it very rewarding. I applied all over, and ended up choosing a law school in Boston for a fresh start.

14 Law School Admission Test

Boston was a culture-shock after Berkeley, and the cold weather of winter was its own unexpectedly horrible shock. I loved learning the law. I sped through my work and made good friends. I was deeply depressed and anxious through much of that time, which led to a relationship with a brilliant, emotionally manipulative, and verbally abusive man. It became long-distance when he went to school in England, although I visited him. We would go out often, and the escalating nature of our drunk arguments made me increasingly afraid of him. Sober, he belittled me.

I took a semester's leave of absence to get my head on straight, decide what kind of law I wanted to practice, help my mother with her own health problems, and finally get my own oft-dislocated shoulder repaired. Despite all of that, those months were a magical time. My mother had returned to California to get her teaching credentials renewed, and it was wonderful to live with her in my old childhood home while we both recovered. I volunteered at the San Francisco Public Defender's office a few days a week. My cousin with the law firm had offered to put off retirement if I wanted to take over her small firm, and I had to decide what direction I wanted to take. I sang in a church choir on Sundays. My law-school flatmate, a very close friend, came to visit. We ate cherries and drank wine on the back deck, talking late into the night about the choices before me. With my mother cooking, I lost a lot of weight, and physical therapy for my shoulder helped a lot too. It was a time of transition, and I healed, feeling I was unconditionally, if anxiously, loved.

Returning to Boston to finish law school took a lot of courage. I had burned a lot of bridges. Instead, that time went well. I was in a new apartment with new flatmates, so my ex-boyfriend did not have my address. With the help of my friends, I took advantage of the distance to break the relationship off, which I did in the only way I felt I could, by basically disappearing. My early experience of moving and leaving each world of friends and supports gave me confidence I could do it again. Although I know that any breakup conversation with my ex would have been too traumatic for me to handle, I still regret the necessity of cutting it off so abruptly, and from his point of view, ruthlessly. It is a regret I carry with a strange kind of pride. This is the only time I can remember having used separation deliberately, after a childhood spent hating it, but in this case, it saved me.

I recovered my love for studying law, and finally made the decision to take over my cousin's law firm, doing public benefits disability law. I started talking more and more frequently with my old flatmate. We started dating, and when he finished graduate school, we moved in together. He got a job in his field, and I became a partner in my cousin's law firm.

We have now been married and living in California for ten years. We still travel and go out every weekend with lots of friends. We love each other and treat each other with kindness. Fortunately, he doesn't want children either. I love kids and I don't know how much of my decision comes from my childhood experience. My little sister is still the one I have nightmares about having to protect or save. I have five godchildren, including my brother's son and daughter. My parents now live close enough to me that we try to have lunch at least monthly. I'm trying to rearrange my thinking to embrace this new reality of being middle-aged.

My area of law, helping people with disabilities prove they are entitled to the benefits they deserve, has been a good fit for me. It is hugely rewarding, and I can interact with people from all walks of life as they confront painful and difficult circumstances. Despite migraines and increasing emotional burnout, I am still able to feel a kindred spirit with my clients, and there is a satisfaction to being good at your job.

I try to return "home" to Thailand whenever I can swing it, usually every year or so. If there is a theme in my life, I believe it is that my parents gave me the love and support I needed to move forward from the choices – both their choices and mine – that were traumatic or mistakes. It is only as an adult I have been able to see the safety net they have always been for me.

* * *

L.J. is a pseudonym. Her story is true.

A.M.

*"And it came to me then that we children,
     pale as ghosts,
would forever wander outside the city wall."*

Rebecca Mackenzie[15]

Too Young to be Parted

THE ARMED GUARDS opened the village gates as we approached, and allowed us to pass through, so that we could wait on the roadside. They spoke to my father in some foreign language that I didn't understand, as all the family walked out – all the family that is except my elder brother, Jim, who was no longer living with us.

We didn't have to wait long in the sunshine, before a convoy of armoured military vehicles appeared and came to a halt alongside us, with soldiers jumping down to guard the convoy from any guerrilla attack. The back doors of one truck were swung open, and I was lifted in, together with my suitcase, to join several other children already there. Within a few minutes I heard my mother call out "goodbye", just before the steel doors clanged shut, and enclosed us in darkness.

As my eyes adjusted, I realised that some light was coming in through the slit windows at the top of each side of the truck, and I also found that there was one lady there, with about ten children.

15   Rebecca Mackenzie, *In a Land of Paper Gods*, Tinder Press 2016.

Then there was a lot of banging of doors, roaring of truck engines, and the convoy moved off into the unknown. As we sped along the uneven roads, it didn't take long for me to become travel sick, so I spent the next few hours alternating between lying down on the hard floor and throwing up into the bucket provided. As I lay there, my mind was reeling. "This isn't fair! Why was this happening to me? Why was I being sent away, in this horrible metal box? Where was I going to? When would I ever see my brother and sister again? Why do they get to stay at home?" I had been told that I was going to go to a new school, but this wasn't what I understood to be "going to school". My previous experiences of going to school had been short periods of attending primary schools in England, walking there each morning and walking home again in the afternoon. I quickly found that this school was quite different! I soon realised I was not going home at the end of the day, or even at the end of the week – instead I was to stay here for several months at a time, amongst children that I didn't know, being taught by teachers that I didn't recognise.

So it was that, at the tender age of five, I arrived at Tanglin Military School, in the Cameron Highlands, in Malaya, during the Malayan Emergency[16]. The school was situated on a small plateau at the edge of the mountain, and was overlooked by a military guard post, manned by soldiers day and night, and this was to be my new home. This is how I started a life away from my parents and family that was to continue, in various forms, for the rest of my days: isolated, pushed to one side, of secondary importance, learning to cope alone, and to keep all feelings and emotions hidden.

Too Bound to be Free

"Where am I? How did I get here? What am I doing here?"

I have just woken up and found myself in a strange bed in a strange

---

16 The Malayan Emergency 1948–1960 was a rebellion by the Malayan Communist Party. Defeated, the rebels retreated across the Thai border into South Thailand where prolonged instability has persisted even today. Note the story by Kerry at the start of this chapter about the killing of two missionaries by rebels in South Thailand.

room. There are rows of beds down each side of the room – there must be about twelve beds in all – very reminiscent of the dormitories at school. My bed is right in the corner furthest away from the door. Some men are wandering around whilst others sit on beds, reading books. There is one older man, in a white coat, who comes over to me when he sees that I am awake,

"How are you doing? Are you settling in okay?"

I ask him where I am, but I am so tired, I don't really understand what he says. He gives me two blue tablets and soon I am asleep again. Next time I wake up, the room is dark, and everyone else seems to be asleep.

As I think back over the last few weeks and months, I realise that I am now a 21-year-old student. Having completely failed even the resits of the first-year exams, I moved out of London to try again, to get a degree at a polytechnic college. I find myself struggling to cope with life – alone in a strange town. A few months ago, I did very seriously consider ending my life. I got as far as spreading out all tablets on my bed before something stopped me – but that's a story for another day.

For most of my life, I have lived in boarding schools and hostels, away from the family, and have been forced to hold in all my emotions and feelings, whilst being bullied for being different from everyone else. Having grown up without any direct caring support from my parents, I don't feel able to share my feelings with them, or with anyone else, for that matter. A few years ago, dad was suddenly flown home from the Far East for major surgery. No one had explained what was going on, but I knew it was serious, as travelling by air was so unusual. For the last thirty years, dad and mum had always travelled to and from China and Malaya by sea.

Now, I find myself alone and isolated once again, alone in a strange place with no one to tell me what's going on. Bit by bit the room gets lighter, people start to wake, and the quietness is broken by the sounds of men moaning and grumbling. After breakfast, which is served at a long table in that same room, I am taken to the office and, at last, someone explains where I am. I am in a psychiatric hospital some miles away from my college lodgings. No one seems to know how I got here, but I am assured that I am here as a "voluntary patient", so I suppose I can leave whenever I want! How that can be is unclear, but it seems that all the others on my ward have been "sectioned"[17], so they have to stay for a specified number of days.

Here I am, incarcerated in this dreary place, with nothing much to do apart from sleep the days away. I spend the next couple of days in bed, sleeping. They have given me some pretty potent meds, and I know very little of what's going on around me. Whenever I am awake, we are either eating meals, or attending group discussions. Everyone else seems happy to say how they feel, but I just sit there in a trance. Over the next few days I learn that I am being assessed to see if Electro-Convulsive Therapy (ECT) would be the way forward. It seems that this resets some of the brain, but that it can also result in a change in personality. I suppose the one good thing about being here is that someone is acknowledging that everything is *not* all right.

No one seems to have visitors, but in the afternoon of my fourth day here, I am told that someone has come to see me. Who can this be? I go to the office and find that Kathy has come. She's a nurse whom I met a few months ago at the church. I haven't a clue how she knew I was here, but we are told we can go for a walk together, so long as we stay within the hospital grounds, so off we go. As we walk and talk together, Kathy soon asks if my mum and dad have been to see me, and the answer is, "No". Since their sudden return from the mission field, and the surgery that dad underwent, he has taken on a job as a GP[18] in an urban medical practice. This involves long hours, including nights and weekends, so he has limited time for anything else. He also seems to have taken this on as a "missionary work", and often gives Christian literature to his patients. From my perspective, dad is firstly a Christian, and secondly a medical doctor. Neither of these allow him to acknowledge, and deal with, mental health issues, particularly in his own family, which leaves me way down in his list of priorities. I found

17   In British Law patients whose mental health makes them a danger to their own or other people's safety can be compulsorily detained in hospital. This is colloquially known as being sectioned.
18   "General Practitioner", i.e., a primary care doctor.

out much later that my time in this psychiatric hospital was kept a secret from everyone – not even my siblings knew where I was. As it is, mum and dad come to visit me once a week, and each time they take me out to an old-fashioned tearoom nearby. It's hardly very exciting, but at least it gets me out of the hospital for a couple of hours. In contrast, Kathy comes to see me whenever she has a day, or half-day, off work, so I usually see her twice a week. The spring weather allows us to wander the grounds on most of her visits, and these are the only times that I leave that claustrophobic hospital ward.

The usual hospital routine continues over the next few weeks, with group discussion sessions, as well as occasional individual meetings with one of the staff. I really don't think that they are doing anything for me apart from dosing me with drugs three times a day. After six weeks of this monotony, I am eventually told that the doctors have decided that I would not benefit from ECT, and that I am to be sent home.

But where is home? Am I to go back to college and to my lodgings there?

No! A couple of days later, dad and mum come on their usual visit, and explain that they are taking me back to live in their house. It seems that I'm not being given any choice in the matter, certainly, there is no discussion about where I am going. So, off I go, still well drugged up, to live in a house that I hardly know, as part of a family who seem like strangers to me. So, although I am being released from this incarceration, am I going to be free? In fact, will I ever be free of this depression that continues to haunt me?

Too Late to be Reconnected

As I look back over my life so far, I can see lessons learned (often the hard way), pains and struggles experienced, as well as some positive outcomes. I am now well into my seventies, retired, with three children (all married) and six grandchildren. Kathy and I will celebrate our golden wedding anniversary in a few months. My parents are both dead and buried, but their legacy continues to impact my life.

As a child, I travelled the world in a way that was not available to others. I lived in foreign lands, saw foreign cultures, ate foreign food. But this came at a price. Initially we lived in western China and, for much of the time, we were looked after by local Chinese servants, whilst dad and mum travelled around doing their medical work. Once I turned five years old, we moved to Malaya, and I was dispatched to boarding schools – starting in a military school and then progressing on to the newly established mission school. Later, I was to spend some years at a boarding school in the UK whilst my parents returned to their primary work on the mission field in the Far East. When my parents did finally return to live in England, there was no family bond, and it was too late to build close relationships. In contrast, Kathy has stood by me – my constant support – through thick and thin. I have not always been the model husband, and our relationship has been quite strained at times. However, it is quite clear to me that I would not be the person I am today had she not been there for me.

In his last years, Dad was hospitalised on a couple of occasions. I therefore made it my duty to visit him regularly, even though doing so meant a four-hour return drive after a full day at work. During my working years, my parents showed no interest at all in my job, or what I was doing. You see, I was the only one of their children who did not spend at least some of their working life doing "Christian" work, and so I believe that I was a great disappointment to them. I have tried to ensure that I didn't follow in my parent's footsteps by making my work life more important than my home life. Have I always achieved this? No, of course not. I can see that there have been times when I have got my priorities wrong. However, I now have three loving and caring children, who are attaining their potential in their various careers, who have their own strong and healthy families, who choose to keep in close contact with us oldies, despite the miles that separate us geographically. So, I can't have got it all wrong! When each of our children went off to university, I ensured that we took them there ourselves, and that we visited them regularly. This wasn't always easy, as they each chose colleges many miles from home. Some visits required starting out from home early, and driving through all sorts of weather conditions for many hours, but we always got to see them, even if we arrived several hours later than planned.

For many years, I worked as a domestic appliance engineer, visiting people in their homes to sort out problems with their washing machines etc. Later on, I worked on the retail shop floor for a major chemist. Through all this, I found that my primary role was in face-to-face work supporting people in various practical ways, and this gave me a real sense of job satisfaction.

When I was approaching retirement, I knew that I would need to find some useful occupation. My face lit up, therefore, when a work colleague showed me an advert for a charity that was looking for volunteers. The aim of the charity is to help victims of crime move on and get their lives back on track. I have now been a volunteer caseworker for nearly eight years. Three or four days each week, I go out to meet people who have had their lives turned upside down by various crimes, and I hear some very distressing stories. I meet with people who are subject to harassment, who have been burgled, or physically attacked. Some have been affected by various forms of domestic abuse, whilst others have lost family members in acts of murder. Each person is different, and each crime is different. I know I cannot change what has happened to them, but I can offer a listening ear – empathic listening, interspersed with words of encouragement, and occasional suggestions for things to think about doing. In return, I get a really positive feeling of a job well done whenever I see clients take their own steps forward in reclaiming their damaged lives.

As part of my training in supporting victims of domestic abuse, I learnt of the many forms this can take. In the past, the crime group was always known as "domestic violence", but it is now more accurately referred to as "domestic abuse". It can take on many forms: violence yes, but also sexual, financial, emotional, neglect, controlling etc. This became very personal for me. I am glad to say that I was not sexually abused, though I did experience physical abuse in the form of bullying at school. However, I do believe that I have been abused by my parents in the form of emotional neglect. Young children have a basic need for an emotional attachment primarily to their mother, but also to their father. Without this early-years' attachment, many aspects of their development will be affected and their whole lives can, and often will, be changed as a direct result.

As I write this, I reflect on my own childhood experiences. I cannot change what has happened, but it also seems impossible to leave it all behind me and move on. Instead, I try to be a support for others who feel knocked down by life's events. Every evening, I take my medication, hoping it will keep my mental health reasonably steady. Every couple of weeks, I go to a neighbouring town and spend an hour with my counsellor, discussing my personal experiences. Some of these experiences reflect directly on my upbringing, and clearly display the symptoms of PTSD. I often ask myself the question "What would life have been like if I had been brought up in a normal family? What if Dad and Mum had had normal jobs within the UK?" I'm not sure what "normal" really means in this context, but it is most unlikely that our family would have existed as such, anyway. Due to the differences in dad and mum's backgrounds (both geographical and socio-economic) it is almost impossible to think that they would ever have met and married in the first place. Had the impossible been possible, and our family had existed in a regular setting, I am sure life could have been very different. I could have had a regular education in a school local to our home. I could have had a closer relationship with my parents and with my siblings. However, dad's personality was such that he would always have been very committed to his work. He would have put in long hours and would never have been a "fun" dad. In a similar vein, mum was always very serious and strict, and hardly the sort of person that I could imagine playing with her young children, or understanding us as teenagers.

So, what does the future hold for me? I cannot change who I am, nor do I want to. My personality has been forged in the fiery furnace of isolation and neglect. I may be distorted and twisted, but with all this, I have developed a special strength, resilience and usefulness.

Can I ever forgive and forget? At present, I am not ready to forgive either my parents or the mission. This may change, but I cannot see this happening in the near future. Can I forget what I have been through? *Never!*

* * *

A.M. is a pseudonym adopted by the writer, who was a missionary child in China and Malaya in the 40s & 50s, to protect identity and family. This contribution comprises excerpts from Chapters 1, 34 and the Conclusion of his book, Alone in a Crowd *(in preparation). Whilst this story is based on real life events, a liberal amount of artistic license has been added in the telling. Names of all characters portrayed have been changed to protect both the innocent and the guilty.*

Bernard

UNTIL NOW, WHENEVER I've been asked about how being sent to Chefoo has affected me, I've said that while it has clearly had an impact on me, it didn't damage me. On the face of it, this is true: I've remained a practicing Christian; still consider myself an evangelical, albeit of a fairly open, liberal variety; I worked as a Church leader for nigh on twenty years; and am – I hope, my wife might say otherwise! – a reasonably functioning human being. Yet I'm coming to see this is a bit of an evasion, a bit of a rationalisation, to avoid doing the necessary reflective work. For, to the extent that Chefoo has contributed negatively to my development, it has surely harmed me. So now I need to do some – perhaps long overdue – reflection.

One thing I think is true, that perhaps I was trying to express by my formulation, there is – to my mind – a danger in TCK circles to imply that we are uniquely damaged as a result of our boarding experience, that our suffering is worse than that of any other children. Evidently this is not the case, as a brief review of the lives of inner city kids, or children born into slavery (for example), makes clear. In fact, as Philip Larkin says, no child reaches adulthood undamaged by their childhood experiences[19]. For myself at least, I don't think my childhood, while certainly different from most people's, was significantly more damaging than many others, and certainly much less damaging than many people's.

19 Philip Larkin, "This be the Verse", first published 1974, available online from www.poetry foundation.org/poems/48419/this-be-the-verse, and many other places.

Another caveat I must make before really getting started is to say that it is hard, nigh on impossible, to separate out the effects of being sent away from home; of the treatment I received at the hands of my contemporaries; and of my own innate character and that of my parents. From conversations with other Chefusians, it seems that my parents were different from many other OMF missionaries, and their ministry rather different. My father was an introverted scholar, not an extrovert pioneer evangelist, and his ministry was, at times, university lecturing, and at other times literature work. His greatest achievement was probably the publication of IVP's New Bible Dictionary in *Bahasa Indonesia*, on which he (with a team of others) laboured for many years. In many ways I take after him: academic – although perhaps not quite so introvert – rational rather than emotional; undemonstrative; friendly and open on a superficial level, but not having many intimate friends; fascinated by history, and theology, and language. Of course there are differences, my first degree was in Engineering, whereas his was in History (I got my name because he studied St Bernard in his final year). I've been fascinated by aeroplanes, in particular, and machinery in general, since before I went to Chefoo, although even there, he had a kind of latent interest in trains and ships. In many ways, my character is a replica of my father's. My dad was brighter than I am, but my interests are broader than his: my knowledge is relatively shallow and broad, whereas his was deeper but narrower. No doubt the experience of boarding exacerbated these characteristics but, given who my father was and how similar our characters are, I don't think I would have developed much differently, even if I had been living at home with my parents throughout my childhood. In fact, I've often thought that not living with my parents for most of my teenage years prevented me from getting too frustrated by them, and feeling the need to rebel against them to establish my own identity.

Some basic biographical facts: I was born in Central Java, where my parents were teaching in Satyawacana Christian University, in June 1964. Six months later they had to flee the country because of communist agitation in the area. My first school was the local church kindergarten, within walking distance of our home, where I was in *kelas nol besar* (Upper Class 0). The school's name was Ora et Labora – Latin for "Pray and Work" – but the teaching was in Indonesian, and at rising five I was effectively bilingual. I was there for a term or two, before leaving for Chefoo in January 1970. My Dad describes the event graphically in a letter to his own mother:

> Well, the 29th January has come and gone. It was quite a day! The plane was due to leave at 8.45am, so I was up at five to prepare breakfast. The rascals did not wake until half-past, so I had a brief time to scan the daily portion. "The commandment I write to you is not a new commandment, but an old... nevertheless it is a new commandment". Old, yet ever new! The words of that old hymn were going through my mind all day. Separations we have had before – so have you: nothing new about them. And yet each one comes with a separate quality of its own, a newness. A new pain perhaps, a new blessing. What would we feel like this evening? But the daily bustle of awaking children soon occupied us. Dressing, eating, the last morning reading together: then a few photos on the porch of our little traveller with his case – his sister refusing to cooperate and beginning to howl when made to join in the pictures. And so off...
>
> Eventually – not before the boys were getting impatient to be off – the call for passengers only. Guy had talked to the chief flight steward and committed the party to him, and he was kind enough to suggest that we all went out to the plane – another highly unusual feature. So we all stood at the foot of the steps leading up to the plane as our little lad climbed up, waved from the top, and was gone... So we waved, and back to the terminal to wave as the plane took off, eventually at 1.45...
>
> By now they should be safely ensconced and getting used to the school. My own worst moment came on Friday morning when as usual I was up to get the breakfast. No fourth place to lay! We had to rearrange the seating around the table to cover up the sense of loss.

One week later he writes again,

> On Tuesday we had a letter from one of the Chefoo staff, sent from K.L. on the previous Friday morning (30th). This is what she said, 'Bernard arrived here this evening, giving us full details of the wonderful experience of flying. He has a beautiful picture of the plane of which he is very proud. All the children are in bed now. Bernard fell asleep as soon as he lay down. He has talked of Mum and Dad being far away but is looking forward to 'writing' you a letter when he gets to school. We travel to school by taxis in the morning.

From my dad's words, I think – and this accords with my own memory of my excitement at flying off to school – that he and mum found the separation much more of a wrench than I did.

Apart from a year at primary school in Bristol during my parents' second furlough (1971–72), I was at Chefoo until I finished Level 6 in June 1975. Terms were four months long, and there were two a year: February to May, and August to November, with two eight-week holidays (December/January and June/July). During my entire time at Chefoo my parents were only able to visit me once; around halfway through my Level 5 year they had a week's holiday in the Bungalow. Unfortunately my Level 5 year was disrupted educationally, as early on in the year I picked up a bug (diagnosed at the time as tonsillitis, although I don't recall being particularly troubled by a sore throat, and I've never had my tonsils out), and I struggled to throw it off. As a result I was in and out of sick bay for much of the year. A week before my parents were due to arrive on holiday I woke up, once again, with a headache. I was desperate not to go to sickbay again, but no, I had a raised temperature, so off to sickbay I went. A week later I was feeling well again, and despite my temperature still being above normal, Aunty Betty, the school nurse, took pity on me and let me out, as my parents were coming. Typical excited small boy, the first day of their holiday I was out riding up and down the school drive on my bike in the rain, showing off in front of them; the next day I woke up with a headache and a temperature again – and back to sickbay I went. I recall vividly that my parents visited me in the sickbay several times, and my dad and I built a Lego airport control tower together – but the holiday wasn't as special as it would have been if I had been well. The story has a tragic ending: a week after my parents' holiday ended, for some reason Aunty Betty needed me to move to a different bed in sickbay. The Lego control tower, which was on a table beside my bed, was moved by another child in the sickbay (I still remember his name, nearly fifty years later, though I'll discreetly not name him here.); halfway across the room he stumbled and dropped it, and it smashed to pieces. I was distraught... That was the only time at Chefoo I recall feeling homesick.

And yet, and yet. Throughout my school years, from the very beginning of my time at Chefoo, I felt something of an outsider. My first term I was the youngest child in the school, and was teased accordingly by my classmates, who called me "Dainty lady". My best friend, I told my parents in a letter, was the oldest boy in the school. Much of the time I played by myself, "flying" my toy airplane up and down the school drive. I had a series of "best friends", but even when I was playing with them, much of the time I was on the receiving end of teasing and practical jokes. I was not in the choir, I was not in the football team, I always came last in the half-term cross-country race, I was not in any of the school plays. Indeed I remember one year going to a lot of trouble – with Aunty Barb's encouragement – arranging an after-play party to "thank" those involved. My efforts were lauded as very public-spirited, but I think they were in reality a desperate attempt to get some recognition from my peers.

Anders, in his contribution, mentions that while at Chefoo he was involved in a revival, "challenging other children whether they were prepared to carry the cross of Christ", and having prayer meetings in the dorm after lights out, until Aunty Barb found out and put a stop to it. As I recall, she called us all into her room and asked anyone who wanted to tell their story. I recall saying that while I wasn't one of those who had just given their life to the Lord, two weeks before-hand I had done so on my own – not for the first time – and this time I had felt a sense of peace I'd never felt before. To this day I regard that experience in April 1973 as the beginning of my Christian life.

In the summer of 1975 I finished Level 6, and after a wonderful family holiday in Bali, "returned" to the UK for secondary education at a boarding school near Bath. Perhaps because I was bigger (just 11), perhaps because it was much further (8,000 miles as opposed to 1,000), perhaps because the separation was for longer (a year instead of four months) I felt the move back to England as much more of a wrench than I ever felt going to Chefoo. My parents sent me off with the promise of Joshua 1:9 as my own: "Be strong and of good courage; be not frightened, neither be dismayed; for the Lord your God is with you wherever you go." I flew home via Moscow in the company of an OMF missionary by name of Dorothy Marx, who was apparently petrified that the Russian authorities would detain her because of her name.[20] The junior school, where I spent the next two school years, was a real culture shock compared with Chefoo's easy-going ways. All those rules! I remember walking and talking with another newly arrived pupil, and being bawled at to get off the grass, as only prefects were allowed to walk on it.

Two years at the junior school were followed by four years at the senior school down the hill. Early in my time at the senior school, I recall describing my faith to the school chaplain: that I felt that spiritually, I was in a desert across which ran the boundary between being saved and not being saved, but I wasn't sure which side of the boundary I was on. This uncertainty resolved itself, quite unexpectedly, the first time I took Communion in the School Chapel a few weeks later – suddenly, I don't know why, I just *knew* that I was saved. Ever since then, though I have had my ups and downs spiritually, I have known I am a Christian.

Which brings me to the major trauma of my time there. I had

20 Dorothy was a remarkable woman, whose life is worthy of a full length biography. Born into a Jewish family in Germany, she lost both parents in the holocaust. Becoming a Christian she joined OMF and went to Indonesia in the 50s and spent most of the rest of her life there, eventually taking up Indonesian citizenship. She had to be begged to take furloughs, and if I recall correctly, the time she escorted me to Britain was only her second furlough in 15+ years!

always been on the receiving end of a certain amount of bullying from my classmates – I remember once throwing a metal bookstand at one boy who had teased me beyond endurance – but this was of a whole different order. There was a boy in the senior school whose life was closely intertwined with mine. When, at thirteen, we first moved from the junior to the senior school, he was the natural leader of our small gang of (over)-zealous Christians. But soon after we started the senior school, he went off the rails, turned against his faith, started drinking and smoking, and generally being rebellious. By the time we left he was doing glue, and what he got into after we left, I don't know – but that is rather to get ahead of the story. I remember my parents bought me a new overcoat when I was about fourteen and he used to "borrow" it – not that I got much choice in the matter – to go smoking in. On one occasion, he even insisted that I come with him around the back of the Latin classroom while he had a cigarette.

We had to do homework ("prep") every weeknight from 7–9 pm. The junior boys – up to Fifth Form[21] – studied together in common rooms, but once you got into the Lower Sixth you were entitled to a two-person Study. For some reason, in my first term in the Lower Sixth, there weren't quite enough studies to go around, probably because of the number of boys staying on an extra term to do Oxbridge exams, I guess, but I don't really remember. This boy and I, as the two youngest boys in the Lower Sixth, had to stay in our house Senior Common Room for an extra term. Another difference between the Fifth and the Lower Sixth forms was that the Lower Sixth formers got several study periods every week, when they weren't in class but were supposed to be studying on their own. In that first term, he and I were on our own during these periods in the common room. That was when the physical abuse started. It started with small things, such as kicking my Bible around the room until its covers came off, and urinating in my box of cereal, but he soon began hitting me. There was one occasion

21 In British boarding schools Fifth Form was the year children did their O levels, generally the school year they turned 16. (In my case it was the year I turned 15, but that's another story). Lower Sixth was the first year of A Level studies, Upper Sixth the second year.

when mum and dad took me out for the day, and noticing my chin was
yellow with bruises asked me what had happened. I can't remember
what I said, something vague no doubt, but I certainly didn't tell them
the truth, and they didn't press me.

A few years ago I wrote about an occasion when God didn't answer
my prayers. This was that occasion. By the end of the Michaelmas term,
I knew that this boy and I would be allocated a study together the
following term, and over the Christmas holiday I prayed desperately
that God would prevent it happening. He didn't. Sharing a private
study together, meant the way my "friend" treated me got worse and
worse. Because I was better at our schoolwork, he would often call me
over to his desk whenever he was struggling with something and ask
me to explain it. But when I did so he would grab hold of my crotch
and – what shall I say? – mistreat me. Whenever I refused to help him
with his work he would wheedle and nag and tell me he wouldn't do
it this time, and how it wasn't very Christian of me not to help
him, until I gave in and came to see what he wanted. It wasn't until
many years later that I developed the security to resist that particular
manipulative manoeuvre.

Although I hated what was happening, I interpreted it as suffering
persecution for the sake of the gospel[22]. But eventually I could stand
it no longer, and about a month before the end of the summer term
started doing my prep in the school library – keeping out of his way
– in other words. But after a couple of weeks, for some reason, I
convinced myself that God wanted me to work in my study with him
(as a witness, I suppose). Naturally, I was just too terrified to do so. So
now I had a rapidly developing crisis of faith on my hands, caused by
believing that I was being disobedient to what God had called me to
do. Eventually, I could take the internal conflict no longer, and going
out for a walk by myself confessed my weakness and repented my sin.
(Mind you, I did wait to repent until after the last prep of term, so that
I would be safe, nonetheless.) I still have the Bible I had then, in which

22 I don't know that I would now – although there may be a sense that my faith functioned rather
     as a red rag to a bull.

I have written inside the front cover "Rebelled, 3rd–9th July 1980, Reconverted and Rebaptised in the Holy Spirit, 9th July 1980."

Anyway, that was the end of the abuse. The following year I was put in a study with someone different. He wasn't a particular friend of mine but by that time I was happy to share with anybody else.

And then in 1981 I left school, and never expected to see this boy again.

But in September 1988, I went to London Bible College (LBC) to study for Christian ministry. The Principal, when I started, had previously been OMF's General Director. Obviously he knew me by name. He also knew the other boy, knew that I knew him, and knew that he was still having trouble. So in all innocence he asked if I would go to see him to try and be some help to him!

Well, I had long since "forgiven" the boy concerned, but it's one thing to say you've forgiven someone you're never going to see again, and a completely different thing when you are suddenly faced with the prospect of seeing them again after all. That was a real test of the genuineness of my forgiveness. To begin with I was very hesitant, but eventually I agreed to go, and with great fear and trembling drove down to the boy's home city one weekend, in (I think) the Easter holiday. I wish I could say that weekend brought some dramatic resolution, but it didn't. I think he was as afraid to see me as I was to see him: we had tea together in a café, he apologised and I accepted his apology, we took a few pictures, and I came away again. I never saw him again. Sometime later, I heard that he had died of an accidental overdose.

Well, in completing that story I've jumped a long way ahead. After school I spent four months unemployed in Worcester, before going to Brussels with Operation Mobilisation for six months. That was a very formative year, that turned me from a boy into a man. Mum and dad returned to Asia at the beginning of the year, and I elected to stay with some friends from the church in Worcester, rather than return to Donnington Hurst in Newbury. I'm still friends with them forty years later. After OM I went to Manchester University to study Aeronautical Engineering, and then to Derby to work for Rolls-Royce for two-and-a-half years.

Which brings me to my time at LBC, and the beginnings of the greatest emotional crisis of my life so far. Just before I left Derby, I fell madly in love with a young woman in the church youth group. We had a brief long-distance relationship in my first year at Bible College, but I put too much emotional pressure on the relationship too soon, and she couldn't take it. Early in the summer term, she (emotionally) pushed me off a cliff. I was broken-hearted and, unfortunately, I took my pastor's advice to try and win her back, rather than accept her decision. All that achieved was to prolong and deepen the grief, so that it clouded the rest of my time at LBC. I sought counselling from one of the lecturers, who basically told me to pull myself together. I sought consolation fancying – and asking out – a sequence of female students in my final year, all of whom turned me down (gently of course.)

Some months after leaving LBC I got a job in a tiny charismatic church on the Welsh border. In name I was the pastor, but actually I found out my role was to be the front man for the church Secretary, in whose properties the church met, and five out of six members lived. Unfortunately for me, this woman had through many difficult life experiences become very bitter and critical. She was a fan of Frank Peretti's *This Present Darkness* – to the extent she almost treated it like a new book of the Bible. According to her demons were everywhere, eventually even in the telephone corrupting my phone calls to my mum and dad. The constant criticism and talk of demons, together with my unhealed heart from college, combined to completely undermine me, so that I ended up quitting after just five months.

As it happened, the Lord brought good out of bad, because a friend of mine invited me to London to stay with him for three months while I pieced my life back together. Twenty-eight years later I have only just left London. But it took several years of counselling, and the kindness of many good friends, to put me back together again. Slowly, I began to realise that God doesn't make mistakes, that he had made me the way I was and allowed these painful experiences for a purpose. Out of these fires I wrote a number of poems, which express better than prose what my faith is about. One goes:

I am the perfect handiwork of the Master Craftsman.
I am the object of the redeeming love of the Son of God.
He desired me so much that he gave his life to rescue me
I belong to the family of God
I am a child of the King
Therefore, I am valuable to God.

These are objective facts: so I don't need to look down on myself, thinking myself unworthy and of no importance, and trying to avoid attention. Neither do I need to strive feverishly to impress others and hope that they'll notice me. Instead I am called to be the person God has made me to be: secure in the knowledge that I matter to God, and that nothing I can do will make him more (or less) impressed with me than he already is.

While another ends

TODAY is Resurrection Day
A day when hope and love came back to life
After the most devastating blow, perhaps
The world has ever known.
Oh Lord, may this day, and those following
Become for me, another Resurrection Day.

There is much more I could say – I've only reached 1992, after all – but time and space are failing. To return to the original question: how has the experience of Chefoo, and of boarding from an early age affected me? I owe it (and my parents) my faith, my love of colour and of travel, my interest in all kinds of things; but also insecurity, loneliness, and apparent lack of emotion. Has it damaged me? Yes, clearly, but it has also made me the man I am.

One more thing I must add. As someone who has married into the UK's Caribbean community, I am becoming more and more aware that along with much good, much pain and harm was also done by missionaries in the name of God across the world, and for this I want to say I am sorry. Having suffered in a small way myself, I stand in solidarity with any who have been harmed by the actions of our parents, their colleagues and forebears, whose intentions, though on the whole well-meaning, seem in the light of history to have been naïve regarding the full impact of their actions.

Interlude 3:
Magdalene Resurrection
Bernard

Death, it has done its work this weekend
The Prince of Life lies dead,
Dead, and in ashes are the hopes of all men
Dead as his stone-cold bed.

Mary comes to the tomb this day,
Despairing, all on her own,
Her life, it has gone, and all she has left
Is the myrrh to anoint him, Farewell.

Early this morning, still in the darkness
She comes to this grass-grown place
Knowing she'll see by the cliff the huge stone
Covering his fresh-hewn grave.

She comes, but she finds not what she expects
The great stone's rolléd away
And there in the entrance two young men stand
Why are you crying? they say.
They've taken away my Lord, she sobs,
I don't know where they have put him.
My life, my love, my hope and my Lord

Now he's gone, Oh where have they put him?

Why look for the living with the dead? They reply
He's not here, he has gone, He is Risen!
But weeping, she turns, despairing and grieving
Lost and alone in her world of depression.

A stranger approaches, out of the dawn,
She runs to him begging, Good Sir
Have you moved him? where've you put him?
Please tell me; please tell me, he's where?

Mary, he speaks, and she falls at his feet,
Master, she whispers, It's you,
Master, you're back, you're alive, you have risen,
Don't leave me alone, don't leave me again.

Lifting her up, he says to her gently,
Don't cling to me now, I must go to the Father,
For much as I love you, you cannot possess me,
What you try to possess only crumbles to dust

Oh Lord, as Mary came, I come
Despairing, distraught and alone,
All my hope gone; my vision shattered
Please meet me and bring me back home.

Like Mary, I cling to the gifts that you bring me,
Trying desperately to grab what you want me to have,
You've promised me good, yet Oh Lord I keep trying
To make it come true, not letting you do it.

That morning you met her, she found out the answer
To her grief, to her loss and her pain.
Oh Lord, when I meet you, I need the same answer
Oh Lord, will you meet me again and again?

4

The Good Times

Children being sent away, lonely, and
vulnerable to trauma was not the whole story.
Chefoo as a school was remarkable. These writers
review their time there with approval.

CHEFOO

Andrew C.

MY FIRST SCHOOL experience was in Australia.

Happily, it coincided with our family's first furlough from work in urban East Asia. Before then, my life had been a school-free zone running around with local lads on the streets near our home.

I went along to North Narrabeen Infants' School, on Sydney's northern beaches, just before turning five, in early 1957. As in many other places, the school and many surrounding houses had been hurriedly assembled from timber kits, to cope with the post-World-War-One baby boom. With skinny brick piers planted in soft sandy soil on Beach Road, and surrounded by Norfolk Island pines, the school had timber walls and floors, broad verandas and a tin roof. It was scorching hot in summer and cold in winter. When it rained heavily, you couldn't hear anyone speaking inside.

After lining up for roll call in the playground each morning, we waited for the teacher at the class-room door. Just as in Asia, shoes were left at the door, lest sand scratch polished floors. Individual desk-and-bench sets were lined up to face the front. Each desk had an ink-well at the top right corner of the ledger. Nobody spoke out of turn in our class, but for the life of me, I cannot remember the teacher's name.

My earliest individual class-room memory is of picking up a pencil to write with my left hand. Clearly on the look-out for any deviant behaviour, the teacher immediately made me sit on my left hand and work with my right. His ruler was there to whack my left hand, if ever it appeared on the ledger, looking as if it wanted to do any writing.

After a time using a pencil to form letters, numbers and words, our inkwells were filled with 'Swan' blue-black ink. We were each given a steel-nib dip pen to start to print out words. Having a go with the dip pen in my left hand when nobody was looking, I quickly realised the teacher's discipline would deliver me from life with a permanently inky left palm.

When Mum brought home a new baby sister, we went and stayed with Uncle Alex, Aunty June and our cousins. Another big event that year was when we all went from school by bus to Brookvale Oval for polio vaccination injections; a jellybean rewarded each one who did not cry. Another day, a Dutchman came to cut our backyard grass with a scythe; mum set fire to the pile of garden rubbish, which blew up into the garage gutter next door, consuming both the garage and the £10 car inside.

At year's end, returning by boat to Asia with the new baby sister, we slunk on board at night, as we two boys had a rash, and mum and dad were scared we would be quarantined from boarding. The ship from Sydney to Fremantle was good, but then we transferred, for the slow trip up to Singapore, onto one of the Blue Funnel Line cattle boats, of all which had classical Greek names. I think it was the 'Gorgon' that took us, and hundreds of cattle, north from Geraldton, Derby and Broome. Passenger cabins were just above the cattle decks; everything was smelly by the time we reached Singapore.

Christmas was spent at the old OMF Home at No. 2 Cluny Road, Singapore, with Santa Claus climbing up a rickety ladder to come in the first-floor sitting room window and distribute gifts to us. When he wished us "Happy Christmas" with an Irish accent, I knew Santa was really dad, despite everyone else telling me to the contrary. As a Cantonese and Mandarin speaker, with most Perak tin-miners being Cantonese, dad was sent there to pastor a small, new-village church. We travelled up on the cream-and-chocolate carriages of the "Day Mail", pulled by a green steam engine with a copper-cap chimney. The livery was supposedly so that betel nut juice would not visibly stain the lower parts of each carriage.

Some weeks later, it was time to go to school at Chefoo. I remember my mum crying as I got on the train to Tapah Road with dad, holding my "Globite" travel bag, to meet up with everyone else "going up the Camerons". It seems incredible to me today, that I could fit all my clothes, toys and a photo of our family, inside a modest-sized bag – in those days, we always seemed to run around in sandals, shorts and shirts, with hand-knitted jumpers, one sleeveless, and one with long sleeves. We climbed into Mercedes-Benz 180D taxis, bags stacked in the back, and there were empty jam-tins, just in case. In my case, it happened a few miles beyond the waterfall, and recurred all the way to Ringlet. I resolved never again to eat and drink before making that trip. Arriving at Chefoo (the old "Bungalow" campus) late in the afternoon, my memory is of wondering how it could both be sunny and cool at the same time.

Meeting a whole bunch of new schoolmates was confusing. Unlike Narrabeen, where most spoke in the same way, Chefoo had a real mix of British, American and other English accents, and all sorts of surnames, some even sounding like expensive cars. Others seemed to be cousins of various kinds. We boys slept up at the end of the bungalow, next to the driveway, on plain beds with kapok mattresses and grey blankets to keep us warm (not). I remember night-time tears for a couple of weeks, but after that, boys' humour and mellifluous nether winds usually kept us going until sleep overtook us.

Evenings were often misty, and I remember mornings as being quite cold, and you never did #2 until well after breakfast, avoiding a cold toilet seat, until someone else warmed it up. Chefoo introduced me to breakfast porridge with milk and brown sugar, and scrambled eggs at times. I learned to eat everything on my plate, and quickly, if I wanted a second helping – it gave a whole new meaning to believing in "the quick and the dead". To this day, I eat porridge for breakfast, and quickly. It seems to me that lunch was often sandwiches and milk, and dinner was a hot meal. We always used cloth serviettes, rolled up in a serviette ring (mine was made of bamboo).

Unlike Narrabeen, memories of teachers in my three Chefoo years are very real indeed, probably the strongest of all my teacher memories from school days. I had two years with Margaret D. and an in-between year with Margaret Q, who was very proud of her Isle-of-Man heritage and three-legged coat of arms. They taught the foundation of all my learning to this day, giving me a love of reading, writing, singing and mathematics. They gave me a visual sense of history, that is in my mind's eye still, with a wall-chart going all the way around the upstairs octagonal classroom above the windows, starting on the far left with Alfred burning cakes, and ending on the far right with Queen Elizabeth II's coronation. They encouraged me to read anything and everything I could get my hands on, and that all learning is in some way connected to everything else. Miss D. even taught us some very basic Latin (*Poeta sum! Quo ambulat nauta?*) and helped us write weekly letters home, without very much censorship at all.

One winter holiday break, dad took me up to Thailand to visit his older sister Nina. Margaret D. told me she had been a bridesmaid for Nina in China, and now she, her Norwegian husband and three children were living and working in a town beside a river, somewhere near Tak. On the way up, we met with Arthur P. and Albert G. I then understood what the lads from Thailand meant by the long train trip down for most, and boats for some, not to mention teak logs, muddy rivers and elephants.

Having a June birthday, a present always came just before the summer holidays – the first year it was *Now We Are Six* by A. A. Milne. The next year it was a battery-powered tinplate model cargo ship, with working cranes. It was taken apart some weeks later by another of the lads I shall not name, to get the magnets out of the motor. The best thing about June, however, was that it would soon be time to go "down the Camerons", meet Dad at the Rest House at Tapah, and get an old bus or train home to Slim River, or later to Teluk Anson, for a happily tearful family reunion.

Summers seemed to pass in a blur. Once or twice, dad took me out with him on open-air preaching evenings, replete with pressure-lamps and indifferent PA systems, helped by a youthful Fred Collard. Dad had gone back to Ireland to visit his elderly mother one year, and much to our delight, brought back his childhood Hornby clockwork train for us to enjoy. Between those and the new shiny green diesels now appearing each day on the Day Mail, trains became a deeply ingrained hobby of mine.

I still remember the day a letter came to Chefoo from mum and dad, telling me that Uncle Alex, in Sydney, had died of cancer, and Margaret D. helping me write an aerogramme with something meaningful in an eight-year-old kind of way, to my Aunty June in Sydney.

Out of classes, play was often pretty rough and tumble, with home-made wide games, or climbing in trees (one day Danny H. used a serrated kitchen knife to saw off a branch that he was sitting on), or handball with "branding" (the mark of a wet ball on a running leg), or roly-poly down grassy banks. Why was roly-poly so popular? Another day, somebody rolled me down the bank too fast, and at the bottom I couldn't move my right elbow. An ambulance arrived and I went "down the Camerons" horizontally nauseated, was met by dad at Tapah, and we reached Ipoh General Hospital late at night. To this day, nobody in our family knows who paid for that ambulance trip. I remember the sickly-sweet smell of inhaling the open ether anaesthetic, to set my elbow fracture, and waking up with a 90-degree elbow plaster – but I got to go home for a month to recover, ha!

Coming back to Chefoo later that year, my younger brother Patrick joined me, and we made the big move across to Lali Djiwa, the "new school". On the day of the move, all of us boys who wished to could walk around there by the road, past the Hong Kong & Shanghai Bank bungalows. It poured with rain when we were half-way there, and as we walked into the new school gates; a bee stung me just above my right elbow. Moving there was great – the new dorms were nice and warm! In the first week, we dammed up the stream and made a great pond for paper boats, until some downstream Brinchang villagers came up to complain that we had cut off their water supply.

But by the end of 1960, mum and dad decided they could not continue to cope with sending two of us away to Chefoo, and the family separation. Although dad was really good at speaking on his feet, and could preach directly from a Hebrew or Greek Biblical text into Mandarin or Cantonese, he was sure his training and qualifications would be even better used in theological training in Singapore, where the family would not need to be separated for schooling, an option not then offered by OMF.

Sadly, the then General Director of the Overseas Missionary Fellowship did not agree with dad. There followed a heated theological debate about whether the sacrifice of separation was either like that of Abraham with Isaac, or like passing children through fire to Molech, the Ammonite abomination, which led to the judgment and ultimate destruction of Israel. No way back after nailing those colours to the mast! We returned to Australia, and a new home, friends and another school experience for 18 months (our elderly male teacher was called "Domine"). Our family returned to Singapore with another sending agency, for Dad to teach theology at Trinity College, and for us kids to attend British Army day schools there.

A decade ago, our older daughter's wedding was held at the Narrabeen Surf Club in Beach Road. The Norfolk Island pines were still there, but the Infants' School has vanished without a trace, with a new Aged Care Centre standing in its place. Visiting there brought me no identification with times past. In stark contrast was the 2018 Chefoo reunion – seeing the Bungalow and the octagonal tower, the new campus, and renewing some long-lost friendships in that context, brought memories flooding back, and introduced Marilyn to a part of my life she had never glimpsed before.

This is not exactly a tale of two schools, but the Chefoo classrooms of the two Margarets helped set a really solid base for my life-long learning. Narrabeen's rigidity meant that Chefoo seemed the better place to me, both then and now, despite the bee-sting, a slightly crooked right elbow and separation from family. Dad's 1960 decision to leave OMF meant that we were delivered from the stress of boarding school during teenage years, having to cope with an unfamiliar country and cultural setting, without our parents being around to help us.

The bee-sting is one of many marks on my skin, a hardly visible white circle now; but each mark reminds me of various incidents and scrapes. My crooked right arm eventually came home to roost in a much more serious way in 2007, with an arthritic bony spur and fibrous band constricting the ulnar nerve, at the funny-bone point on the inside edge of my elbow. I was noticing increasing clumsiness playing a keyboard, worsening handwriting (common enough in a doctor, to be sure) and was losing muscle bulk in the small muscles of the little finger and edge of my right hand. A friendly neurosurgeon relieved the pressure by de-roofing the ulnar nerve tunnel at the elbow; fortunately, almost everything recovered over a couple of months.

Perhaps because of the separation from family while I was at Chefoo, I later grew especially close to my dad in teenage and college years. We walked together with our blue-heeler cattle dog "Horror" each evening, when we both needed a break in the fresh air, away from our studying – theology for him and medicine for me. It wasn't until near the end of medical studies, in my mid-twenties, with periods of time spent away from home at different hospitals and residencies, and with marriage approaching, that dad and I talked in detail about what the time of Chefoo separation had meant for us. Fifteen years after the event, dad asked forgiveness for what had happened in my early primary school years. Poor "Horror" had some of his longest walks ever, in those following weeks.

Sixty years on, my Chefoo years look extraordinarily educationally formative. I never had opportunity to thank Margaret D. and Margaret Q. for what they gave me, and upon which all the rest of my schooling and professional education has been built. But I have had opportunity to thank my parents for the difficult choice they made, between work and family, which spared me the teenage separation and boarding school experience that seems to have been so destructive for many of our Chefoo peers.

* * *

Andrew C. was born in Sydney. When six months old, his parents went to East Asia, to live as pastoral workers in Chinese and Cantonese speaking churches. A polyglot school experience resulted: Sydney northern beaches 1957; Chefoo Malaya 1958–60; Sydney downtown 1961–62; Singapore Army Schools 1962–68; and finally North Sydney 1969–70 (after his family returned to Australia). Science Medicine studies followed at Sydney University, where Marilyn and Andrew met. Married in

1978, four children came along, while Andrew did specialist training in Sydney, and Marilyn taught in secondary schools. The family returned to Sydney in late 1996, after six years' work in Taiwan. Andrew has worked since as HammondCare's Chief Medical Officer and a conjoint Associate Professor at University of New South Wales. Marilyn retired as a High School Head in 2016 and has worked as a high school education consultant since. After over 40 years of marriage, their family includes seven grandchildren and a geriatric Border Collie.

Christine

IN LATE HIGH-SCHOOL, I attended a camp for missionary kids. The speaker shared some of the characteristics of those who attended overseas boarding schools compared with children who lived with parents in their own culture. He mentioned both positive and negative characteristics, such as, early independence, being flexible and quick to adapt, difficulties dealing with grief (from constant losses), difficulties forging close friendships and relationship difficulties with parents. Some of what he said resonated, but I have found it difficult to untangle the threads of what might be attributed to my personality, my own culture (including family culture), generation and even birth order. It would be much easier if I could have pushed rewind on my early schooling and lived it under two different contexts – a day student in Australia or a boarding school in Malaysia – leaving the variables of personality, generation, birth order... the same. As I cannot live my life under scientific test conditions, I am left to reflect as best I can.

At five years and eight months old, I went off to Chefoo School, a boarding school in Malaysia. Every term was four months long and then we had two months of holiday. At eleven, I transferred to boarding school in the Philippines. There we had one long holiday and one much shorter, a pattern I found much more difficult. Even those who now look back negatively at the boarding system concede that the education we received at Chefoo was top rate. When I arrived at Chefoo in the mid-70s, there were six classes with about twelve children per class. All my teachers were good, and some were superb; and we had a far better teacher-student ratio than most in our home countries. Our environment was a children's paradise: a private valley, surrounded by tropical jungle and with its own stream and, if you disliked the outdoors, then there was plenty of indoor space and activities too.

When I set off to fly from Taiwan to Malaysia at age five, did I find it difficult? I'm sure I did but I don't have any memories of those first goodbyes. I do remember always feeling sad for the first night or two, but I never remember feeling abandoned, or that my parents didn't love me, or that they loved their work/Jesus more than me. Why didn't I experience these feelings? Was it because of my personality, or that my parents prepared me well and somehow succeeded in assuring me of their love? What part did prayer play in protecting me? Or did I simply make friends and enjoy school and so didn't have time to think about such things?

Did I cry? I don't remember ever doing so. However, there were at least a few reasons for that. Firstly, I seemed to instinctively know that this was hard for my parents and that my mother, in particular, was determined not to break down. I followed suit. In high-school I clearly remember feeling a sense of responsibility for my younger sister. In line with the era – mid-to-late 70s – I would have been urged to be brave for my siblings and parents and to look after my younger brother and sister. Was this destructive to my emotional well-being or to theirs? Possibly. Certainly I cannot ever remember crying at school (I once faked crying to gain the dorm aunt's attention.) and I do remember the isolation as a seventeen-year-old, when everyone else seemed to be crying at graduation and I couldn't. But at that stage I simply accepted that that was the way I was. Was it caused by the fact I went to boarding school as a five-year-old (and therefore children should never go to boarding school so young)? Maybe, but it could just as easily be a factor of my own personality as an oldest child, whose first instinct was always to think and problem solve rather than respond emotionally.

Certainly, the grief of constant goodbyes did impact me. Having worked hard, in my earlier years, to "be brave" and look after my younger siblings made me a tearless child. The relief of tears was not granted to me until my late twenties when I attended my first conference as a missionary. One of the missionary children was leaving for tertiary studies and I broke down in tears, well beyond what was normal for the situation. One of the leaders questioned if I had emotional problems (implying that perhaps I shouldn't be a missionary). I simply told him that this small goodbye had almost nothing to do with my tears. I was crying for a lifetime of losses. Was I distressed at the time? Not really. More relieved, believing it was something that I needed. Since that time, I have been more able to cry when needed.

If not boarding school, then what were the other options? In light of recent research into the impact of early boarding school on bonding between parents and children, much criticism has been levelled at our organization for recommending this educational option. Suggestions have ranged from only allowing singles to be missionaries to insisting that some other way of getting us educated would have been better for our emotional wellbeing. I've found it helpful for myself to take a step back (I did say I was a thinker rather than a feeler) and remember that parents of every era want the best for their children. They make decisions that they feel will allow their children the broadest range of options for their future.

Way back in 1880 Hudson Taylor, the founder of the China Inland Mission, saw the healthy environment at Chefoo in Shantung Province. Several of his own children had died of disease in inland China and he saw the benefits of being on the coast. Plus, being in a school would allow children to be educated together, rather than their parents struggling on as best they could, in a context where there would have been no outside help like resources arriving by mail. Did parents agonise over sending their children? They must have. The distances travelled meant that they seldom saw their children. They had to entrust their children to the care of other members of their organisation. Children at the original Chefoo were prepared for the Oxford-Cambridge exams, then the most highly regarded curriculum in the world. Even during World War II, when the school and its teachers were interned in a Japanese concentration camp, those children "sat" the examinations. At the end of the war the stored exam papers were submitted and the majority passed.

By the mid-70s, when I was growing up in Taiwan, the educational options and resources may have increased but the desire of our parents was unchanged from those parents of earlier generations. The possibilities for primary (elementary) school were:

- *Do some sort of home-schooling.* This was a fairly unsupported system in the 70s. Mail was unreliable, and many parents weren't equipped to do the teaching. There were also issues of differentiating the parent-teacher roles.

- *Attend a local school in the host country.* The huge advantages of this were being able to learn the local language and being able to live at home. This was also the cheapest option. However, not all local governments permitted foreigners to enrol in their schools, or were willing to accommodate children who were different. Many Asian countries included religious ceremonies and religious worldview frameworks that missionaries did not want their children being influenced by.

- *Return to your home country and board at a school or with relatives.* This happened at high-school level, but I don't believe anyone did it for 5–11 year olds.

- *Foreign* schools *in the host country.* These were mainly schools for diplomats, business and military children. These schools were not only expensive but, in many countries (like Taiwan), used the American curriculum. The Australian system was closer to the British and we needed to be prepared to return to our home country. It probably didn't matter at primary school age, but it certainly did for high school.

Those making the decision (mostly parents themselves, and thus with a vested interest in getting the best solution) chose an option that was not only healthy, but set out to make the best possible education for children.

How were my friendships and other relationships, affected by Chefoo? What effect has this had on me in later life? Relationships between the children and the staff at Chefoo seem to have been deep and healthy. However, as children matured, they were faced with multiple goodbyes. The pain of these goodbyes led to some children choosing to avoid deep relationships and to withdraw emotionally so that the pain of goodbyes was lessened. These seem to have been the children who have suffered the most in later life.

I had particularly good friends as a ten- and eleven-year-old, and only one close friend and a few others accompanied me to high school. I had also been close to several of the staff, both on the teaching and dorm side. I continued to write to six of those staff for the next forty years, although two of them died along the way. Although maybe this was "odd" in the sense of not a common thing, it has been nothing but blessing in my life. As I became an adult, the relationship changed and now we meet as equals to encourage each other.

Sometime in high school, I made the conscious decision that I would pay the price of painful goodbyes, because it was better to have deep friendships which tore my heart when we parted than to keep everything superficial. My choice led to pain but also moments of great joy; but I saw the alternative of choosing superficial relationships as only leading to isolation and a sort of grey existence. I have never regretted my decision. The grief of goodbyes has been balanced by the joy of deep friendships and many hellos, and makes heaven more real to me. For me, one joy of heaven is a place where there are no more goodbyes. I believe my friendships and relationship with my parents have hugely benefited from my experiences. To this day I can quickly develop strong ties to people.

Relationships with parents. Adult missionary kids have commented that it is the relationship with parents that suffered most from early age boarding school. Issues raised include an inability to communicate with parents, a sense of emotional distance and ongoing resentments, One other area is that, when the time came for the missionary child to be a parent, they struggled to parent primary school aged children because they had not experienced a consistent, full-time model themselves. I did not experience these difficulties and I'm not sure what made the difference. My mother wrote wonderful weekly letters, full of news and little drawings appropriate to our stage of life. As someone who writes to different age nephews and nieces, I know it isn't easy to write to young children. My mother had been an infant teacher (five-to-seven-year olds) which must have helped. My dad seldom wrote, which made his short paragraphs even more precious. During our school holidays, my parents made a big effort to include us in their work, and I remember many camps and church visits where we helped sell Christian books. One of the disadvantages of boarding school was that I didn't speak Chinese and I loved adding up the prices and using the few words of language (mostly numbers) I had to give change. My parents also took all their holidays when we were able to accompany them. Thus, one quarter of our time at home we had their undivided attention. Walks, swims in rivers, and picnics were all highlights of my childhood. It is tempting to blame family, relationships, emotional and parenting difficulties on early boarding school but I suspect the reasons are more complex. It is easier to blame an institution than to admit that it could be due to other factors, like our own parents and their inadequacies, or personal factors. My parents certainly weren't perfect, any more than I am, or any other human being.

Would I recommend that children be sent to boarding school at age five? No, not if there are other better options.

Do I regret that I was sent at age five? No. A resounding no. However, this is because the particular school I attended was not your run-of-the-mill boarding school. My high school does not evoke the same feelings at all. It was a good school with good staff, but I would never describe myself as "belonging" to that school. However, Chefoo School was different. To this day, when I meet a graduate there is a deep, emotional link, even if we were from totally different eras. I have travelled to Malaysia twice for a reunion. Each time I've come home full of joy and thankfulness that I had the privilege of going to Chefoo.

I find it hard to identify what makes the vast difference. Maybe it is because the primary school was much smaller. It had more of a family feel. This may also have been because over 90% of the children were from one missionary agency. Many of the family attitudes and values were similar, even if we went home to holidays in different countries. Maybe it was the quality of the staff, or a few outstanding individuals, who made the school special. I don't know. Did they pray more for their students and love us better? I don't know. I just know that I loved it and to this day pity people who did not attend Chefoo.

One thing that has helped me process my experiences is my Christian faith. Believing in a God who loves and can be trusted has coloured my world. It has enabled me to concede that no matter what my schooling/family situation there would be challenges. That is simply a matter of living in this broken world. If I had grown up under another education system, there would still have been challenges and issues. Not necessarily fewer or even easier, just different.

The hardest parts of my education were the years I attended public schools in Australia. I appreciated having my parents around at those times, as surviving in a place where I was bullied, and taught by teachers who did their job but were a pale reflection of the teachers in Malaysia, was much more difficult. Chefoo School was an environment in which creativity was encouraged and fostered. I look at the schooling nowadays and feel sorry for the students in comparison with what I experienced. Yes, we lost out in terms of music (there were only three instruments available to learn) and other opportunities (no ballet, horse riding...) but other pursuits – craft, inventing games, drama (with homemade props and costumes) flourished.

Looking back from the perspective of middle-age, I do not regret going to Chefoo School. I loved it, and regard it as one of my life's privileges. If I could live my life again, I'd still choose to go to the same school in preference to any of the other options that were available.

* * *

Christine attended Chefoo between 1975 and 1981 and then went on to board at Faith Academy in the Philippines. Her parents served in Taiwan from 1964–87 and she has two younger siblings. At seventeen, Christine returned to Australia to complete her secondary schooling and attend University. She worked as a physiotherapist, then attended Sydney

Missionary & Bible College as she had always intended to go overseas as a missionary. She joined OMF herself in 1999 and is still serving in Taiwan as a church-planter. Bible storytelling, training others and writing fill her days. Her first books were ministry related non-fiction, but she is now writing Christian fiction, see www.storytellerchristine.com.

Elwyn

I WAS ENJOYING the warmth of the sunshine as I hung the washing on the clothesline behind our home when I noticed the two policemen standing, hats in hand, at the bottom of the cobbled driveway outside the Karuah Road office of OMF New South Wales. They were hovering at the doorway talking to the receptionist. When they turned and looked at me my chest tightened. "What now," I asked myself! They asked me where my parents were. I hurried inside to find whoever I could.

Uncharacteristically, most of my family had been back under the same roof for the previous six weeks following my father, Neville C's double heart attack, at the age of fifty-six. I was in my mid-twenties and had been overseas to study and travel. My parents had been in the middle of moving house, to live in the vacant old Karuah Road property (formerly an OMF Mission Home, then a hostel for missionaries' children), when my father had suffered his stroke. Now, roughly a year later, he was recovering from two heart attacks, probably brought on by him continuing to drive himself to maintain his workload as Australian Home Director for OMF while paralyzed on the right side from the stroke. On hearing of his father's heart attacks, my brother Rhon, (otherwise known as Rhonsley to those who had started school with him at Chefoo) had caught the next available airline flight back to Sydney from Queensland to be part of the family.

You see, my sister was in hospital, a different hospital, at the same time as my father was admitted. She required surgery to remove a tangle of plates, pins and screws, which had been installed in her left leg and arm, following a massive car accident only two years previously. So we took it in shifts to visit one hospital and then the other. While in hospital recuperating, dad had asked for his old diaries to be provided and he had reflected on his years of ministry with OMF, starting from the beginning, and God's call on his life from his days in Bible College.

Rhon had been the chauffeur when our mother brought dad home from hospital. He had left his job in Queensland, helping a friend set up a new gym, and was at a loose end. He caught up with old friends but had been in quite a reflective space for a few weeks. An old friend who worked in a radio station gave him several cassettes of music from our teen years and we danced and sang together and felt nostalgic for the "good ole days" in the Philippines. I remember he reflected on his life and told me, "I'm brighter than you, Elwyn, but what do I have to show for my years? You have two degrees and I haven't even finished one!" He surprised us all with his mellowing attitude and newfound thoughtfulness. Where was the egocentric bodybuilder, obsessing about his image and getting the ladies? It was lovely to see my mother smiling and hopeful, despite her concern for her husband. It was encouraging; her prodigal son seemed to be finally returning.

A couple of Rhon's friends approached him to join their road trip to Adelaide to watch the first ever Australian Grand Prix. Somewhat reluctantly he agreed to attend. The noise, the fumes and fracas of the Grand Prix just didn't hold the appeal that it had once. But, commitment to his friend, who had only recently netted an enviable position as a sports journalist, won him over. They had embarked on their road trip before dawn on the Friday morning. I remember hearing the rear fly screen door bang as he departed.

Now it was Monday morning – mum came down the stairs to meet the police. We were ushered into a nearby room and told to sit down. The tension and gravity of the moment was immense as we searched the faces of the policemen for a clue of what they were going to tell us, desperate for better news than we feared. We had been in a not dissimilar position in a hospital emergency room only two years previously, following my sister's MVA.

Apparently, Rhon's friend had, they think, gone to sleep at the wheel of the car and driven it headlong into an oncoming truck, in the early hours of the morning as the sun had been rising in his face. The young men had taken turns and driven all night, in an effort to return to Sydney in time for an interview the journalist had at midday Monday. We were to learn that Rhon had been in the back seat of the car, probably asleep after taking his turn at driving, and would have been oblivious to what unfolded. All three young men had been killed in the impact.

My mother's response was to moan and cry out, "No God! No! You promised!" I alone knew to what she was referring. She had been desperately interceding for my wayward brother's soul for many years and, at one point, she felt that the Lord had assured her that her three children would all call themselves after the name of the Lord (Isaiah 44:5), and now he was gone... she was bereft. She had never seen this brilliant, personable, strong-willed young man using all his latent talent to glorify the Lord. She felt abandoned by her God as well as all her motherly aspirations for her precious only son.

By this time we had found my father, who was sitting in a warm sunny room on the opposite side of the rambling house, reflecting on his diaries and the journey of his years in ministry on the mission field; he had heard the commotion and intuitively began to prepare himself for bad news. The next few days are something of a dazed blur. First the newspapers turned up to get a more detailed picture of the friend of their journalist colleague. A couple of my uncles kindly volunteered to travel the hundreds of kilometres to the site of the accident and identify Rhon's body, sparing us the added trauma. Then there were consultations with the funeral directors, and composing of an obituary, and commencing plans for the funeral. I remember a procession of well-wishers and phone calls, flower deliveries, hot meal deliveries and constant busyness for my sister and I. Extended family began appearing from interstate and, bunking down in the rambling house, trying to be as supportive as possible but forcing us to suspend any expressions of grief. Mum was a shell of herself, going through the motions but lost in a world of pain. Dad numbly retreated to his office, his diaries and composing a eulogy for his only son. What would he say?

I have never known such emotional exhaustion as I did that week. A day or two later, mum had collapsed for a "siesta" after lunch, and suddenly appeared with an intense expression on her face. She recounted to my sister and I how she had been sleeping heavily and just as she was rousing she found a line from the story of the Prodigal Son (Luke 15:20) was repeated over and over to her in her mind. It said, "and while he was yet far off the father saw him and ran to him". She wondered whether it was a message from the Lord. A message to assure her that her prodigal son had been taken to his heavenly Father. A message of reassurance and comfort from her loving Father.

I pounced on this insight and recounted to her the supporting evidence that Rhon had been "on his way home" to getting himself right with the Lord. We had all witnessed how he had mellowed and become more thoughtful, less selfish and I told her of my conversation where he'd been expressing regret for the wasted years. Though sad, we drew comfort from her revelation. Suddenly dad emerged from his office, limping from the effects of his stroke. He was holding a flimsy piece of writing paper on which was the scrawl of a young child's handwriting. His face held a quizzical expression. He said, "Look what just fell out of my diary when I turned the page today," he held up a precious letter written by Rhon as a young lad while attending boarding school at Chefoo school in Malaysia. Despite the childish spelling mistakes the message was clear. God so mercifully uncovered that note at the perfect moment when the boy's earthly parents needed its message. It said, "Daddy, I learned to know God at school after the story of William Carey. Jesus is in my heart now today and forever. Rhonsley". We could take heart that this lad's heavenly Father was committed to honouring the contract He had made with the boy that day.

So, thanks to a letter from Chefoo, I believe I will see my brother again in that place where there are no more tears, no more heartache, and no more goodbyes.

* * *

Elwyn attended Chefoo Malaysia 1966–68, Chefoo Philippines 1968–70, boarded in Sydney OMF hostel for children of missionaries early 1973 & 1976-77. Attended Faith Academy Manila 1974–76. Today, blessed to be a wife, mother of five, Occupational Therapist and Counsellor.

Edmund

WAKING UP TO THE SOUND of glorious birdsong early each morning, nestled among the jungle trees of the Cameron Highlands, Malaysia, has given me a real appreciation of God's creation, the ecology of natural habitats, and such joyful childhood memories. Our many guided tours through those jungles gave me a sense of direction and exploration skills that came to good use in more recent adventures. I found our lodgings were so cool, not just in the low temperatures, but in the sleek architecture of the buildings we resided in. The central building of the school was different, a much more interesting construction in warmer colours, yet with the bold lines of Tudor architecture. Compared to most other schools I have seen in Australia, I have come to the conclusion that Chefoo was the most beautiful establishment anywhere! To add to this were the sprawling greens of the football pitch and the streamside playing areas. I miss that stream, as Australia has barely any running watercourses, unless you go into the mountains. Well Chefoo was in the mountains at any rate, but Malaysia is mostly mountainous anyway, with equatorial rains all year round.

A beautiful setting, it had, furthermore, a beautiful staff group of teachers and dorm carers. They gave such calming and heart-warming welcomes, I soon got over my fear of tigers, and was entertained by the whoops of a gibbon swinging through the trees. I marvelled at the nature studies presented by Mr M. that illustrated godly character. It was fun to get off-campus on the weekends and see some of the town, the palace-side golf course, and go to church in an arched roof building with a granite facade. All small steps to being able to do business in the outside world. School tours of industries like tea plantations, a Tin Dredge, a pewter factory, or even the Post Office and Fire Station, gave a sense of industriousness needed for later work applications.

Chefoo's sport programmes did prepare me for high school efforts, and I've kept fitness throughout my working life as a result. Soccer was a great sport, though I was not as fanatical as some about it. I opted instead for the wrestling team in High School. What was really cool though was Chefoo's swimming pool, and I have been more of a water-sports person in adulthood. It was rather chilly for swimming half the time, but we had some great times, and even had school gala days. I was the champion slippery pole wrestler. I could still brace myself for cold water when I started surfing in Australian winters, wearing a wetsuit conveniently. I still laugh at myself, remembering how I was a fast sprinter on field days but would come third last in a marathon. I enjoyed hurdles and long jump too, like a kangaroo.

Being Christian involves forgiveness and acquittal of wrongdoings, so I'm not about to bring up all the faults of people at Chefoo, or even of myself. I can say that Dr P. inspired tenacity to the faith on his preaching visits, and an appreciation of historic Christian scientists and explorers. Dianne W. gave a general understanding of relationships and psychology as my dorm parent. Mr M. gave good instruction on sexuality, and was honourable in many other ways. Mr P. was a very accepting gentleman and encouraged me in both sport and study. I liked the British atmosphere of Chefoo better than the American atmosphere of Faith Academy, and I try to maintain that British honour in my heart here in Australia. "Honour God and fear his command, for this is the whole duty of man," concludes Ecclesiastes.

Coming to Australia from Asian countries was a breath of fresh air. Much more sparsely populated, Australia has much less pollution, but I think the people are calmer too. I found it grievous, however, that I would have to separate from friends of my youth, as they all went to Britain and America, save one I continued to go to church with in Sydney. He was very accepting, and we had fun exploring the Australian bush, but also attending music concerts. I had been into rock and roll, ever since hearing Cliff Richard and The Shadows at Chefoo, so the rock scene was not a shock to me and I played in a band. Luckily, my Christian education had steered me clear of the drinking and drugs associated with it.

Far from trying to please people due to peer pressure, a book by Dr Carson instilled the resolution to be faithful to God, despite all opposition, even to the cross, so to speak. So, while I had some adjustments to make with new people groups, the problems were not at the feet of Chefoo, or to be blamed on my upbringing, but were rather the faults of Western society. I may not have had the charisma to make it to fame and fortune, but Chefoo gave the basis to a faith that will transcend the world!

While I have not yet become a clergyman, I am well aware of what it is like to be separated from parents for the cause of the Church, much like the prophet Samuel was. His mother Hannah dedicated him to temple service from a young age. Going to Chefoo was quite a stressful ordeal, with three-day journeys by train and taxi, even without the heartache of missing family members. However, it was understood that it was for a good cause, for Christ no less, and the cross we bore in the process was endured, much like Samuel, in separation from our family. I thank God for the mercy I found at Chefoo, learning to trust and obey Christ, whom I had accepted on the mission field. I would say that primary schooling does not have as big a bearing on adulthood as high school, but Chefoo did have a great influence towards love and purity in my life.

Interlude 4:
The Journey to School /
Going Home
Jemimah

The Journey to School

MY JOURNEY TO SCHOOL began on the sleepy train from Surabaya to Jakarta. Daddy came with me and my little friend Anna. Bunk beds in a moving carriage – what fun! Lying on my narrow berth, the regular juddering of the engine made it feel like the carriage was falling sideways down the hill. When I woke up the next morning, we were in a new place. The next part was the plane to Malaysia. After goodbye hugs with dad, we happily tripped up the escalator holding hands, escorted by the air hostess onto the plane.

We were met by a member of staff and spent the night at the KL mission home. As we arrived at the guest house, we were greeted by many old friends who had all arrived the same day. We were piled up in one bedroom, eagerly whispering our news to each other. A teacher had to sit outside the door of the bedroom to make sure we all quietened down and got to sleep. The next morning, I made sure I had a big bowl of the chunky homemade breakfast cereal. You can't get muesli like that anywhere else on the missionary kid school circuit.

Next came the best part. Four hours in a taxi with a teacher, who had a plentiful supply of plastic bags, toilet paper and polos[23]. When a boy in our taxi suddenly said, "I feel sick!", out whipped a plastic bag which was promptly filled, along with appropriate retching sounds. We disposed of this at the next rest stop, where we each trooped off to the toilets with a couple of squares of toilet paper in our pockets. Then we got to choose a soda pop to drink with a straw, and a coconut bun. Mountain Dew was the most popular choice, so I expressed my rebellious ways by going for Seven Up.

Further up the mountain, our teacher issued everyone with a polo, "Let's have a competition to see who can keep a polo in their mouth the longest without breaking it!" That came in handy for keeping the taxi quiet for half an hour.

After four hours, we bundled out of the cars into the cool air of the highlands school, greeted by hugs from our dorm aunties and warm beds with blankets on them. I loved snuggling up under the covers after the heat of the equator.

A couple of weeks later I realised my parents were not around.

---

23 A well-known brand of ring-shaped mint boiled sweet.

Going Home

I come from where the rain falls hard
and the crickets sing loud
and the heat sticks to you.

I have seen a lifetime of beautiful sunsets
and cockroaches sleeping under my bed
and children begging on the streets.

I would go home
to the land of cold winds and frosts,
and comfortable carpeted rooms,
and people who look like me but

I am myself
to no-one there.

Everywhere I go I search
for people who will listen
and then I try to make them into people who will
understand.

5

Relationships

How hard is it to stand on sand in waves?
A childhood based on family separations for
religious reasons may not have been a firm
foundation for such standing. Adult relationships
were affected in these two essays.

Anonymous

WHAT WERE WE TAUGHT? What did we learn that we were not taught but gleaned? What did we learn for ourselves as we grew up? What tripped us up? What are we still learning?

Sex is a good thing created by God for a married couple to enjoy.

You may ruin the experience of sex with your husband if you have sex before you are married – whether with him or with someone else.

You will go to hell if you have sex before or outside marriage.

You should not tell your parents if you are having sex with a boyfriend, and you should expect to be put into separate bedrooms if you and your boyfriend stay at your parents' house (however old you are).

Sex is a powerful force and needs to be managed.

Men cannot control their sex drive as it is so strong, so it is women who have to "apply the brakes" and manage situations which may get "out of control".

If someone wants to have sex with you outside of marriage, they don't respect you.

Women and girls should not leave underwear lying around as men and boys may not be able to control themselves.

Women should dress discreetly and not flaunt their sexuality because men cannot control themselves.

Women should wear a petticoat which shows just a little under their skirt or dress as this is feminine and alluring to men.

Any attempt to be feminine or to enhance one's appearance with make-up is female frippery and we have to accept ourselves as we are and as God made us.

So

I regret not enjoying my young and attractive body and feeling so disconnected from my own body for so many years.

I regret feeling I had to suppress my sexuality and feeling that I had to take responsibility for men's.

I am sorry that I didn't sleep with more men when I was single in order to learn more about my sexuality.

I am still learning that it is ok to feel sexual and to express sexual desire.

I still have a lot to learn about asking for what I want in a sexual relationship.

I still need to feel more comfortable bringing the sexual and the emotional together.

I love having a man in my life whose body I love to touch.

I am still learning to fling my bra onto the bedroom chair rather than hide it under other clothing.

I would like to feel lighter and more playful about sex. It doesn't have to be serious!

Rosie

WHY DID I MARRY a man who didn't really love me?

This question has haunted me down the years.

The man I married was intelligent, an Oxford classicist, cultured, a former choirboy with an artistic bent, a talented photographer and handsome. I thought I was the luckiest girl on the planet.

So, years later, why did I leave him? When we first met, he courted me devotedly, was romantic, charming and we enjoyed debating about everything. I did not realise that there was another aspect to his personality.

Should I, could I, have known what he was really like? After years of retrospection the first clue to my choice is the location where I met him: Hong Kong. Away from any anchor points of family or community, yet achingly familiar for me. He was there for a year post-Oxford working for Help the Aged. A man with a sense of adventure and a charitable heart. Like my father, I thought. I was in Hong Kong for different reasons: having grown up all over South East Asia (born in Jakarta, Indonesia; schooled in the Cameron Highlands of Malaysia; as well as living in the cities of Manila and Singapore), I had longed to return to my homelands, so had secured my first job, teaching in a Sixth Form College in Hong Kong.

In those days the approach to Kai Tak airport was spectacular: flying low over shantytowns and the infamous Walled City, adjacent to high-rise tower blocks, wings dipping from side to side before pulling up to a very short runway heading straight out to sea, followed by a dizzying sharp turn back inland. I can still remember the sensation as I stepped off that plane as a twenty year old: mixed diesel fumes, smothering humidity and heat that glued your clothes and hair to your body, mingled with the pungency of childhood memory – steamed rice, ginger, chili, five-spice, soy. With one breath I was transported back to my five-year-old self. This smelt like home.

It held many associations for me too, as my British father and Canadian mother, who had met as young missionary language students in Chungking, China, twenty-eight years before, had been evicted to Hong Kong by the Chinese government. They married there, with friends but no family in attendance.

So when I met my husband-to-be at the international church we both attended, it seemed significant. The first time we spoke was at a house party on the nearby island of Cheung Chau to the sound of waves crashing onto a jagged coastline – the very place, the same shuttered, veranda-ed retreat that my parents had honeymooned in. I was intrigued: an educated, literary Englishman discovered so far from our homes, in this Asian setting that echoed my childhood countries.

A year later I showed him the places I had grown up in: the amazing complex of offices and flats in the heart of Embassy-land opposite the renowned Botanical Gardens (my childhood playground) in Singapore; the slums, sewers and shipyards of Jakarta; and my beloved jungle-school in The Cameron Highlands. Our extraordinary education there inspired in me a lifetime of teaching. Learning was fun. Books were plentiful and reading a joy for this bookworm, especially when we lay on the floor to listen to a story. Plays, poems, projects – all were coloured by the fabulous rainforest we lived in. School trips were to rubber plantations, tin mines and even to stroke a newly deceased tiger. Free time was spent climbing trees, munching on stolen sugar-cane, sipping nectar from colourful flowers, collecting rubber bands, three-legged races, playing hare-and-hounds in the surrounding jungle and, on occasion, wandering off alone to the stream to shed silent tears of loneliness. It meant so much to share these precious places with the man I was hoping to live my life with. This was not just sentimental nostalgia for the past; I wanted this man I had met to understand where I came from and who I was. I knew instinctively that these places were deeply laced into my identity.

Whilst visiting Chefoo, we stayed in a beautiful colonial building, known as The Bungalow, that had been a holiday home for visiting parents. It was a stunning location, overlooking valleys and fern-clad hills, surrounded by roses and orchids, and a real haven of peace, filled with happy memories of precious holidays with my parents. Imagine my amazement when I discovered that my mother's Canadian bridesmaid was also staying. When she heard years later of my divorce, she wrote to me, recalling a day during that visit when she had found me in tears, and was very concerned that the relationship I was embarking on was not a tender one. She had seen my father courting my mother, and no doubt shared my mother's confidences, so she could have made an example of my parents' relationship but, as an unmarried woman, didn't feel qualified to counsel me, and so said nothing until that sad letter – a first warning delivered too late.

One strange aspect of this incident is that I do not remember the cause of the tears. Along with so many other early memories it remains, to this day firmly locked up in my subconscious. Others amongst us have memories seared with incredibly painful detail. Dare I say, I almost envy them the opportunity they have to face up to their realities? I wonder if my healing would be more complete if more of those early traumas returned to sharp focus. Or should I be grateful that most of the negative associations have been lost, leaving me with a rather myopic, sunny vision of my childhood?

Thirty years later, I returned to Asia for a Chefoo School reunion in those verdant hills of Malaysia. I was grieving deeply for my parents who had both died the previous year. I was also five years post-divorce. On my first evening there I met a fellow adult missionary child, who had been in Hong Kong with her parents while my former husband and I were there, and she remembered us both. She confided that her father had been concerned about my relationship and thought that I needed to go back to England to spend time with my father. Another undelivered warning. I was stunned at this insight from the past. Why had he not spoken to me? And if he had, would I have listened? Although I adored my father and had a very close, empathetic relationship with him, I had spent a total of not more than five childhood years with him. Parenting was largely remote – by letter, with intense bursts of family life for all-too-short holidays. He had not had many opportunities to filter my responses to other people, to guide me, to reinforce my better instincts.

My vicar in Hong Kong, whose family I had become very close to, did try to intervene, I believe, when my young man headed back to England. Unfortunately, his advice was to not become engaged then, which neither of us had any intention of doing at that point, so the more relevant conversation about our compatibility never surfaced. Three potential warnings, not clearly given and not understood.

So why was I impervious to the misgivings of the adults around me?

At the age of twenty I was fiercely independent, like so many other Third Culture Kids. My parents were working in a country I had not previously lived in, but which was in many ways familiar. Confident, articulate, I was keen to live life to the full. My colourful childhood stories, retold with relish, marked me out as exotic. I would not say that I was impulsive, I gave our relationship a great deal of consideration. I read books on the subject. I sought Biblical guidelines. I dreamt that my godly grandmother gave us her blessing from heaven. Even my literature studies were insufficient to alert me to the potential problems in our relationship.

In many ways we seemed well suited: both highly educated and articulate, fond of travel, churchgoers, and even both with parents in adjacent English counties, despite meeting at the other end of the world, I had high hopes for our life together; buoyed by youthful enthusiasm, inspired by the unconditional love of my parents for each other and us, and assured that we were a strong partnership. Naively unaware of the misgivings of others, I did not seek the opinion or approval of the people I trusted most: my parents. Three years later we married. In a few years I entered into motherhood with delight – compensating no doubt for the absences I had experienced as a child, and rose to the challenges of expat life in America and Ireland, making several homes and gardens with joy. Life was full: I was happy in every respect except for the most intimate relationship of all.

Before our marriage I had been unaware of the impact of traumatic relationships undergirding his experience of family. Equally, I was unaware of the effects my own upbringing had had on what I brought to our partnership.

That first Chefoo reunion was the start of another difficult journey of unravelling how my childhood had impacted on my adult life and my marriage: what I may have inadvertently brought to the mix of a failed relationship. Over the past five years since that first reunion there have been other opportunities for my peers and I to come together to process our extraordinary childhoods. We were privileged to have gifted and professional advisers such as Ruth van Reken (MK, author of *Letters Never Sent, Third Culture Kids: The Experience of Growing Up Amongst Worlds,* hugely influential co-founder and researcher of the TCK movement.) and Ulrika Ernvik (MK, author of *Third Culture Kids: A Gift To Care For* and inspirational therapist.) to guide us through experiences we were too young at the time to understand, let alone deal with adequately.

So how and why had my marriage gone wrong?

One factor may have been the impact of a boarding school education, first in Malaysia, and subsequently in North Wales, UK.

There were undoubtedly benefits: a strong sense of independence, self-reliance, adaptability and creative problem-solving have all served me well in later life.

My entire schooling was at boarding school. At the age of four, not quite five, I flew from Manila to Kuala Lumpur to travel up to Chefoo. My older brother and sister were, by this time, at secondary schools in England. I barely knew them, in many ways I was an only child. Joining my parents for holidays in Singapore, where they had relocated, was an experience I only shared once with my older siblings. At nine, I returned to England to attend a girls' school, in order to be with my sister for her last year of school. I think she has felt a burden of responsibility for me ever since. I am indebted for her unwavering kindness, but I wish, for her sake, she could have just been my big sister, not my surrogate mother. Sadly, I have hardly ever lived in the same country, let alone the same house, as my brother. It was two years before we saw our parents again. I was beside myself with excitement anticipating their return – I believe the whole school knew! The reality, however, was that when they did appear, they were familiar strangers. I felt shy with them. They had turns of phrase that I had forgotten, but recognised with a shock of loss.

We had to rebuild trust within our face-to-face relationships, subtly different to our pen-pal personas. I was fortunate that my parents were emotionally warm and absolutely focused on working at making our family time together special. Despite this, I feel it would have been emotionally healthier for me had I stayed at Chefoo, spending holidays with my parents until returning to England at the age of thirteen. The reality was that I needed my parents even more than I needed my siblings.

As I was growing up, because my parents were not on hand as advisers, I learnt to manage by myself. After all, this was our default behaviour, learned when we first started to live, for months at a time, away from our parents. I did write openly to them about many things, but they were unable to filter my responses to the daily incidents of life. In addition, there was no one at school to make me feel special. There was no tender touch. I did not feel safe, as I did with my tall father. I missed the warmth and gentleness of my mother in those spartan surroundings. I did not feel understood for who I was. I became unnaturally shy and quiet. Had I grown up with my parents, I would have embraced much earlier my natural outgoing persona. So I grew up in the only way I knew how, not expressing my needs, my thoughts, my concerns. I grew up alone in a crowd of other lonely girls. I promised myself that my children would grow up with spontaneity and warmth – and they did. But sadly, I married a man who increasingly couldn't engage with his own emotions – an all too familiar reflection of those earlier boarding experiences. Had I unconsciously sought out the very opposite sort of man I should have been with? I learned to express my needs to him, but he was unable to support and care for me in the way I yearned for – as my father had.

Another aspect of boarding school life that impacted me deeply was the food I was expected to eat. As a very young child in Malaysia I developed an aversion to the porridge that was served. I could not tolerate the slimy texture, the sour taste of reconstituted powdered milk, but especially the lumps. I could not, would not swallow them. So I sat there, in tears, often after everyone else had left breakfast, unable to force it down. I was not allowed to eat anything else until I'd had my porridge, so I was unable to enjoy the homemade bread, which I adored. My aversion is surprising, because my mother was a life-long porridge devotee, purple porridge being her specialty in later life, made with gleaned English blackberries. Had I lived at home, I am sure I would have learned to love this healthy food, but to this day I cannot bring myself to try it. At my English boarding school the dish of hate was also served at breakfast: fluorescent, sulphuric-dyed kippers; so salty they made me sweat. Here too I was made to sit staring at my plate for what seemed like an eternity, forced to stay until I had eaten something I viewed as unpalatable.

What did I learn from these "culinary" experiences? That my choices, my preferences, even in something as personal as my food choices, did not matter. Such choices are often asserted by very young children as their first declaration of independence and individuality. I understand that in institutions food has to be prepared and consumed communally, but there was no leeway for really strong aversions. What I felt did not matter. This subordination of my will, reflected in a thousand other rules surrounding clothing regulations, length of skirts, colour of summer dresses, bedtimes, and so on, may have led to self-discipline and an ability to deal with deprivation, an absence of spoiling. However, I now also understand that at school, away from my parents' loving influence, it became "normal" for me to be forced into behavioural patterns that violated me – a sad precursor in later life to becoming abused.

Reading *Boarding School Syndrome* by Joy Schaverien[24] in

24 Joy Schaverien (2015) *Boarding School Syndrome: The Psychological Trauma of the 'Privileged' Child*. London, Routledge

conjunction with listening to a lecture by Ulrika Ernvik I came to another shocking realization: a childhood of boarding schools had not only created independence, it had also inured me to rigid rules, often rules I disliked, but was compliant with. Growing up outside the family home without my parents' support, my instincts that this was unacceptable were not confirmed. I had learned to obey, rather than rebel, as a very young child. With that, however, came the suppression of my will. I was forced, finally, to confront the very uncomfortable truth that this was a toxic combination. Obedient by nature, despite a strong sense of justice, I had also been trained to submit, as well as learning to be self-effacing, this toxic combination had set me up as the perfect candidate for an abusive relationship.

Looking back, I also wonder if the fact that I did not belong to any one community made a difference to my life-choices, especially as none of these groups remained part of my life when I embarked on adulthood. I belonged both everywhere and nowhere.

I grew up in communal mission homes, boarding schools, then university. I lived entirely in a succession of disparate communities until I married. Large international groups were my norm. I learned to connect easily with a wide range of people. Hearing a conglomeration of Aussie, American, Swedish, Chinese and English voices remains familiar and soothing. Diversity is something we took for granted from a very young age.

From the formative age of five to eight, in the school holidays, I belonged to an international mission community, as well as to my family. There were benefits as well as deprivations with this lifestyle. We had the privacy of our own flat, but meals and playtimes were shared with the other resident families. A sheltered community, where I knew few men. The one man I knew best, my father, was a wonderful father to me: thoughtful, kind, passionate, fun – I felt special with him, and very much loved.

Once I returned to England, at the tender age of nine, I belonged to another type of community: a girls school, known locally as "The nunnery on the hill", where the majority of staff were female and unmarried. This was not the healthiest environment for a teenager's development. Educationally tepid for the most part, socially restricted, it stifled my individuality, my creativity, my ability to explore who I wanted to become. It gave me no role models for the sort of woman, wife or mother I wanted to grow into. I missed my mum.

At university I enjoyed choosing the communities I belonged to. I flourished, enjoying the freedom at my disposal, nurturing not only my need to belong, but welcoming others who needed a home from home. Stimulated intellectually and socially, I came alive. I was ready for life! But these were three short years, after which the pull of Asia drew me back, severing much of the community I had built up for myself. Changing worlds regularly is a familiar cycle to the TCK, and has cost many of us dearly. The habits learned in childhood persist, even subconsciously. We were used to changing friends, schools and countries with alarming regularity.

Another question I have had to address is what was the impact of long separation, not only from my parents, but also normal family life?

I did not grow up for long in my family.

My sister was at boarding school when I was born, I was two months old when we first met, my brother soon followed her to school in Malaysia and, when I was three, to England.

Family life was a rare treat for holidays: and for those of us growing up fifty years ago, the cost of travel to the other end of the world prohibited being a family for years at a time. So, in my secondary school holidays, along with up to thirty other missionaries' children, I lived in a grand old house in Surrey, cared for ably by a team of adults *in loco parentis*. But they were not my parents. I was one of many children, and I still felt alone. I had few visits to my English relations, and barely knew my Canadian family. Yet again, our basic needs were met, but love, touch and individual nurturing could not flourish in such an environment. I was fortunate that my parents returned to England when I was a teenager, sharing our home in order to fill that same role for other MKs.

My parents had, despite the long separations, lavished me with love and we enjoyed real closeness as adults. I adored being with them. Sharing my mother's recipes and her passion for colourful flowers;

discussing my set texts with her, listening to my father's enthusiastic retelling of stories and lively debates around shared meals; trying to beat my mother at Scrabble, or my father to the crossword puzzle answer; going for walks to pick blackberries, or harvest apples; picnicking on their ancient, green tartan rug; watching Kent play cricket at Canterbury – we all did our best to make up for our lost family time. As an adult, it gave me deep joy to integrate them into our family life – Christmas, Easter, birthdays – we all gathered together at any excuse. It was healing for my siblings and I to share our children with our parents and, in some measure, give back to them what they too had missed out on while we were boarding. It is not surprising that my sister, brother and I all chose to be very involved in our own children's care, no doubt each of us attempting to heal our own lost childhoods.

The night my father died, most unexpectedly, closely followed eighteen hours later by my mother (who had been gently fading for some time), I re-experienced, for the first time since childhood, the grief of being utterly alone and unprotected. I wept tears of deepest anguish that night, once again the little girl of four who could not run to her mother for comfort, or feel safe in her father's arms. My early traumatic memories remain locked away, but that night was a visceral re-entry to the emotions of my tiny self. This separation was far more powerful for knowing that there could never be a reunion in this life. This time they had gone completely from my life. My childhood fears were realised: my adult nature unable to deal with the compounded pain of that earlier incomprehensible loss. Maybe I still had not outgrown my need to be parented. Perhaps a childhood lived as a family would have made that inevitable separation easier to bear.

However, with the loss of my parents I was at last able to grieve for the little girl who had lost her family; the lonely teenager, confused and bewildered by the cold, grey world she'd been displaced to. That mourning process was long and painful. There were many tears and much heartache.

For many of us, in adulthood, the Chefoo community has become our surrogate family. With each other, we feel an instinctive sense of belonging: no effort required. No need to try to blend in. We can be our colourful selves with a freedom of abandonment that most of us have not experienced in our adult lives. We can share the deepest and darkest recesses of ourselves and still receive comfort from each other. But when, on the cusp of adulthood, we were making formative life decisions, we were scattered in different hostels, in different countries, often without parental support, adrift from the communities we'd been raised in, inadequately prepared for the worlds we were entering. Exotic, but naive, yet with deeply ingrained independence: many of us were ripe for personal disaster.

So how and why had my marriage gone wrong? What was missing?

Intimacy. Soul sharing. True partnership of spirits and shared purpose. For instance, the role of money became a touch point. As an MK I appreciated our financial status, gladly sharing our home and hospitality, but as the child of missionaries, I also knew how to be prudent. However, my Accountant husband had a different fiscal focus. So the split between able, multi-cultural adventurous parents who were financially poor, and middle-class, well-heeled Surrey stalwarts, may have contributed to the rift between their offspring. Blending status was not as easy as it first seemed. But perhaps the most fundamental difference occurred in our understanding as to what it meant to have a faith. My husband became uncomfortable with the familiarity of my relationship with the Lord I'd learned about with my mother's milk. Possibly he felt at a disadvantage. As the years passed, it became sadly clear that our priorities differed.

Our relationship became increasingly shallow. He withdrew from me early on in our marriage. I tried everything to win him back, to support our marriage, as I had been taught. Without forensically unpacking a twenty-five-year marriage (that's a book in itself), the man I married became increasingly unreasonable towards me, although he could be perfectly charming to others. I was utterly perplexed and confused. What had happened to the man I first knew? Perhaps my independence frustrated him; he needed to feel important, whereas I craved companionship with an equal. I also believe he may have been jealous of my close relationship with the children. Passive aggression gave way to something far more damaging: coercive control. With hindsight, this was a reflection of his own lack of security, but I didn't know it then. I now know that he had deeply hidden insecurities. I remember challenging his behaviour, explaining that it was killing my love for him. The look of blank incomprehension in his eyes showed me that he could not grasp what I was saying. I wonder if there was some form of disassociation in him: the clever, capable man at odds with the unreasonable treatment I received.

It took me a very long time to understand that, in some way, I might find unfair subjugation in my marriage to be familiar, courtesy of those early experiences as a boarder. Which might also explain how long I remained in that unhappy union. More fundamental though, was the fear of breaking my marriage vows to God. I knew that our marriage vows were broken, but for years I was terrified of incurring the wrath of God. I know I am not alone amongst my peers in that mindset. Very belatedly, helped by David Instone Brewer's research mapped out in *Marriage and Divorce in the Bible*[25] I understood that God had intended provision to be made for those who suffered, whether it be an absence of cherishing, or emotional, financial, verbal or physical duress. God is not a coercive controller. He has compassion on the crushed, the broken, the defenceless. I am also grateful to Paul Young for his insights and insistence on this truth. With a great deal of painful soul-searching, and virtually no human support, I eventually came to the conclusion that I was not breaking my marriage vows by leaving the man who had not fulfilled those same vows for years. My resolve strengthened, alongside my independence of spirit and belief in the strong relationship my parents had demonstrated, knowing this marriage was not what I had signed up for and that our children should not be exposed to further trauma in their home. So, just short of our twenty-fifth wedding anniversary, my children and I left our home, our belongings and our financial security behind with him.

Thankfully, once removed from the daily experience of their parents'

25   Instone-Brewer, D. (2002) *Divorce and Remarriage in the Bible: The Social and Literary Context.* Grand Rapids USA. Willian B. Eerdmans Pub Co.

distress, our children were freed to rebuild a better relationship with their father in their adult years. I am immensely proud of them for their forgiving spirits.

Another question I ask myself is whether I would have had a happier marriage if I had lived within my family for longer? My parents certainly set a wonderful example of a close, loving marriage for sixty-three years.

Did I need more years with my father to learn how to discern what qualities I required in a man? I think so.

Did a secondary boarding school comprised almost exclusively of single women prepare me for the choice of life partner? I doubt it.

Have I blamed myself for making a bad choice? Often.

And yet...that choice seemed marvellous at the time. I certainly was blissfully unaware of the heartache that was to follow.

Returning to that first reunion at Chefoo another shocking realization came to light: there was a higher incidence of failed relationships amongst us, the children of God-fearing missionaries, than in the general population. On the whole I would say that the majority of us are personable people: friendly, fun, creative and good at relating to others. So why this dreadfully high failure rate? In addition to the separation and will-breaking that I have personally identified with, I suspect that many of us have been unable to find a partner we can fully share our early experiences with, someone who instinctively "gets" us.

I had hoped that meeting my husband in Asia and showing him my homelands would ensure that, but sadly that was not the case. As the common ground receded, my sense of "otherness", my "foreignness" grew. Rather than enjoying my exuberance, I was increasingly rejected for not conforming to his idea of "normal". I expect he wished I was more conventional, more compliant, more conservative.

Had I stayed with my husband, I would now be a wealthy widow, but I dread to think of the further damage that would have been inflicted on my psyche and those of our children. My upbringing had hurt me, but it had also given me the independence and courage to do the unthinkable: to leave financial stability and social acceptability and head for the unknown in a desperate bid to protect us all from further emotional harm. I chose peaceful poverty over solvent strife. I chose to be true to myself, rather than continue to live the lie of a marriage which was no real union. So the irony is, without my childhood experiences, I would most likely have remained in a stifling, loveless relationship; but had I had more time with my family, I might not have made such a damaging marriage in the first place.

I do not blame anyone for my choice. I do not blame God, my parents, my schooling or the mission. Blaming others is an abdication of personal responsibility. The choice was mine and I chose, for better or worse, the father of my children. It would be easy to blame him for having promised so much but delivered so differently, and believe me, I have. Yet I choose to believe that he truly did not know what he was doing to me, and as such, I must and will continue to work at forgiving him. Sadder and wiser, I have learned a tough life-lesson.

The clock can't be turned back. I have two lovely children whom I couldn't entirely protect from harm; but they both know how to love and are loved in return. I am grateful for their support despite the drastic steps I took ten years ago. My former husband rebuilt his family life through marriage to a lady who suited him and gave him joy for his final years. Our young adults have now had to process the death of their father at a much younger age than I. And me? I have had to mourn, all over again, the loss of my hopes and the love I once had.

And now? Now I embrace my differences and indulge my connections with Asia. I teach from home, using those wonderful childhood memories to enrich other children's lives, welcoming pupils from many backgrounds. We laugh a lot. I indulge in frequent storytelling. There is something cathartic about caring for them and taking some of the strain from their parents. My wounded child is healed a little more with every pupil I nurture. I now have the freedom to fully embrace and integrate my Asian, Canadian and English cultures in my garden (orchids, a jungle, roses and a profusion of scented flowers), my friendships and my cooking. Most wonderfully, I am looking forward to sharing these enthusiasms with my yet-to-be born grandchildren, the first of whose arrival is eagerly anticipated this coming summer.

I have been deeply wounded, yes, and the cracks still show, but I am now able to be truly myself.

Looking forward I know that I will only experience fully that sense of belonging and acceptance I've yearned for throughout my life when I reach my forever home and finally meet the father of all fathers.

* * *

Rosie was born in Tikini Hospital, Jakarta; lived in Manila and Singapore, and went to primary school at Chefoo Malaysia from ages 4–9. She moved to the UK aged nine and boarded at Clarendon School, North Wales until seventeen. After her first degree (BA (Hons.) English) she taught in Hong Kong in a sixth form college for two years, before returning to the UK to take an MA in Renaissance Studies and a PGCE[26]. She taught, married, survived encephalitis and had two children, living in Washington DC and Dublin. Divorced just before her 25th wedding anniversary, she set up home as a single parent, left her job (Head of English), started a tutoring business, saw her daughter married, and buried both parents, all in one year. Soon to be a grandmother!

---

26 "Post Graduate Certificate in Education". A British teaching qualification

Interlude 5:
A Small Boy Waiting
Andrew

I didn't notice him at first,

The small boy sitting on the bank above the playing field.

A hunched figure in a striped shirt and brown shorts, no more than five or six,

His blond hair flopping down over his eyes as he picked distractedly at the grass.

Around him, the other children laughed and played

In the late afternoon sun as the jungle sang cheerily around the bowl-shaped valley.

At first, I thought he wasn't doing anything in particular.

But as I watched, his behaviour began to take on a pattern.

He seemed unconcerned, disinterested even by anything going on around him.

Balls flew over his head, a girl called out to him from the wall below his feet,

A butterfly landed just a few feet away from him.

But nothing stirred him as he stared sightlessly at the grass, plucking at the stems.

Then, quite suddenly, his head jerked up and he stared intently at the driveway.

I had not heard it myself, but he had. A car was coming.

The small boy's eyes narrowed, and I thought, just for a moment,

That I saw hope in his eyes.

He shifted his position slightly, the better to see the approaching vehicle,

Which sounded its horn as it crested the bend in the drive.

But it was not the one he was waiting for, and his head dropped once
more.

A short while later, another engine could be heard in the distance

And again the boy studied its approach, only to curl back up into
himself

As his hopes were once more dashed.

An hour he sat there, two, his desperate hope now almost tangible.

Finally, a horn sounded from down by the gate and the purr of an engine

Betrayed the arrival of one more visitor to the school.

Still hope shone out bravely from the small boy's eyes,

Right up to the moment when the car came into view.

Then the boy slumped back against the bank, his eyes now moist with
tears,

His face drawn with frustration, grief and hopelessness.

Somewhere, a bell rang, and the other children began to move towards
the buildings.

But the small boy sat on the bank, eking out the last few seconds

Before he would have to leave his watchtower and abandon hope for
another day.

The sun dipped down behind the mountain, leaving the valley in shadow.

Only the tinkling of the stream and the relentless cicadas

Disturbed the peace of the oncoming night.

The small boy drew his arms around his tiny body in a desperate embrace,

The only one he would receive that night.

Mummy and Daddy would not be coming to get him now.

Many years later, I returned to that boarding school in the jungle.

And there on the bank, still hunched in foetal expectation

Was the small boy...waiting...waiting...

Waiting...

6

The Borderlands

"You see, I am what some might call an adult Third Culture Kid (TCK), somebody who has spent a significant portion of their childhood in countries or cultures outside that of their passports, and has had to create their own unique blend of personal culture – a third culture, if you will."

Joshua Tan

These essays tell of lives marked by those cultural differences.

Joshua

"WHERE ARE YOU FROM? You don't sound local."

That is often the first question I am asked, whenever I meet somebody new. I always answer with a bit of a laugh, because – to tell the truth – I have never really sounded local, no matter where I have been in the world, no matter how much I would have wanted to. You see, I am what some might call an adult Third Culture Kid (TCK), somebody who has spent a significant portion of their childhood in countries, or cultures, outside that which issued their passport, and who has had to create their own unique blend of personal culture – a third culture, if you will.

"So, where are you from?"

Like all TCKs, I have a short answer to that, and a long one. It often depends on how much time I have, or how interested the listener might seem. The short answer is that I am from the small, sunny island of Singapore.

The long one? I am a missionary kid. I was born in Singapore but moved overseas when I was just six months old. I grew up in small towns amongst the dusty roads and green paddy fields of Thailand, went to Chefoo international boarding school in the middle of the lush, tropical jungles of Malaysia, where I picked up my mish-mash of an accent from other missionary kids from all over the world. I spent my teenage and early adult years back in Singapore, and now find myself in the United Kingdom.

For the first nine years of my life, I moved, on average every 6 months, between towns, countries and communities. On one hand, it was an incredible privilege to travel, and to see so many cultures. It made me adaptable, open-minded and curious about others – traits that I think are so important in today's modern world. But there was a dark side to it too. Growing up, it was hard to make lasting friendships in a world of goodbyes; to find a place to call home; to feel like I belonged, *truly* belonged.

Looking back, I wish somebody had told me that life is not just about "belonging" or "not belonging". Perhaps there is a space in between those two seemingly polar opposites, a space which we are constantly journeying through during the course of our years, months and days. It is a place that I call the "Borderlands of Belonging" – that hazy period when you move between cultures, countries or even communities. It is the time when you feel on the fringes, part of a place, yet not part of it. The term "culture shock" often seems too harsh to describe this slow, agonizing search to settle, and resettle.

I am wary of attempting to give a textbook definition of "belonging" here, given how personal, and often emotional, a lived experience it is for everyone. I would like to think that one does not need to just be a TCK to experience the Borderlands of Belonging. Maybe it comes from moving from one city to another for university, settling in another country for work, or marrying into a different cultural community. Deep down, at some point, I believe that many of us have longed to belong to somewhere, something or someone. We have all been on the Borderlands of Belonging.

In writing this, I hope to share a little bit of my own journey through the Borderlands of Belonging, following my time at Chefoo School. There are so many aspects to my ongoing TCK experience, and I would like to use just one small part to illustrate this journey – my accent.

Stage 1: Entering the Borderlands

We often remember when we first enter the Borderlands. I can clearly recall one of mine. Aged nine, I wake up in the dark at five o'clock in the morning, and smell the most peculiar, sour and earthy scent. I can only describe it as the smell of rotting chicken soup. It is a smell I will come to know very well. It is the distinct smell of fear.

I have just returned to my "home" country of Singapore for "good". But it is so different from what I have known growing up. I am struggling deeply, but as a child I do not know how to say it. But my body knows. It is so stressed that I vomit every single day for the rest of that first week of school. I distinctly remember throwing up on the steps of my school bus one morning, earning the scorn and disgust of fellow schoolmates. We often say that children are resilient, but research increasingly shows that to be not completely true – they simply do not have the language to describe their experiences, nor the ability to process them fully by themselves.

It is the oddest thing. I have my standard uniform, big school bag and awful haircut. I am an Asian TCK back in Asia, back at "home". I look like everyone else, so therefore, I should fit in. But one thing gives me away the moment I open my mouth – my strange quasi-British boarding school accent, courtesy of Chefoo School. A classmate comes up to me and asks in Singaporean English, "Why do you speak like a newscaster?"

Then it hits me. To him, I speak like the foreign-sounding television anchors on the nine o'clock news. For the first time in my young life, I realise I sound different from everyone else around me. As a child, I had no idea I was different. I had simply assumed everyone was the same. It is then that I realise that I cannot successfully *code switch* – that elusive skill when people can change, for example their accents, depending on their environment or company. I am a chameleon that cannot change its colours.

Suddenly I am back on the Borderlands. And so it begins: the journey through these Borderlands for the next one and a half decades.

Some people think my accent is fascinating, others think I am pretending to be posh and tell me to stop faking it. I get bullied on the school buses and teased down class corridors. Singaporean Chinese strangers on the street scold me for not knowing Mandarin, my "Mother Tongue".

"You should be ashamed of yourself," they say.

The truth is, I *am* ashamed. I am ashamed that I am not local enough. I am ashamed that I am *never* really local enough, no matter where I am in the world. That shame becomes anger. Anger directed inward becomes a teenager's struggle with depression and anxiety. I withdraw into myself, but like any good TCK, I look fine on the outside.

"Thoughtful," my teachers will say of me, "but quiet".

When you are that age, I think most people will understand what I mean when I say that all you want to do is just fit in. You do not want to be on any Borderlands – you just want to belong. Each journey on the Borderlands, I think, begins with this struggle.

Stage 2: Establishing Life on the Borderlands

So how does one establish an identity and build a life on the Borderlands? Many TCKs will tell you that the key is to accept your multi-faced identity: that you are a mix of many experiences, places and people. It took me years to learn to accept who I was, and to see my differences, like my accent, not just as weaknesses, but strengths. It took me years to celebrate what made me different, embrace my identity and establish some sort of life on the Borderlands.

Age eighteen, and I do not know any of this yet. I have withdrawn so deeply into myself that I flunk my national GCE A-level[27] exams. I am drafted for my compulsory Singaporean military service, where my officers notice that I speak rather well and make me the Master of Ceremonies (or "emcee") for our base's promotion ceremonies and events. They give me training and guidance, and I emcee event after event.

When I finish my military service, I head back to school and study Mass Communication, determined to one day be an announcer/presenter, to use this voice as a strength and not as a weakness. I join the campus radio station and start to get gigs as an emcee, or host for

---

27 Generally taken around aged 18, "Advanced Levels" have been the upper level of secondary school education in the British system, and elsewhere in the anglophone world, since the 1950s.

public events. Over the next decade, I keep working hard at accepting myself and honing my craft. Most importantly, I meet incredible people in the industry who see my potential and mentor me, and I start to get larger and larger gigs. I speak to crowds of 100, then 1000, then 10,000. At the peak of my career, I play host to an audience of over 40,000 at Singapore's National Stadium. There is nothing quite like the thrill of making an announcement and hearing the crowd roar. Yet, deep down, something within me still does not feel fully at home.

It is the strangest thing. Despite spending two-thirds of my life in Singapore, after embracing my differences and even building a career around it, I still feel like I do not fit in. I had attempted to accept who I was. But perhaps there was more – a need to go, to reach out to others, and to do meaningful things with our life on the Borderlands. To not just put down roots, but to grow.

Stage 3: Growing in the Borderlands

Looking back, my time on the fringes of cultures has made me so much more sensitive to those around me, those who do not belong, or are struggling to.

Age twenty-four: I am longing to do something meaningful with my skills in art, but also communication. I start volunteering at a weekend art class, for the most amazing individuals with Downs Syndrome and other intellectual disabilities. I hear their stories from their Borderlands of Belonging. One mother shares with me that when her child with Downs Syndrome sits down on trains, strangers next to them get up and move away. I dig into my experiences of being on the fringes, and empathise with their shame and sadness.

They never once ask about my accent. I go for one session, and then another, and then another – I have never felt more at home. After some time, they ask me to take over as their art teacher, and I end up teaching them for three years. During that time I see, first-hand, how art can give a voice to those who do not always have one in society. At the end of the three years, I know that this is what I truly want to do with my life – to use art to work with others on the Borderlands. And something inside me knows it is time to move on.

Age twenty-seven:. I pack my things, take my life savings and travel to Britain to pursue a postgraduate degree in Art Psychotherapy. And so my journey through the Borderlands begins again – the all-too-familiar stages of struggling, establishing and growing.

The Continuum

In my current field of study, one of the things I particularly appreciate is the idea of the Mental Health Continuum. It is the idea that we are not just "well" or "not well", but that there are a lot of stops along the way. It proposes that we exist along a scale, a continuum of health, on which we are moving up and down constantly during the course of our day.

Likewise, I would like to suggest that it is not just about "belonging" or "not belonging". There are many stops along the way – the Borderlands of Belonging. In each new group or environment, we find ourselves at different points in the borderlands, in different stages of struggling, establishing and growing. Perhaps we see a friendly smile in a strange place, and we move up the scale, or a colleague makes a remark that makes us feel uncomfortable, and we move down.

My A-level art teacher, Mr C, once did an activity with us that I will never forget. He gave my classmates each a different Lego figurine, and then asked us to take a few minutes to negotiate and swap parts with one another if we wanted. Some parts we swapped with glee, others we liked and kept. At the end, I had a real mix of a character: a werewolf's head with a policeman's top and a fireman's trousers. "This is a bit like life," he said, "We often wonder what our identity is, where, or to whom, we belong. The truth is, we are a mix of many things, many people, and sometimes, many places. When we interact with other people, we give something of ourselves to them and vice versa." What if being on the fringes, on the Borderlands, is not so much our loss, as it is our gain, and each other's gain?

So to those reading this who are journeying through your own Borderlands of Belonging, whether at work, school or home, may you know that you are not alone. Know that these Borderlands of Belonging are not as bleak and lonely a wasteland as we think they are. Know that they are rich with potential, sowed with the seeds of struggle but filled with the colourful lives of so many others. Know that you will find your place, in your own time, in your own Borderlands of Belonging.

* * *

Joshua is an ex-OMF missionary kid born in Singapore but raised in Thailand. He attended Chefoo School (Malaysia) from 1996–99 before returning to his passport country for further education. A former event emcee, art facilitator and graphic designer, he is currently pursuing his postgraduate degree in Art Therapy in the United Kingdom. The piece published here is based on a talk originally delivered at TEDx University of Derby 2019.

Anonymous

I'LL START WITH my life before Chefoo, for no one comes to Chefoo as a clean slate. We arrived in Malaya when I was nearly four and my parents were assigned to a Cantonese speaking New Village. It was at the end of the Emergency and the area was still something of a terrorist stronghold. My parents set about learning Cantonese, having learnt Mandarin in China in the late 40s. I picked up the language more quickly than they did, through playing with the village children. When these village friends disappeared off to the local Chinese school I was sent there too, and had the distinction of being the only white pupil.

The reason I give this background is that the village was a scary place. There were crocodiles in the nearby river and indeed when the Malay soldiers went on forays into the jungle, they often brought back large creatures they had captured, sometimes only half dead. These included: a wild boar; a crocodile, which opened its eye when touched; a tiger, and a thirty-foot-long python, which had been captured because it had swallowed a dog. Another scary aspect of the village were the missionary posters which used to adorn our front door. The most nightmarish was the Sinner's Dream, which depicted a man running from a tiger, climbing a rope over a river, below which was a crocodile. The rope was being gnawed by two rats, one black and one white, representing night and day. As well, the atmosphere in the village was very oppressive at times. I still recall a festival with a Lion Dance that progressed slowly up the street and passed our closed double front doors.

I still remember quite vividly the day I left my family at Kuala Lumpur station, boarding the train with other OMF kids. I recall the shock as we pulled out of the station and the realization that I was leaving my family. Part of the trip up the mountain by car was in convoy with a military escort because of the continuing danger from terrorists. When we got to Chefoo it was misty and I ran around outside The Bungalow in the mist. Apparently, I was crying, but I have no recollection of that. In fact, I have very little recollection of how I felt at Chefoo; especially, I cannot remember crying. I remember shame at times, and anxiety on the day I left just before I turned eight, but very little else in the way of feelings. Nevertheless, I have quite strong memories of Chefoo, its surrounds and events that happened there.

I probably would have been perceived to have "settled" at Chefoo. I think I probably developed my own "Survival Kit" – strategies I developed that have come to affect me even to this day. These include a sensitivity in social contexts – a carefulness to read such situations and a belief that "if you obey the rules you will be alright"; a belief that strong emotions could "betray" me; as I did not like one particular teacher expressing knowledge about my family, I developed a feeling that knowledge about me gives power over me – which is partly why this narrative is anonymous; not liking feeling uncomfortable – to this day I have a tendency to try to control my circumstances so that I won't feel uncomfortable; a dislike of conflict.

Coming to Chefoo as "illiterate", I learned that letter writing to parents could not express what you felt. Our initial letters were dictated to teachers, and we then traced over each word. Later letters had to be checked for neatness etc., and often included a comment from the teacher. This had the effect of making me cease to confide in my parents – fortunately, at the age of twelve (I left Chefoo just before I turned eight), I started to share with mum again. Linked to this is the memory that, when I first went to Chefoo, I stored up events to share with mum, only to realise after a few weeks at school that this was hopeless. The holidays were just too far away, and once they came, there was neither the opportunity, nor inclination on my part, to share intimately – by then these events had become irrelevant.

One thing that Chefoo taught you was a certain degree of independence (not to be confused with self-confidence). By the late 50s my parents had moved to Hong Kong. At the age of six or seven, I flew on my own from Kuala Lumpur to Hong Kong, via Bangkok and possibly Saigon. Once I almost got "lost in transit" as I did not understand the difference between "disembark" and "transit". When I was nearly eight, I travelled on my own from Singapore to Sydney, via Jakarta and Darwin. In spite of this I came to enjoy travelling by air on my own.

There were good things about Chefoo – the activities such as hikes and sausage sizzles; treacle tart cooked by our housemother; lots of friends to play with; trees to climb; the girls' and boys' hideouts; games such as King and Kick That Can; Guy Fawkes Night[28] – I can still smell the burning rubber from the guy's plimsolls[29]; the birthday parties; Merdeka[30]. I learned to appreciate beauty at Chefoo – it has always been a thing that has helped me survive. I loved the flowers, both native flowers such as monkey cups, and English flowers such as violets. There were good things that encouraged faith – I loved a few of the songs we used to sing – but there were other things that to some extent undermined faith, such as the frequent question, "Have you given your heart to Jesus?" I did a number of times but I never felt any different. I used to be worried how I would cope as an adult because I could not find that hymn in the hymn book in time!

After leaving Chefoo, close to my eighth birthday, our family had a year's leave in Australia. I remember the culture shock, including trying to cope with the concept that not all white people were Christians. School did not make much sense and I had to read *Milly-Molly-Mandy*[31] after school with mum, as I was having difficulties. Indeed, I did not read for pleasure until Grade 6.

28 On 5th November 1603, Guy Fawkes and a number of other conspirators were caught attempting to blow up the King at the Opening of Parliament. It has since become traditional in the UK to celebrate every 5th November by letting off fireworks and burning an effigy of Guy Fawkes (called a "guy") on a bonfire.
29 A variety of soft shoe with a canvas upper and rubber sole, sneakers.
30 Malay for 'Independence'.
31 A series of children's books written and illustrated by Joyce Lankester Brisley, and the main character of those books.

After a year, our family went to Hong Kong, where we lived in a mission flat and went to a local government English-medium school. At some point I started to feel anxious and this developed into separation anxiety – I became afraid my parents would die. When my parents attended the mission prayer meeting, in the mission office, I would stay awake till they returned. Our flat was on the third floor, and the OMF office and shop were on the ground floor, where prayer meetings were held at night as it was still cool from the air conditioning.

While we lived in Hong Kong no children were sent away to Chefoo. They all went to local schools. This may have been partly because OMF's first Asian missionaries lived in Hong Kong and sent their children to Christian Chinese-medium schools. My two younger siblings stayed with my parents all the years they were missionaries.

When I was twelve, I was sent back to Australia early for the sake of the school year. I was accompanied on the ship by a sixty-something, female missionary who spent a lot of time ripping up old petticoats to make mats as gifts to friends in Australia. I don't think I felt it, leaving my family, but in Australia I again experienced culture shock. The kids in my high school were so different from my friends in Hong Kong. In addition there was such a disconnect between life at school and life in the very small mission hostel. The hostel mother was kind and tried her best, but it was a dark, cold, gloomy converted house that had been used for aged care. Resources had to be carefully managed as there were "old ladies who had given of their meagre resources to the Mission". Bath water had to be reused. Seconds went to the chooks[32]. I remember being taken to a Disney movie about the Vienna Boys Choir by my aunt and grandma. I found the hostel parents did not approve. The four months I spent there were very long – I remember the lonely sound at night of trains leaving the Surrey Hills Station.

That furlough passed fairly uneventfully once my parents returned to Australia. As a family, we had to get used to how quiet Australia was after Hong Kong. It seemed boring by comparison. We adjusted to the different culture, and changed our accents yet again, to fit in with

32 Chickens

our Australian peers. What really was life-changing for me, occurred at the end of that year before we returned to Hong Kong. The Mission expected that children in their secondary-school years would stay in the "home country". In Melbourne's case, that meant living at a small hostel, run by a different couple, but people we knew. The Mission would not fund my boat fare to Hong Kong, or my school fees in Hong Kong. Nevertheless my father gave me the choice of whether I wanted to stay in Australia or go back with them to Hong Kong. I spent a trial weekend staying at the hostel and decided I wanted to go with them. Providentially, my father found he was entitled to a war-service pension for injuries sustained and this paid for fare and my fees. I never once regretted that decision. Although adjusting was hard, when I finally returned to Australia as a sixteen-year-old, it had still been the right decision. Fortunately, my father retained his faculties and lived long enough, for me to thank him for what he did. This I did after the Chefoo Reconsidered One Conference in 2014.

My teenage years in Hong Kong were largely good years. I started to achieve academically, and I began to love painting and drawing. The Cultural Revolution affected Hong Kong with riots, bomb scares, mass strikes and then mass sackings. But this did not worry us – only mum, who went through a bad time. As my final years of schooling approached, it became obvious I would not be able to complete them in Hong Kong. I hit on the idea of returning to Australia to finish my last two years of high school. It was therefore my choice.

Family friends, with five children aged from 13–22, kindly offered to board me. This family was a breath of fresh air, but very different to other Christian families I knew. They did not have a fortress mentality ("Of course you should go to the school dance!") They also did not believe that it was a good idea to send your children away. In many ways, I took on their approach. In some ways I transferred my loyalties to them, but when my family came home and I did not see much of them, I felt a certain degree of rejection. I also clashed with the mother. Her children were very different – socially adept and attractive, whereas I was more bookish, wore glasses and was quite overweight (when I left school I weighed nearly 12 stone[33]) – which led to conflict. This discord was something I had to get through, though we were reconciled at a much later date.

In my last two years of school, I changed schools twice: I went to a government high school for my second last year, and for my final year I attended a private girls' school that was very academic. The latter I found difficult, I had been at co-ed schools all my life and this felt quite unreal. I had learnt good study habits and, in some ways, studying and achieving was one way of compensating for other areas where I felt inadequate. I did not respond well to the pressures within the school. Events in Hong Kong, which affected my family, also did not help my adjustment to the new school.

My mother and siblings came home later that year, just before my final exams. My mother was fragile emotionally and I felt responsible for her. (My father had to stay in Hong Kong to complete their term.) Needless to say, my exam results were disappointing, and I chose to go to primary teachers' college, a seemingly easy option that offered the payment of fees, a living allowance and a job at the end for three years.

When I left school, I entered into a period of quite severe depression. This continued for a number of years and into my three teaching years. My mother said later that she thought I would have a breakdown. I did not get medical or psychiatric help. The support of my Christian friends, whom I could ring up and ask for prayer from, and with whom I could talk honestly was really what helped me through. Other things that also helped through this period were travel, painting and drawing and eventually pursuing something that challenged me more intellectually. After school I travelled to New Zealand; Fiji; an Aboriginal Reserve in Northern Australia, where I drew illustrations for SIL[34] primers; Canada, to visit my Canadian relatives; Hong Kong, to work in a home for severely disabled children, run by two women who had taught me Sunday School; and after I left

33   12 stone = 168 lbs = 76 kg.
34   Summer Institute of Linguistics is a Christian non-profit organisation, whose main purpose is to study, develop and document languages.

teaching, to Canada, the States, Europe and the UK. When I returned from this last trip, I went to university as a mature student, to study linguistics, and was blown away by it, ultimately doing postgraduate work (on a topic connected with Hong Kong) and then teaching at university.

I did not marry till I was thirty-one. I feel I struggled with negative thinking. I thought I wouldn't be happy if married. I also felt I would not be a good mother, partly as I had struggled as a primary teacher. I married a lawyer who, though a Christian, was not an evangelical – he says he tried it at university for a year, but it did not work for him. Providentially for me, he also had been sent to boarding school at a young age. I had two children in my thirties, a boy and a girl. My husband used to talk about his cases, which stimulated my desire to study law. I still work part-time as a lawyer.

Chefoo Reconsidered, reading about Third Culture Kids, and the discussions since have helped me to process my history. I have come to a greater understanding of why I react as I do in certain situations. I value my cross-cultural upbringing, particularly now that Australia has become multicultural, and there are so many Chinese people here. I feel I can connect with them and it is great to be able to use my "domestic Cantonese" in the Chinese Shopping Centre near me, and with Chinese friends.

I think to some extent my upbringing has made me enjoy change. I remember thinking as a teenager that if I did not like my circumstances, they would be changing soon anyway. A coping strategy that I developed when I changed school, was that I knew I would feel uncomfortable for the first term, but after that things would improve. Also, I did not live in the one place for more than three years until I was thirty-four. Although I have now lived in the same street for many years, I have had three careers.

I felt the benefit of not being left with a "one-size-fits-all" Christianity. My parents left the Mission just as I finished school. My father told me this was partly because he had seen "too many missionary kids go off the rails". Both he and mum had also felt that the Christianity that they were experiencing in their missionary work was not enough for them, or for effective ministry. They had become interested in the Charismatic Movement. This created some sense of uncertainty in me but in the long run, has been beneficial and helped me find my own level.

Belonging has taken me decades. In the last ten years, I finally feel I belong in Australia and not Hong Kong. I think that it has a lot to do with belonging with a close-knit group of people, even though I can feel different at times.

Anders / Undies[35]

NOT ATTENDING a boarding school would obviously have meant that I would have stayed with my parents and siblings in Penang. Our years in the house on 280 Circular Road, on the hill of Bukit Gelugor, were some of the happiest times of my life.

My first four years in Malaysia, as an infant, had been spent in Kuala Lumpur and Port Dickson until we went for our first furlough in 1966. Those were good years. I had spoken fluent Tamil with my neighbouring friends Krishnan and Ganeshan, as with the members of the sexton S's family. My parents were working with the Evangelical Lutheran Church of Malaysia and Singapore, which was a predominantly Tamil speaking church, but in Penang almost everyone spoke English. I had already lost all my Tamil during the year-long furlough in Lund, refusing to speak it when surrounded by Swedes. I'm sure the impact of those early transitions shouldn't be ignored when considering my present state. A language carries both a set of communication skills and a world of cultural outlook.

Penang isn't a UNESCO World Heritage Site for nothing, with the world's largest Chinatown, among other things. As one of the original Straits Settlements it has an important history and a fantastic mosaic of the great Asian cultures and the remnants of British colonialism. I've always felt fortunate, having grown up in its warm embrace. Bukit

---

35 'Undies' was a nickname Anders was given at Chefoo because of its similarity to pronunciation of 'Anders'.

Gelugor was originally a community of customs officers and their families, and there were people of every ethnicity and creed, Malays, Tamils, Sikhs, Chinese plus a very few Westerners. Every door was open, including our own, and my siblings and I roamed freely about with our friends. My sisters and baby brother were all younger than me, so I was the first to start schooling at St. Christopher's, twenty minutes away by car. It was an international and very British day school: although PE[36] was a joke, its pedagogical standards were outstanding. Most of the kids were Malaysians from rich families, but we could enter because the school had a missionary discount. Except for a run-in with the headmistress, who nearly expelled me in my first term, I flourished.

Upon completing Levels 1–4, there were numerous other local primary and middle school options in Penang that would have allowed me to keep on day schooling and remain in my family context. One of those, yet bordering on a Chefoo experience, would have been Dalat School, recently relocated from Tanah Rata to Tanjung Bungah in Penang. Although Dalat was only 20 minutes further away from home than St. Christopher's, we would probably have had to move closer to the north coast to make commuting less of a hassle. That would have meant keeping us together as a family, but uprooting us from our familiar community. (By the way, that happened anyway a couple of years later, when a politician took over the lease of our house). The only logic in selecting Dalat, however, would have been a compulsion to attend a missionary school, or to socialise with Americans. Neither of which was the case.

A number of my neighbours on Bukit Gelugor attended quality schools such as Penang Free School, St Xavier's or the two Methodist Schools. Those choices would have meant staying in the neighbourhood and maintaining existing friendships, even becoming school mates for the first time with a number of them, and would also have widened my local network. Instead, I almost lost touch with them, beginning with my disengaged attitude when we met on holidays.

Admittedly, this may have begun for other reasons too. A couple

36 Physical Education

of my closest friends were Eurasian neighbours who had attended St. Christopher's with me, and I grieved when they moved to England in 1970, to attend Christ's Hospital[37] in Horsham, and we lost touch. By this time, I think separation was becoming an issue, having left friends and relatives already in Kuala Lumpur, Port Dickson, and Lund. A few months later we went back to Lund for another furlough. Although we were subsequently returning to Bukit Gelugor, those six months of distance didn't exactly help.

As it happened, the Malaysian government had just passed new legislation, limiting the maximum time for foreign professional visas to ten years. My parents had originally planned to spend their whole careers abroad, but this may have been one of the factors that changed their minds. The languages they spoke were Tamil and English, and by then India was already closing down its borders for missionaries. So, while hoping for some extension, they set their sights on moving back to Sweden within three years. In Lund, I had attended a Swedish school for the first time, and it seemed to make sense to avoid too much of an interruption having begun.

That was the main reason I came to the Swedish School in Kodaikanal in southern India, straight after the furlough in January 1971. After some family sight-seeing in Delhi and Accra, we flew to Madras and Madurai in Tamil Nadu and then drove up the 2000 m elevation to the school, surrounded by the old holiday settlement of Swedish missionaries. The number of pupils had been dwindling for some time, now totalling just twenty-one, ranging through Levels 1–9, half of them being kids of industrial expats. I was in Level 5, and I soon found it all miserable.

The truth is that we had stopped by once before, on the way to a previous furlough, meeting the Swedish Bishop of Tranquebar and other missionaries there, to follow-up the events of the recent independence of the church in Malaysia, branching off from the one in Tamil Nadu. Visiting the school as a young boy, it seemed to have the atmosphere of an amazing fairy-tale, especially with all the dance

---

37 A prestigious boarding school in the south of England.

and merriment around the maypole on that occasion. That impression
stuck with me, and I had actually implored my parents to let me
come back and be a part of it. The mountains were also a bit like
the Camerons, where we had spent many wonderful family holidays
before. As a huge bonus, I felt safe having Uncle Olle and Auntie
Regina as dorm parents, as they were former missionaries in Malaysia.

But when my family left after the first few days, the excitement
faded away and I was rather forlorn. I can't imagine what it would
have been like if I were five years younger and put on a train to an
unknown place... This was different from a furlough, although I was in
a Swedish cultural environment, because the family wasn't there. I did
well in class, as always, but in my free time I often spent time in Uncle
Olle's office. He was calm and his pipe smelled like my Dad's. Some of
the kids were great, but there were unfettered bullies too. I seemed to
be the odd one out, going on about Malaysia, and not having much
of a clue about Swedish fashion, rock music or dating. Three guys, all
four years older than me, kept swiping at me verbally and physically
whenever I was around and adults weren't. So I had to look behind my
back most of the time. But they managed to drag me to the basement
once, where they laid me on the high jump cushion and proceeded to
jump at full weight. If not before, I'm sure that's when I developed my
hyper vigilance, always prepared for some assailant around the next
corner and trying to practice some basic jiu-jitsu moves.

I wish every parent would realise that a child can't really imagine
what it's like without their presence, even though the child seems
sensible, independent and excited about the adventure. Not to mention
the effect of growing apart from the other siblings.

Anyway, my parents really listened when I came back to Penang
for summer holidays. In the same garden swing where we had watched
the astronauts of Apollo 11 land on the moon two years before, I told
them everything between the sobs. They took me to see Dalat, which I
didn't like, and then Chefoo. I was given the choice. I really appreciate
that, to this day. But we never considered the other options in Penang,
which I do regret for the reasons mentioned above, missing out on
strengthening my local bonds. I would mull much less over this today,

had we tabled all the alternatives, but I have no idea whether or not that would have altered my verdict at the time.

A few days ago in Gothenburg, we went for dinner with family friends who have a Malaysian chemistry student staying with them. It turned out that she comes from Gelugor, only a mile away from my childhood address there, and that she had attended the secondary school SMK Hamid Khan just across the street from our Lutheran Church nearby. It's funny how I've never even thought of that school before. But apparently it must have been OK, because here she was, a very bright postgraduate, even speaking good Swedish!

I must have blended into the cultural context more than OMF kids, simply by having been immersed much longer before I began boarding. My roots and memories are strongly Malaysian, and I'm grateful for that, but a big chunk is missing despite my many trips back as an adult. I still get to see some of my old friends, and I relish that, but they're not as many as they would have been if I had stayed home.

So what advice would I give my younger self? Should I refuse boarding, stick to my friends and to my Penang identity, perhaps eventually becoming fluent in Malay, or pick up some Chinese? There is a big difference between simply moving from place to place, and breaking up from a culture and language environment. As aforementioned, a language carries with it an entire outlook of the world. Having said that, Chefoo meant reconnecting with the English language, which had been an integral part of my life in Penang. What's more, without Chefoo I would certainly never have encountered that many Americans, Canadians, South Africans, Rhodesians, Australians and New Zealanders, and probably not that many British either. Meeting them, and getting acquainted with their cultures, has certainly been life changing in a good way. I value the great benefits of that trade-off, while grieving the other losses.

The way I made friends before and at boarding school was similar, with the exception of Kodaikanal, and any real difference would appear later, which may have more to do with circumstances in Sweden. I had always loved playing with large groups of children, physical games like tag or hide-and-seek, or hikes or any kind of building project. I seemed to have no problem joining in the fun and taking elements of competition very seriously. So, Capture the Flag was one of many new games at Chefoo that made me very excited, as did jungle trekking, and the Drama and Art Clubs. Another activity worth mentioning was the yoga practice in our dorm before bedtime. With 104 kids, it was the perfect place to have a lot of fun, especially with a Headmaster as imaginative and caring as Mr Miller was.

Also, I had always had a few intensely close friends, in whom I confided one or two at a time. Robert D. and I were real book worms, and as we plunged through stacks of stories, we shared them and speculated together in depth about life and more. There were others too, but I mention him specifically, because it was so heart-breaking when he left for England after my first year. I joined the Thai party on the night taxi convoy to Butterworth, where the others continued North by train and I was picked up by my parents for the ferry ride across to Georgetown. At the platform we were separated by an iron gate and, until they all disappeared from sight, I clung to it in gruelling fits of tears.

I was eleven by then, but was thankfully granted an extra grace year at Chefoo. Even when I arrived for the first year, I was one of the big boys in Level 6, but almost everyone had been boarding for much longer than me, and most of them knew each other well. Something that amazed me was the number of kids with teddy bears, but at the same time they were tough and outgoing.

I found coming home for Christmas and summer holidays quite boring, especially after we had to move to an unfamiliar semi-detached on Jalan Tembaga. By the way, I still don't know how that eviction came about. Well, not only did I have to walk a couple of kilometres along a busy road to see my old neighbours, but there wasn't much to do in the daytime at home except reading. My siblings were in school and my parents were working. In the old days on Circular Road, I would always find someone in the neighbourhood at home. When we didn't play or go exploring, we read endless amounts of their D.C. and Marvel comics or war comics, or watched everything running on T.V., Disney and Merry Melody Cartoons, Wanted Dead or Alive, Star Trek, the Twilight Zone, Zorro, Film Noir matinées, Malay melodramas and horror, Chinese Kung Fu action and Bollywood extravaganzas. It's quite ironic how my Mum was convinced, years after, that I was brought up without any television, just because we didn't have one. At Chefoo we were allowed to watch Scooby Doo, but not M.A.S.H.

For my second year, my sister Eva also entered Chefoo but, regrettably, I never paid her any attention. In the next summer holidays it was time to graduate from Chefoo and I spent the two weeks I had, listening with headphones to a double vinyl album, twice a day on our living room sofa, before embarking on a new attempt at the Swedish school in Kodaikanal, this time together with Eva. It was Jesus Christ Superstar, the first real rock I'd listened to, except for some of the Beatles songs. I brought a cassette recording with me. And when Eva and I landed in Singapore for transit to Madras, I realised that we had at least four hours before the next flight. A last chance to see the L's and the K's, and maybe play them some of the music too. Eva needed some convincing, but we grabbed a taxi to Cluny Road and had a wonderful surprise visit.

The next surprise was discovering, at the airport, that the departure time on the manually written flight ticket was incorrect. Denis L, who had kindly taken us there, called our parents in Penang and managed to ease the panic they were in, having received a telegram that we weren't on board the flight. For us, the surprise was very welcome indeed, allowing us another two days with our dear friends! As a bonus, the only available tickets were by first class on Singapore Airlines. We were served lamb stew and Russian caviar on real plates, and offered champagne.

That final year in India was very different from the last time. I was older and surer of myself, now a boarding veteran. And I had become a natural link to the guys at the huge and exciting American high school, Highclerc[38], a few kilometres away.

---

38 The school name was 'Highclerc' until 1972 when it became the first international school in India and was renamed 'Kodaikanal International School'. Formerly, it had been an American school with a Christian curriculum.

But moving back to Sweden was painful. Trying to avoid the inevitable, I wrote to my parents, thanking them for everything they had done for me and asking them please to let me stay in Asia, where I would take care of myself from now on. The distance that had grown between us had nothing to do with hostility, but we had an evolving difference in identity. To begin with, their home country experience wasn't mine and, while boarding, I had seen other role models and tasted other flavours of behaviour and faith.

At Chefoo, I had loved the Sunday evening hymn singing, in dressing gowns, and the interesting variety of morning devotions. The dorm devotions and the quiet times with Scripture Union notes were quite different from the formal family prayers we had at home, led by my Dad. I had been brought up with those, and with Mum's more personal bedtime prayers, and stories from the Children's Bible by Anne de Vries. As much as I had appreciated that before, my new experiences made me feel frustrated with their lack of expectation for contributions from us children. The level of ambition at Sunday School, where we made our way through Genesis and Romans in a year, was only surpassed when I studied theology at the university. And a really strong impression had been listening in the dorm to *Run, Baby, Run!* Eschatological speculation was nothing I'd ever come across before, especially not of this American brand. Also, I had come to admire the commitment and faith economy of the OMF, as opposed to the steady budget of the Church of Sweden Mission.

Around my twelfth birthday I found myself in a revival, and some of us began walking around the school grounds challenging other children whether they were prepared to carry the cross of Christ. It was all very genuine, but quite misguided. We made three groups of our dorm beds and had secret devotions after lights out, until Auntie Barb discovered us and identified me as the ringleader. She gave me a stern wake-up call, and it all took a healthy ending.

If some of my convictions had become fundamentalist at Chefoo, I received somewhat of an antidote in Kodaikanal, which was quite the opposite environment. Someone scribbled graffiti in my Bible, tore it up and threw it in my waste basket. And the school devotions were apathetic and rather shallow. As a believer, I had to get by on my own, more or less. And I had more of that coming in Sweden. All very harsh, but wholesome in the end. The way I see it, for both Eva and me it was very beneficial to experience other faith perspectives than at home, however much I respect my parents, because it has helped us distinguish our own faith, and to better discern between parents and God.

Without the ten-year visa limit, I'm not sure what my teens would have been like. Times and attitudes had changed by the mid-70s, and Swedish missionaries were already less inclined to send their children back to Sweden on their own. Anyway, we all moved together, from the bustling excitement of life in Asia to the Technicolor tranquillity of near death in our passport country. I felt uprooted and lost, however exotic and beautiful things could be, and however much I wanted to see my grandma, my uncles, aunties and cousins. As far as I was concerned, my childhood was gone. Malaysia was on the other side of the planet, and there was no feasible way of coming back. Even my collection of 3000 bottle tops was left behind. I didn't want to end up like Lot's wife, so I firmly decided to look ahead and make myself at home, except I did dream of opening an *Ais Kacang*[39] stall eventually. I kept a notebook with Chefoo signatures, but with very few addresses, and I didn't write much.

I was quite ignorant about a lot of things in Sweden, which had more to do with having lived in Malaysia than with boarding as such, and even my parents had lost touch. But they would have known, at least, that football was played there. I was extremely surprised to find Sweden advancing to fifth place in the World Cup of 1974, and that England hadn't even qualified. At about the same time, I had to re-evaluate my first impressions of Björn Borg and Abba too. I made numerous misjudgements, behaved awkwardly and sometimes my misapprehensions were hilarious. We spent the first summer driving through the country, and my Dad would frequently pick up papers at the "Pressbureau", which I took as command centres for

---

39   Ais kacang, literally "bean ice", is a popular desert in Malaysia and Singapore, made of shaved ice, red beans and/or other flavourings.

Lutheran priests. Another time we passed a bus labelled "Christers", which seemed to me like an outreach team, when it actually was a popular dance orchestra. Christer turned out to be a common name, corresponding to that of Hristo Stoichkov[40].

But it took me a very long time to understand the psyche and values of Swedes: perhaps I still don't get it. For starters, my sense of fashion was non-existent at that point. My corduroy trousers weren't keeping up with my growing legs and I wore batik shirts and one in glistening gold, all buttoned up. My hair was long but not the bangs. The fact that my gait and manual motions were inspired by Don Martin didn't help. Nor did being a year younger than the rest of my class in eighth grade, but two years ahead in most subjects. And they thought I was showing off with my English, when in fact I was still thinking in English, and did so for the next three years. What really set me apart was not swearing, not drinking, not taking snuff and not dating. Quite a number started calling me a gay, but I didn't have a clue what that meant.

While survival mechanisms had been at play in earlier periods of my life, they certainly kicked into overdrive now. So they thought I was a bit odd? Well, I'd give them a real oddball! So, between classrooms I would always walk backwards, sometimes intentionally tripping over the legs of people seated on the corridor floors. I would respond nonsensically to any statement or question asked at breaks, but never in class. I would keep my voice at a squeak pitch and, when teased, sometimes feign fright and lock myself into a lavatory. The safest way to hide was behind this clown character that wasn't me. In many ways, it was actually quite difficult not to feel superior, knowing too that I was consciously putting them on. They thought my red school bag was funny, which truly amazed me, because they all brought their books in plastic shopping bags.

Sources of relief were cycling to and from home, as we lived three kilometres away in the countryside; mowing the lawns; reading books; sketching inventions; drawing; evenings at the Youth Fellowship; and,

40   A Bulgarian football (soccer) player, famous in 80s and 90s.

most significantly, spending a lot of time with a couple of close friends. One of them was a Marvel nerd like myself, and the other brought me into what became my musical world of refuge and indulgence. Taking off from Ian Gillan and Deep Purple, I let myself soak into Queen and Genesis, Gentle Giant and other prog rock. The imagery, quirkiness and raw power was a window to my soul, especially of its English identity.

A few years and a family move later, music provided me with a breakthrough moment when I was grappling with an identity crisis. I found myself in limbo after three good years in high school, where I had behaved normally again, much to the astonishment of some. My hopes to leap across to Seattle for further studies had floundered, because I forgot to actually send the application papers. So, here I was stuck in a dreary commuter town in Sweden and didn't know what lay ahead. Truth be told, I was also suffering from a secret heartbreak, because nothing ever happened between me and a beautiful girl in class, whom I had covertly been in love with for five years. At Chefoo, I once vowed at the dining room table never to marry, although I found some of the girls very attractive. My discretion was such that I suppressed my own interests and accepted the office of postman – stealth deliverer of love-letters – between other kids at school.

Anyway, I had now finally come to a point where emotional suppression was taking too much of a toll on me. Rationalizing, intellectualizing and generally going numb had helped me get through thus far, but it had in effect turned me into a zombie. But I felt a strange sensation, this time, when the pickup entered the groove of my latest album purchase. I had been catching up on the Beatles records for months, but with *Abbey Road* something happened within me. Particularly the B-side medley took hold of me, and I listened repeatedly until I flooded into tears for the first time in ages. It was like opening a wormhole back to my childhood days in Penang when these songs were ubiquitous.

In my adult years I have been working on getting to know myself better, by rediscovering Malaysia and managing, more or less, to bridge the distance to my siblings and parents. How much have my personality traits been formed by epigenetic effects from boarding, and how much was already there, as my very early striving for independence suggests? Anyway, I have come to identify as an Enneagram type Seven personality, if that tells you anything, and breaking the comfortably numb cocoon is a significant step forward. I even managed to escape my cool reserve sufficiently to surprise Ulrika with my interest in her, but it's a long-term process to completely come out of the shell.

* * *

Anders attended Chefoo in 1971–73. His parents were missionaries in Malaysia with the Church of Sweden Mission from 1962–74. For the last 29 years he has been a pastor in Göteborg. His wife Ulrika is a deacon, and they have three grown up children. Currently, they are both working for the Church of Sweden Abroad on a three-year contract in Southern Thailand, catering for Swedish expats.

Barbara

WHERE DOES COMPASSION come from? On Wikipedia the answer to the question "Is compassion innate?" drew the response: "Compassion is both innate and can be learned and enhanced." One of my earliest memories is of my mother shooing me and my sister up the stairs of our home as she saw a middle-aged Thai woman come in under the house. The woman was carrying a bunch of bananas, which she offered to my mother, who gave her some small change in return, then sat and chatted with this lady. I somehow knew this lady had mental health problems and could be unpredictable, but my mother showed no fear except for us children. I was never afraid, or disgusted, by the deformities experienced by people with Hansen's disease (leprosy) because my parents frequently welcomed these people into our home and showed them love and concern. They cared for the poor and the outcast.

Some may say that my parents lacked compassion towards their own children by sending them away to school, but I never felt that. What I felt was love: at Chefoo from teachers and dorm aunties, from my parents through the letters received from them and what we did together during holidays. Yes, I got smacked at school, always because I was talking after lights out, but my memories of that time are generally happy. I had close friends, and loved learning, playing and exploring. I was fortunate in that I had an older brother at school before me, and younger siblings who joined me after my older brother left to go to boarding school in the UK.

Looking back on my early life, I see that many major decisions were made through wanting to express compassion in action. From a young age, in fact while I was at Chefoo, I decided to become a nurse because I wanted to help people with Hansen's disease. I also wanted to be a midwife, though I do not remember what prompted this idea. So when I reached the time when I needed to decide what subjects to take at school, I decided on those which would take me on that path. I loved nursing and midwifery, loved looking after people, making them feel less fearful in difficult surroundings and painful, frightening circumstances. I felt confident in my workplace, focusing on putting patients and women at their ease and encouraging them. Outside work this confidence dissolved, leaving me shy of meeting new people. I have always been able to get to know people best if I live or work with them on a regular basis, a reflection of the situation at boarding school.

Being content in whatever circumstances I found myself was true for me from a young age. Back in the United Kingdom, I loved school, and saw no reason to flout rules as I was happy and fulfilled within them. Although I think we "missionary girls" were a lot less privileged than many who attended the school, I more often felt blessed than envious: someone gifted my sisters and I with fruit, enough for every day; one of the staff, who had been at Chefoo in China, treated us to Chinese meals in her flat on *exeat*[41] Saturdays when we had no one to take us out; when mum and dad were around to take us out, we went and stayed with friends of my parents and enjoyed the local Welsh countryside and coastal towns; we had an exotic-looking Grandmother, who was always delving into her handbag for sweets and money to give to us and our friends; my sister and I were gifted with a complete duvet set each (matching fitted sheet, duvet cover and pillow cases) when duvets were just coming in!

I would say my only feeling of despair came from my plainness: having straight, thin, brown hair, having to wear glasses from the age of ten, and having a bottom that stuck out, and did not fit into the

---

41   Latin for 'let him/her go out'. Used by many public (i.e., private, fee-paying) schools in the UK to denote a day or a weekend when parents are allowed to take their children out of school during term time.

stiff jeans of those days! At an all-girl's secondary school this was not a big problem, and I do not remember being teased about these things except by my own siblings. However, I was a shy teenager and was happy to spend time by myself in the holidays, mostly reading, though I joined in all the games and outings with the others in the hostel, who felt like my extended family.

My third ambition was to become a "missionary". In those days I was not aware of non-government organisations, but ended up applying to and getting a job with CORD, an organization that worked with refugees. This work was in Thailand, so rather than being anxious and culture shocked, I immediately felt at home, returning to the land of my birth, and moving into a team situation, where we shared houses and worked closely together. I was able to help others on the team to adjust to the changes – though I had not realised to what extent, until five people from the team, at a recent reunion, came and thanked me for helping them settle in. Over the five years I worked there I was on the team with fifty others, only one of whom stayed for more than two years, so I became familiar again with the comings and goings of people in my life, as I had known in much of my childhood. I have kept in contact with three-quarters of these women and men; it is only with them that I feel able to talk about that time, when many of us suffered from compassion fatigue and discovered, often for the first time, that we could not trust everyone.

My time in Thailand came naturally to an end as the refugees prepared to repatriate to Cambodia. I returned to the UK where I was able to get a job back at my old hospital, getting "my hands on some women" again (I had missed that in my mainly supervisory role in the refugee camp). I was doing a clinical teaching course (previously I hated teaching – having to stand up in front of everyone, with all eyes on me, was so outside my comfort zone – but in the refugee camp I had an opportunity to teach and found I enjoyed it immensely) and working for six months in the community – that gave me great joy and a feeling of freedom I had not experienced before! Three years after returning to England I was off to South East Asia again, this time with a development organization, with the aim of teaching traditional birth attendants about safe delivery, and criteria for referral to the, at that time, skeletal health services.

Although Cambodia was a new country for me (in fact I had never heard of it before watching the film *The Killing Fields* at my orientation for going to work in the refugee camps), I was excited at the challenges facing me: a new language, a new culture, a new team and helping people to improve their health. For the first time I was actually living in the same house with Asians. Although my English boarding school had been multinational, and I had had a few Thai team members in Thailand, I had never actually lived with Asians in Asia before. The Filipino and Burmese women who shared my house were so kind and friendly, and accepting of my weird Western behaviour. And I loved learning about the many differences in culture between Westerners and Asians, especially when it came to pregnancy and childbirth. Some things were not so enjoyable, such as the lack of hygiene and sanitation among the local people. I had always thought such things were common sense, but discovered they were learned behaviours – for me from a young age, both at home and school – that had become habits.

I moved on from that organization fairly quickly and went back to working with CORD, who were now trying out development work in Cambodia. Once more, I was in a team situation, living with expatriates but working with local Cambodians. It was a steep learning curve, but, again, I would say, I did not have culture-shock because of my childhood experiences. Most of my language was learned on the job and, because of the language barrier, I was supervising trainees rather than teaching myself. The staff God gave me were amazing, quick to listen, and learn new methods of teaching, to make classes in primary health interesting for the local health staff who attended. In the dry-season months we went out to visit our students in their districts, trying to make sure they were using their skills, as, at that time, there were few health centre buildings and very little other supervision. Almost everything was fun: travelling on dirt roads with huge pot-holes and boggy puddles in our 4-wheel drive Land Cruiser, sleeping on mats on the floor under mosquito nets in the homes of villagers, cooking together using food, either brought from the town with us or foraged for, showering in the dark in the evenings at the communal well, using games to try and get the health staff to remember the knowledge they needed to do a good job. The one thing I was not happy with was that there were no toilets and I had to get up before dawn with my trusty trowel and dig a hole somewhere to do my business. I lost 10 kg over two years because I ate so little on those trips.

After a few years, the Cambodian government started improving the health services and did not want NGO staff helping with training as, I think, it might have meant monitoring of the funds given them. So my team moved out to one particular health centre, servicing thirteen villages, and spent the next three years helping the staff there improve their services to the community.

In my first year of this work I fell in love with one of my Cambodian team members, totally against my inclination. I had been brought up in Asia and chosen to live there as an adult, but never intended to marry a "foreigner". I loved and missed England and had envisioned returning to live and work there. My parents had retired from Thailand in the early nineties, and I had thought that when my work was "finished" in Cambodia I would return to England to be near them. I waited a year and a half to be sure that this man was the right one for me. I don't consider myself a risk-taker; I was cautious, but, in the end, love won! Ottamo's first wife had died, quite suddenly (possibly from meningitis), three years earlier and he had two young daughters, who were living with grandparents from both sides. I met them; they were terrified of me, especially my eyes (blue), which to them looked like the eyes of a ghost. We planned to marry within a couple of months of deciding to get married.

And just two weeks before the wedding I found out he had HIV.

I remember being given the information at the laboratory where they had taken the blood. I felt numb, shocked. My up-to-then protected heart felt shattered. My husband-to-be was in Thailand on a course at the time, with no means of communication except letters. As I cycled home, I knew I had to talk to someone. I was passing the house of the pastor of the International Christian Fellowship in Phnom Penh and stopped to speak with him. As I voiced my fear, anger, disappointment, I knew that I had to go through with the marriage. My heart was still filled with love but now also with compassion. In the following days and weeks the few people I told advised me to consider carefully whether I should still marry him. I could not consider doing anything else; my love had not weakened and I thought that, when the time came and he was sick, I needed to be there to look after him, as I knew how people with this disease were treated in Cambodia.

I wrote to Ottamo and when he returned a week later, his plan was that we go ahead and marry and then live separately. In his disorganised thinking this would prevent others from knowing he was infected, so he would avoid the stigma that was so prevalent at the time. We went ahead and got married but, of course, lived together and slept together, always using protection. He told no one until a year later when he got very sick and almost died, then he told his father, brother and a couple of friends. His brother did not come to see him for three months, despite the fact he lived next door to us, and did not allow his wife or daughters to visit either. Ottamo got over that first sickness, but with no treatment programme in the country at that time, he gradually succumbed to AIDS.

We had eighteen months of joy and sadness together. Then he was gone, and I was overwhelmed with the grief and unfairness of it. Miraculously, my mother was in Chiangmai at the time, looking after the OMF guest house, and was able to come to stay with me for a couple of weeks, after which I went to Chiangmai, to be with my parents for a few days. I had my work and I had my two stepdaughters. I do not remember having any huge grief in my life up to that point. Yes, leaving my parents to go to school in Malaysia, and later in England, was hard, but I did not dwell on the sadness and there were many distractions. If I was unhappy, I generally shed my tears in private, and communed with the Lord and my soul until I felt comforted. A friend had once asked me, "Do you have any problems? You always seem to be OK, and never share any problems with us!" Now, once my mother had left, I found it hard to cope with the grief. Cambodian people do not like storms of tears and kept telling me to stop crying or I would get sick, but the tears flowed in private and public, and I just let them. I was able to have counselling with a Canadian lady, and I had a small expatriate team to support me. I believe the independence I had learned as a child kept me moving on through the fog I lived in for the next eighteen months. Taking care of my daughters also helped me enormously.

One morning, eighteen months later, as I sat on my veranda, I saw, in my mind's eye, the fog lift and roll away. I knew life would carry on and I had to make decisions for myself and my girls.

At that time many people asked what I intended to do; in other words, would I return to the UK? I felt very strongly that I wanted my girls to remain Cambodian. From what I had seen, young people who emigrated rarely wanted to return to their roots, and often even forgot how to speak their mother-tongue. We applied for UK citizenship for the girls, but the stipulation was that they would have to go and live in the UK for at least a year. I was still working with CORD; the girls had no English and I felt it would be too hard for them to get into school and life in England only to return to a much poorer set-up in Cambodia. I also wanted my daughters to keep in close contact with their relatives, especially those who had cared for them after their mother's death.

So I made the decision to stay on, even after my project was handed over to a local NGO. I was able to get paid work with NGOs for a few years, as well as leading the children and women's work in the local church.

My girls left school, each spent six months in the UK (where they had visited my family a number of times) mainly to improve their English, then each in turn attended a Youth-With-A-Mission Discipleship Training School (DTS) in Cambodia, before going on to University in Phnom Penh. My older daughter studied Sociology, and my younger one has become a midwife. Both have chosen Khmer (Cambodian) men to marry, and I have an adorable Cambodian grandson. My older daughter has become a "townie", seldom coming home to the province since going to University. This, I think, is due largely to the fact she met her husband, who was from Phnom Penh, at the end of the DTS and they have spent all their time together since.

I have been surprised that neither of my daughters seem to have kept in contact with their school friends, although they went to the local school for ten years. I had always assumed that children who did not move around a lot made close friends and stayed in touch. They have a huge extended family (I never know who is who) and keep ties with them. They are closer to University friends and people they have worked with since.

The decision to stay on in Cambodia has made life harder for me. By this I mean that I have few close friends in Cambodia. The closest are two with whom I worked on the team in Thailand. I still find it difficult to chit-chat with people, especially when with my Khmer friends, and they speak as they would speak to another Khmer, not understanding that I cannot keep up. There are a handful of expatriates living in the province where I live, but no British people to share a cuppa with, or talk books or films or English politics with. I get asked the same thing every time a local finds I can speak Khmer, "Do they eat rice in England?" Cambodians do not understand English reticence and ask personal questions (How old are you? Are you married?) loudly, so that everyone around can hear. Children yell "Hello!" when I cycle by, but if I stop to chat in English they clam up, that being the only word they know. I find the minutiae of their lives tedious, which I know is unconscionable, but I cannot help it.

I have always disliked standing out from the crowd, but now I stand out every time I step out of my house. Although when I arrived everyone thought my white skin was beautiful, I have since become quite blotchy from the sun. My brown hair has always been considered ugly here, and called grey even before it started to turn so; my eyes (which I considered my best feature) have never been complimented, but rather considered spooky. When I got married I was very thin, but put on weight once I passed the menopause; previously the Khmer thought fat was beautiful, but now I am larger it is no longer considered so, as many women my age have high blood pressure and incipient diabetes and are being told by the doctors to lose weight.

At the time of writing this I feel aimless. It is hard for foreigners to get jobs in Cambodia and much of the advisory/consultancy work I have done in the past is now taken on by younger folk who are much better qualified. One of my weaknesses has always been that I have not felt clever enough to try new things, to branch out, and so opportunities have passed me by. Many of the church activities I initiated I have had to stop, as local people get busier and have less free time, and older or sick people have passed away. No one drops in on me and I do not know the reason for this, except perhaps, that my home is alien to them. It makes me feel very isolated. I have no team to live with, no fellow-workers. Keeping in contact with people far away has never been easier, but I hanker for letters in my post office box that prove that someone loves me enough to take the time to write something longer than a comment, or an e-mail, to buy a stamp and go out to post the letter.

I do thank God for many friends who live all over the world, but sometimes I'd like to have an intimate friend living near enough that I could drop in on them whenever I feel like it. I often have a video of a TV series playing in the background so I can just hear someone speaking to me in English with an English accent. I enjoy many things about my life in Cambodia: my children and grandson; my cat and dogs; the exotic plants surrounding me in my garden; the local food. But I miss walking; views and scenery; comfortable bus travel and being able to travel by train, if I wish; fresh milk and cheese available from a local grocer; local places to go on holiday; being greeted with a "Good Morning!" when I meet my Cambodian housemate in the morning; having an in-depth discussion on current world affairs, or an encouraging verse from the Bible; a compliment after I've been to the hairdresser. My childhood, surrounded by other people, with whom I basically fitted in because of shared experiences, did not prepare me for this isolation.

Isolation is whittling away at my compassion, tolerance and acceptance. Where once I had patience, I now feel quickly irritated. Once I was understanding of cultural differences, and the ways of people in an under-developed country; now I find myself saying, "Well, in England we would ...," before I can stop myself. I get annoyed with the people who shout, "Hello" at me, at the way the local people latch onto rumours, old wives' tales, and anything that is posted online as if it is all true, and the continued petty corruption that is rife at every level. I am critical, rather than supportive, of local church leadership. I dislike the hierarchy so obvious in the society, and feel little respect for local authority.

I need to find community in those around me again, not be so concerned with my own comfort and priorities, not allow myself to be offended. I do have community with my girls – though one lives in Phnom Penh, three hours away on public transport, and I visit once or twice a month, especially to play with my grandson; the other will marry early next year, after which, we are hoping, she and her husband will move home with me, if she can get a transfer from her distant government Health Centre. I share with them a lot more than I ever remember my parents sharing with me until I was much older.

But I need more than this, so... I could visit my in-laws more regularly out in a village just over an hour away, on a bad road. Perhaps I will find community with the children in the local children's home, Hope Village. Most of them are not orphans, but have been separated from their parent(s) because of circumstances (mainly a single, poor mother having to find work), and/or so they have a better chance of an education. I hate that they are deprived of their family, so I fought for them to keep coming to our church Sunday School, so they are part of more than just the children's home. I try to go and hang out with them once a week. I can find community among the local Khmer Christians, if I can have the patience to visit with them, and accept that they will probably not be interested in my life, because they do not understand it and they are very insular. I can have community with the few local expatriates in my provincial town, and others in Phnom Penh. Finding and living in community takes hard work, so I need to get out there and try!

* * *

Barbara was born in 1959 in Angthong, Central Thailand at home by the light of an oil lamp held by her Dad while Dr John H. did the assisting. Her parents both came from Liverpool, England, so she is British. She is planning to try and get Cambodian citizenship this year but will keep her British Passport. Dates are a bit hazy, but she thinks she was at Chefoo between 1965 and 1970 and at Clarendon School (first in North Wales and then in Bedford, England) between 1971 and 1977.

Interlude 6:
See-through Jelly
Jemimah

I'M NOT A FUSSY EATER. I generally eat all my greens. I finish everything on my plate like we're supposed to. Sometimes I have trouble with beetroot, but I don't usually think about whether or not I like something. I just eat it.

But that day I had met my nemesis. See-through jelly. Not sweet, fruit-flavoured jelly. Savoury, see-through jelly, with some kind of grain spread about inside it. With the main course. To this day, I have no idea what it was. We each had a spoonful on our plates and I just couldn't stomach it. I tried. I really did.

It wasn't that I didn't know what it was. I don't mind eating things of unknown origin, or of ambiguous identity. I don't mind trying new things. I tend to like weird, flavourless, colourless, strangely textured Asian delicacies. But I didn't like this one.

As my dorm mates finished one-by-one and were released outside to play, I was left sitting there, becoming more and more distressed, staring at the see-through jelly. Aunty Barbara was encouraging me, "Just a few more bites! Look, everyone else has gone. Let's get going now!" She could see I wasn't being obstinately rebellious. She knew I usually happily ate up everything on my plate.

I ate another tiny bit. I just couldn't do it. Something in me revolted against that taste.

I'm feeling a bit lonely now. The dining room is emptying and it's just me and Aunty Barbara, staring at my plate, and that last forlorn spoonful of … what is it? Oats in jelly? Help!

Finally she had pity on me and let me go. What else could she do?

I slipped noiselessly across the dining room, flew swiftly out the door and round the corner in one well-practiced move, out into the fresh air.

And we never saw see-through jelly again!

7

What about faith?

As shown already, to be sent far away from family,
was difficult. To grow up as a Third Culture Kid
had enriching, as well as negative, aspects. Growing up
as a Missionary Kid in a mission society, passionate
to tell others about Jesus caused pressures too.

But for these writers, being sent away in the
name of God caused a unique twist to the
recipe for lifelong effect.

Ann

It was the doctrine of sacrifice that finally did it for me, maybe seven or eight years ago now. I had one of those light bulb moments where I looked at what God was requiring of me and I thought, "Why? Why is so much required of me? If God loves me why am I constantly in a state of guilt and striving to do better? Why do I have such a deep need to wear a hair shirt?" It was not making me any happier and I certainly did not feel God loved me. Amazing grace rang very hollow.

My entry into the Kingdom of God was through fear of hellfire and damnation. As a three- or four-year-old I was much impressed by the calamity that awaited my soul if I did not make sure that Jesus lived in my heart. I never really moved from that position, although Jesus was always very real to me, and a friend when there were no others. During dark nights lying awake in the boarding school dormitory I would hold long conversations with Jesus, telling him of my joys and woes. I would pray often, and with completely innocent intensity, that I be allowed to die while still a child. I looked at the world of adulthood and did not believe I would manage, and that my life was of no real importance to anyone, after all my parents had important work to do which obligated me to be out of the way, so better to die before any real harm could be done to me or by me; and of course heaven was an agreeable destination! A strange prayer for a child of five, six or seven. I probably stopped asking to die at about fourteen, when it felt that my journey into adulthood was pretty inevitable, and that it seemed less daunting than I had first thought. I must add here that I was never depressed or suicidal; I just thought that it would be a sensible solution to a difficult problem; which is the way Peter Pan felt maybe?

I remember a time in my preteen years when the family finances were so tight that various cost-cutting measures were being discussed at family meals, and we were asked to each pray about it. One of my solutions was to stop spending any pocket money so that it could be ploughed back into the family purse. On mentioning this some years later to a sibling, he told me his reaction was to spend his pocket money as fast as possible so it would not be taken away. I wonder why I felt the need to be sacrificial, but he did not? Other solutions were found, and my pocket money was given to me.

The doctrine of sacrifice – giving my all for God because he gave his all in the death of his Son, Jesus, has been the bedrock of my life. I cannot recall a time when I did not believe that the superior life was through self-denial, and having an open purse, hand, heart and life. I was taught that this is what is pleasing to God, and that I would find joy in living this way. The privilege to give all I have and am in order to make a pleasing offering and sacrifice to God was my *raison d'être*. It was the way of life I had witnessed in the mission; it was what I heard preached each Sunday. I was doing all the suffering and sacrificing I knew how, but I began to feel God must really dislike me. My life was full of rules to be obeyed, sins to avoid and luxuries to forego, all in order to meet the exacting standards that God required of me, which would give me such pleasure and fulfilment at having pleased him, but often did not. Hudson Taylor[42] spoke often of giving everything for Christ and the joy it gave him. "The stamp of men and women we need is such as will put Jesus, China, souls first and foremost in everything and at every time – even life itself must be secondary." Yes, even life itself must be sacrificed.

My husband became a Christian in his twenties; he was from a Hindu family and so he had been brought up with some similar ideas about sacrifice and working for salvation. At any rate, we found in each other kindred spirits. As an early example of our sacrificial living, even

42 CIM/OMF's founder, born Barnsley, England,1832; died Changsha, China, 1905

at the start of married life, we both felt the right thing to do was to give back to God in everything we did. I had saved all my working life but, being a nurse, I still didn't have a lot but wanted to blow it on a honeymoon to India. He had given up a good, well-paid job he enjoyed, as he felt called to mission and was living hand-to-mouth while reaching out to the unsaved. While considering the use of those savings he felt that it was too self-interested to spend so much on ourselves and I agreed, so we gave the lot to the church building fund. Later we went to Bible College, in order to prepare for mission, and the church was persuaded to help fund us, to the tune of the exact amount we had given to the building fund. We have given away 10% of any money we have ever had as gifts etc. We have enough and have been blessed in many ways BUT we have five children, two of whom are adopted, and one of whom is disabled. We have struggled almost every day to make ends meet and for many years my wardrobe was renewed at the charity shop. Friends thought I liked looking like a bag lady. I thought so too. I thought I was living the life God asked of me.

Then I began to look at all my sacrifice and how hard life was, and I wondered why others, particularly Christians in my local church, did not see the need to live that way. Why were so many people in my church happy to go abroad on holiday instead of giving the money to the poor? My sacrificial living was causing me to die a little bit more each day; but not a dying to self, more a dying to life.

I mention some of these moments in my life to help illustrate a way of thinking that started very young, that deeply influenced my actions and decisions, but that was not necessarily the same as my siblings believed or felt. This I find interesting, as we grew up in the same family but were separated for much of our early years and experienced very different influences as a result. This is a legacy not often thought of by those who send children in all directions, in order to be free to carry out God's work. The sacrifice the parents made was always lauded as somehow ideally spiritual whilst forgetting that children were the unwitting sacrifices.

I am the third child in my family and the eldest girl. At various times I have been the youngest, the second eldest and the eldest. These changing positions in the family required different things of me which were difficult to navigate successfully as they were in a constant state of flux. The fact they always required that I conform to an expectation from others meant I often lost all sense of who I was. I finally settled on the role of eldest daughter, no matter who was present in the home. This role was often mandatory and so I decided to let it be my part to play, as well or as badly, as I saw fit.

There are two moments that I felt happiest in the family; first when I was the youngest child with two brothers who had been present all my life; and second when, for a brief time, we managed to be a family of seven and I sat in my rightful place as number three. Those who have not experienced the family disruption that I speak of will not understand what a sacrifice we each made, living with the decisions that our parents made, as God had directed them to do. God did require so much of young parents and children; but only the chosen ones, and I was chosen.

So, I have begun to question why I was asked to sacrifice so much not just then but now. I have sought God's direction all my life. Each step I have taken I believed has been divinely directed. It can be hard to understand some of that leading. Somehow it has always led to living on a tight budget; maybe being a missionary child has uniquely prepared me for this, or brainwashed me into thinking this is a higher spiritual calling?

I can see God's hand in my life, but I can also see a strange doctrine of sacrifice that I thought was required of me, and it began to make me angry. Adoption is essentially a selfish act; to have a child in your life. They do not ask to be part of your family, and have no need to thank you for your sacrifice on their behalf, as they did not ask it of you. That is the bottom line, but why did it have to turn out so hard in our case? Well I guess it is hard for many parents and who am I to expect different? I just feel like I have been sold a promise of happiness ever after as long as you go through the wringer first. (Having adopted children has also given me quite an insight into what happens when our primary attachment is disrupted, and the lasting scar it leaves. I have also realised that I was what would now be described as being a looked-after child.) There is a strong sense that I must follow an ideal, set by Victorian men, or be damned to hell and so I strive to enter the kingdom through works, believing that this is part of my salvation, while knowing that Christ's sacrifice is all sufficient.

I can honestly say there have been some amazing high points in my life, where I have felt God very close and providing and caring for me and my family. The constant playing of that record in my head, of denying my needs, keeps me from being able to truly accept and enjoy those wonderful things I do have, because I must sacrifice all, must I not? Where is the God who loves me enough to die for me? Where is grace? What about eschatology? I seemed to be neither in the now or the not yet. Muddled? I'll say!

Now I search in places away from sacrifice but are still holy. I keep coming back to the Celtic traditions where life is more of a whole, with both hardship and plenty. Of thin spaces and dark abysses. And maybe a God who loves me and sacrificed himself, so I did not have to. I cannot quite let go of a Creator God who has some interest in his creation. I would like to meet him as a friend more than foe. The Celts, unlike the Romans, were relational in their spirituality, not rational. They sought inspiration in their everyday not institutions. Sometimes we can think we know too much, and sometimes we just need to learn to be. I do not say that I expect a life without suffering, but I look for more acceptance and less judgement. Ah, judgement, another whole can of worms...

My allotment has become my place of worship. The work of my hands in growing and providing is creative and soothing. The vagaries of the weather add to the constant need to live in the now. I am starting to understand the work of grace and not the grace of works.

> May the blessing of the rain be on you –
>   the soft sweet rain.
> May it fall upon your spirit
>   so that all the little flowers may spring up,
> and shed their sweetness on the air.

May the blessing of the great rains be on you,
    may they beat upon your spirit
and wash it fair and clean,
    and leave there many a shining pool
where the blue of heaven shines,
    and sometimes a star[43].

Ann went to Chefoo School, Malaysia from the age of 5 for three years in the 60s. These were exhilarating and frightening years with deep friendships, confusion and loss. Ann's teenage years were spent in Rhodesia in a time of war. After finishing high school in Glasgow, Ann went on to train as a nurse and then a midwife; and she has worked for more than 40 years in the British National Health Service (NHS). She is married to Shaylesh and is mother to five children and grandmother to four grandchildren.

---

43 *Celtic blessing* © John Birch, 2016, www.faithandworship.com/Celtic_Blessings_ and_Prayers.htm

John C

THE SMALL BOY, his pale face set with determination, found his water bottle and wrapped himself in his cardigan. Unnoticed he marched away from the dormitory, down the crunching driveway towards the school gates. The stone pillars stood tall, solid, unchanging. He muttered under his breath. "This is not right. I must get home." He felt a terrible unease, a wrongness, a loneliness, a powerlessness; not that a six-year-old knew what he felt in words. But those feelings were compelling him out. He reached the school gates unseen, then shuddered and stopped. The dense jungle greens, the noises of cicadas and birds were overwhelming. Recent stories of armed rebels, wild animals, snakes – and tigers – chilled his heart. Fear! He froze, then curled up outside the right pillar and wept. Home was 1500 km away. He was alone truly. Slowly that strong determination to return to his family leaked away, and two hours later he trickled, defeated, back to the boarding school.

Why? – Story One

That boy was me. In 1959 I was five years old when I was sent to Chefoo School in the Cameron Highlands of Malaya. My parents were missionaries with the Overseas Missionary Fellowship (OMF), working in a river town, Wiset, in central Thailand. My father was the doctor at the clinic there. For months they had been preparing me to be sent to the mission school, Chefoo. I had been told how good it would be to have friends there to play with every day. The heat and humidity of Thailand would be replaced by cool mountain air, 5,000 feet up in one of the world's most beautiful places. The frequent illnesses I had in Thailand would be less in Chefoo. Most importantly, going there was my part to play in God's plan to save the lost people of Asia.

The day came to leave. My brother was born two weeks before, then our family travelled by bus and train down to Bangkok. After my dental abscess was drained, I joined a small party of older Chefoo children and teachers on a train, for two nights of travel to get to Chefoo. That carefully orchestrated goodbye was devastatingly sad, though mum had wrapped a present to be opened after we departed, and that helped distract me. After a ride on a second, Malayan, train we got off at Tapah station, where there were diesel taxis ready to take us up into the highlands into the darkness. The road was winding, with 500 bends. I vomited, and so did each occupant of each taxi. I arrived. There was a welcoming bustle of arrival, a settling into a strange cold-sheeted bed, and I was there.

My parents had gone to China in 1948 to spend the rest of their lives as missionaries there, and they knew that the mission policy was for children to be sent to the mission school at Chefoo, for education from grade one until they reached tertiary level. They knew what missioning meant for their family-to-be. However, along with about 900 other China Inland Mission missionaries, my parents were expelled from China by the new Communist government, after they had been in Shanghai for just two years. After leaving China they came back to live in Brisbane, Australia, where dad set up a private general medical practice.

Now here is where the story goes a little deeper. You see, mum fell pregnant, but my older sibling, David, did not have a heartbeat at birth. This was a searing, scarring tragedy for them. Dad, I think, had a sense of incomplete business with mission work after the China setback, and he promised God that they would return to the mission field if the Lord gave them a child to keep. That child was me, born in 1953. Even that event was a drama. Mum's doctors had advised a Caesarean delivery. Dad believed God had spoken to him warning against surgery and for a natural labour and delivery. Dad wrote soon after, "I knew my stand could end up with the death of a second child, but I rolled the responsibility onto my Lord, and we waited." Two weeks late, I arrived safely, naturally. Faith justified!

I was often told the biblical story of the infertile Hannah: delivering a son Samuel, who was given back to the priestly school at a young age, as another justification for my being sent away. I was a Hannah's child. But the overt reasons for sending me away were simple. God required it as a service of sacrifice. Could my parents hold back when God had given his only son, Jesus, to be crucified for the sins of the world? Jesus himself said, "he that loveth son or daughter more than me is not worthy of me... he that loseth his life for my sake shall find it[44]." Abraham had earned accolades through generations because, when God asked him, Abraham put his longed-for son Isaac, the promised son after infertility, onto the altar and prepared to slay him. God, satisfied, provided a substitute and Isaac was spared. Prior to going to China, my mother had recurrent dental abscesses, so she had all her teeth removed and dental plates put in. She understood sacrifice. That was what God wanted.

There was one more critical strand. My father had come from a broken home and had been "saved" when he heard that following Jesus would bring blessing on his life, to his family, to his children, and to his children's children. Dad had a very strong faith, relied on God's guidance, preached the gospel to many of his patients, and was convinced that, in sending me to Chefoo, he was blessing me, and our family. The faithful God he knew would honour his sacrifice. *Jehovah Jireh*, the mission motto – the Lord will provide – was a promise to mum and dad. God himself would watch over me and keep me from harm.

So as a four- or five-year-old, I would pray for each central Thailand mission station by name, asking God to save Thais. I knew that what my parents were doing was critical to the salvation of many souls. I was on board for going to Chefoo. This was my part in The Great Commission.

44 Mt 10:37,39; KJV

But none of that was in my consciousness as I sat outside those gates some weeks after I had arrived at my new "home". I ran away that day because of a deep feeling that a terrible mistake had been made. I returned, defeated, to anxious teachers. Looking back later, I had learned a new skill that day. I put away the pain and determined to just soldier on. Sadness and crying were put there too – I do not remember ever getting so upset again. I had formed my first internal walled compartment.

"Kids adapt." And I did. From that place, I made my life. Chefoo was indeed a good school to me and prepared me well for returning to the Australian system – though knowing the kings and queens of England never gave me any advantage! I left the school and my family just as the mission wished, at the end of grade six. I flew home alone to Australia, where I lived with my grandmother and aunt in Brisbane, until midway through grade eight, when my family returned for a twelve-month furlough. Fitting together again was hard, but achieved.

Mission directors advised that my sister and I should be sent to the mission hostel in Melbourne for my parents' following term in Thailand. That was 1800 km from my grandmother's home in Brisbane... in a city strange and distant. With critical and timely insight, my parents fore-saw the effects of further separation on their children and decided to leave the mission, and settle back in Brisbane as a whole family.

My life flowed on into an Australian pattern. I completed medical studies, married Wendy, specialised in Obstetrics and Gynaecology and set up in private practice. We had four children and they grew, amazingly, into adults we liked and loved. I remained a keen Christian – of the Baptist variety – and was involved in church work for most of those years.

Looking back, I see two principles by which I worked. Firstly, I knew that God wanted to be first in my life, above work, family, friendships. I had learned that lesson from age four. Secondly, I believed that God had "called" me to Medicine; and wanted me to work with my patients, being Jesus to them. There could be no limit in my willingness to sacrifice for them. Oh! – and there was a third underlying principle for me. It was this: I was a "golden child" because I had been given to God in a painful, sacrificial way when I was five years old onwards. God therefore blessed me. God had provided. Jehovah Jireh. I prayed often that the golden glow would cover my children and then their children. I suspect many parents know that prayer.

I rarely thought about my Chefoo childhood; indeed I could barely remember it. If asked, I said that perhaps some kids found it difficult to be at Chefoo, but I had developed resilience. I had no idea that my life river was heading towards an unseen waterfall, down which I was about to be thrown, into a turbulent cauldron.

The Cauldron

As my fifties ended, I was aware that something was changing for me. I became impatient with the rigidity of the church. I saw that Christians seemed to be judging others, rather than showing love. In my work, I accepted same sex-partners for fertility treatment on the principle that love rules. That was a big change for me. I noticed also that I was crying easily. Hymns at church, any emotional events, would turn on the leaky eyes – even toilet tissue advertisements on television. I became adept at hiding that "non-male" behaviour.

Then, in 2014, I received the letter from the OMF. Among other things, it said:

> While one generation may think that they are doing the wisest thing possible, a subsequent generation is dismayed by their actions. ...the emotional effect on children of lengthy separations from parents was not given appropriate consideration... We expected that all children would go to one of the Chefoo schools. ...We recognise that whilst there are necessary sacrifices for the advancement of the gospel, the care of the family that God has given is also a Christian responsibility.
>
> While there are those who found their experiences nurturing and positive, there are others for whom such policies resulted in feelings of alienation, rejection and pain. The current leadership deeply regret that such policies have resulted

in varying degrees of heartache for the parents and children who went through the system. Looking back from our present vantage point, we recognise that some of the pressures put on parents were not God glorifying. We now recognise this and ask for forgiveness of all who suffered because of it. We want to open the doors of reconciliation and healing.

I was bemused to receive it; no, it was not for me. I was okay, a golden child. At our Sunday lunch I read out the letter to our family – and broke down crying. Hmm! The following week, I read it out to my eldest son, who had been away the first time. The same result occurred – tears. I knew something deep inside was wrong though I knew not what. I decided to accept the invitation to attend the first Chefoo Reconsidered (CR) conference, back at Chefoo in Malaysia, in October. I asked Wendy to come with me – "we will register, then skip off so I can show you this wonderful place where I was schooled."

That letter was a hinge on which my world turned. And is still turning. Far from skipping off, we attended every single event. From the first night, I knew this was to be the most significant event of my adult life (except, of course, marrying Wendy). Ulrika Ernvik, a counsellor and invited speaker, played a game with us. In a large room, she allocated different areas for different countries. Then she called out the years starting from the early 50s and we walked to where we spent most of that year. The room was a mass of moving ex-Chefusians. It was remarkable. For our childhoods, there was no geographical stability. There was no opportunity to retain friends. We went from one culture, with astonishing speed, to another culture, then to another. Families were transitory, furloughs random to us, friends ephemeral, and cultures a bewildering mélange.

In the following days another speaker, Ruth van Reken, presented her work on Third Culture Kids to the group. Suddenly, behaviours I knew as just mine, were shown to be something usual in mission kids sent early to boarding school. So many effects became clear. The ability to bury emotions, the repression of memories, social strategies for frequent changes of social groups (such as being a chameleon – I knew that one!), of cutting off pain, of poor goodbyes, of being a "watcher", emotional blunting, of seeking love, the need to stay in control – these were not so good. On the other hand, many had "good" lives, often in caring professions, were confident travellers, and had wide world views.

It was not just the talks though. The amazing part was the mirroring effect, of seeing sixty or so other adults who had been through similar childhood extremity. Seeing oneself is hard for us all. Walking into CR was akin to entering the changing room in a department store. You may know this feeling – you see yourself in one mirror, but from a different perspective. Then another mirror shows a completely unrecognisable person. At CR 2014, I noted especially that the males were "gentle", by which I mean they had no hard edges, they were socially adept, sensitive, kind. I could "see" the effects of a common childhood very clearly. Our attachments, our characteristics, our behaviours had been laid down by those common childhoods.

When I first went to Chefoo, the school was in its last year at the original Cameron Highlands location, which subsequently became The Bungalow, a rest home for missionaries. This was the scene of my failed attempt at running away. An excursion to the Bungalow, for afternoon tea, was the most significant experience of the CR week for me. We walked through the dense jungle and, in an event of great symbolism of this process of reconsidering our past, were helped by group members down a steep slope, from the jungle onto the road outside the gates... yes, the very gates that I had remembered, with no emotion, all my life. My dam burst that afternoon. So much sadness flowed, so much loss. Something had opened inside me that I had no idea was there. Here I was, sixty years old, crying desperately over an episode of sitting at those gates fifty-five years before. As contributors, we were asked to write about how our boarding experience has affected us. In that incident is my answer: very deeply.

Yet understanding what that flood meant took me another five years. I signed up for counselling, attended another five CR gatherings, did a lot of reading, writing and reflection. I sought out others journeying a similar path, and found an extraordinary band of missionary kids, seeking to untangle meaning from being sent away/abandoned by our parents, in Jesus' name. Others have written about peeling the layers of an onion, in trying to understand causes and effects. That was my journey too.

Firstly, I worked on the Third Culture Kid aspect, using that CR mirror to understand and see how I was shaped by that experience. Intertwined with that was the pressure we all knew of growing in an evangelical hothouse of belief and behaviour.

Secondly, I started seeing a counsellor, and worked on my sadness. I realised I had a locked compartment, inside which were my accumulated losses. Like a bucket full to the brim, it only took a drop more of sadness to overflow. So I set out to release the sadness, by finding triggers. Old hymns, songs by Andrew Peterson, and melancholy choral pieces were my favourites. I grew to love that bittersweet release of singing songs from that past that had been left behind by most. Many times I would be driving (alone of course) with the volume up high, tears running down my face, exulting. Weird, hey? This phase lasted about a year. Gradually, the tears settled, the bucket emptied, and at the second CR at Chefoo, I was able to walk through those old gates without sadness.

With help, I saw that inside that locked compartment was a small boy, thin, almost translucent. Slowly, I realised that my medical "me" was a mask, carefully, unknowingly, constructed to be pleasing, effective and convincing. The second cause of my sixty-year-old angst was that the real me, my ego, if you like, was in danger of disappearing, and that was causing my deep alarm and discomfort. I could not say what I myself wanted. That boy needed to be let out.

My problem was that medicine requires the mask to be secure. When patients disclose their issues, doctors need to have a way of walling off their personal feelings from that disclosure. Medicine promotes compartmentalisation in practitioners. Yet I needed to break my walls down. I fell into a pattern of putting on my superman mask during the working week, then trying to "open" on weekends. I had reached the stage that if I did not open, I would start to sleep poorly, and to become depressed. I knew I had to deal with this internal pressure definitively. So I retired from work. At the end of 2017, I ceased being a doctor, took off that mask forever, and set out to grow the small boy. I had an image in my mind of climbing over a wooden farm fence, and standing – looking over a flat field at the sun just climbing over the horizon – with no clothes on. Naked. And that felt so good. I felt light, free, open.

Thirdly, there was another deep strand yet to work through. My parents were very clear. I was sent to Chefoo because God demanded I went. He had promised to protect us. When I met ex-Chefusians *en masse*, it became apparent that not only had I been damaged by the experience, we all had, to one degree or another. One counsellor at the first CR said afterwards that "there was carnage". That is true. Broken lives, relationships, families, chronic ill health, psychological problems, many with lost faith. There had been twenty-three deaths that we remembered at CR, including suicides; then through CR there came to light sexual abuse by a dorm master. That was after my time at Chefoo, but we were all so very vulnerable. In my reading, I came across the evidence that autoimmune disease is increased following childhood trauma. When I was thirty-three, I developed Type One diabetes, which is an autoimmune disease (which, significantly, I had left out of my "Golden Child" story). The incidence in Australia is 12/100,000/ year. I am aware of three of us affected, in the approximately 300 Chefusians in CR – 1/100. Those figures are not significant for a statistician, but they are suggestive. I had to conclude God had not protected us. No human can see from God's perspective, but sixty years of living gives that finding some validity.

God had not protected us. Oh! Even writing that hurts. Because behind that shocking finding are life changing conclusions. I cannot believe that God wanted children to be hurt. Jesus' words on that were very clear. So our parents were wrong to send us away in God's name. I could see only three explanations:

Firstly, God is not trustworthy; he does not keep his promises.

Secondly, the God we were raised believing in is a false human construct. Over hundreds of years, our understanding of who God is has drifted from reality, and fallen into a culture or pattern of belief that directly led to sending children as sacrifices. An evangelical "culture" had developed that had drifted into error. Maybe the true God is far, far bigger than our human conception, and cannot fit into our boxes of understanding.

Or thirdly, there is no God at all.

After I retired, I set to trying to sort this out. My whole life structure felt undone, a shambles. I had believed and was complicit in a story about my boarding, a construct that was untrue; and I had collaborated in hiding truth from myself. How could I trust myself again? I wrote a poem about feeling lost at sea, limitless dark depths under my flailing feet. I could see that my parents were caught in a mission system, a theological system, that said what God wanted of them – but that was the wrong human construction that ended in damage.

To lose belief in a made-up god is no tragedy. But even if God was not bound by my parents' belief structures, surely he could have looked after us, we children, who had been given so trustfully and worshipfully to his work. By mid-2018, I had become angry with such a God and eventually concluded he was just not there. The whole faith story was made up from human neediness for meaning, purpose and security. That was the darkest place I have ever been in.

At that point I went to the third CR event at Chefoo Malaysia. The speaker talked about the ways trauma affects children. Ulrika Ernvik gave us her notes, as follows:

> 'How did our childhoods affect us? We got traumatised.
> Children need to be seen with glad eyes,
>   to breathe with someone,
> to deal with emotions with someone,
>   to get needs met,
> to get a deep sense of value and love,
>   and to feel a sense of significance...
>
> When we are in a situation where we feel lonely, scared and helpless, we first look out for safety – is there a safe person, or can this person be safe? Without a safe haven, children are easily traumatised by things happening to them, as no one is there for them. So, if we

cannot find safety, we start the "fight or flight" response. If that is not possible, we freeze, or we collapse.

(This accurately described my running away incident). *The trauma is something that happens in the body, it is a bodily reaction. Talk therapy doesn't really help. To survive our traumatic experiences, without the help of safe adults, we developed survival strategies:*

> *Hide,*
> *Smile,*
> *Keep busy,*
> *Obey,* (and others not so relevant to me).
> *As adults, we have added some more survival techniques.*
> *I think about our childhood as "my other life" that has nothing to do with me now.*
> *I forget what I have experienced.* (That was me).
> *I blame others for what I have experienced.*

To heal the traumas, we need to go back to the traumatic event, and bring in safety, by going back to the memory and imagine the little child there, feel in the body what the little child felt, then invite someone safe into that memory.[45]

I saw myself clearly in some of what she said, so I asked Ulrika for an individual session, where she reworked my worst memory, and invited me to bring someone safe into that memory. Of course, the memory was the one of me running away in my first term at Chefoo, and cowering (freezing) behind the gate. I told Ulrika I could not think of anyone safe to take there. My parents had deliberately sent me there, and I was very unsure of God. Undisturbed, she said, "let's just go there and see who comes." I told the story, and we waited at the gate, feeling once more the sensations of helplessness. In this session, my mum surprisingly came around the corner, and cuddled me, and said

---

45   Quoted by permission of Ulrika Ernvik.

she did not know how much our separation was hurting me, and she would take me back to Thailand, where we had a family conference and decided we would all go home to Australia. Talk about tears! That was the most amazing release for me. My anger against God disappeared that afternoon. I just needed my mum.

I left Chefoo thinking I was not sure about whether God exists, but not believing was too dark, empty and meaningless, so I would believe in him. And I do. That treatment for a childhood injury has held firm, even until today, as I write. And it confirmed that the need for shown love by my mother has underlain this journey. The five-year-old needed to know he was loved, though the sending away gave the message that the work, God, the mission came before him in importance – that I was not loved enough to keep. That trauma has been structural for me. It was buried because the fear of not being worth love hurt too much. My faith, my work all helped cover over that deep hidden pain. Now it has been opened and drained, like an abscess, and the relief has been huge.

Why? – Story Two

I started this account off with the story I was given and swallowed hook, line and sinker for my whole life, until age sixty. I conclude with my new story. I was the loved son of a missionary couple who were in an evangelical cult in which sacrifice, including of their children, was sought as a statement of commitment to God, an error in Christian culture and theology. Already distressed by changes of culture and the dangers in the new country, I was sent to boarding school from age five, and significantly traumatised by that. In fact, I was abused by the evangelical church system. In self-protection I locked away the deep memories and pain from that time. I pursued a successful life as a husband, father, doctor and "evangelical" Christian. Yet the deep buried pain bubbled through the internal walls at around sixty years of age. The childhood trauma was hidden by a "necessary" faith in a false image of God. Through the Chefoo Reconsidered process, I have been trying to unpick the distorted system error of who God is, and see truly the real God, whom I have decided is there and loves me. Writing about that would take another chapter! The process of growing the small boy into a man of independence and strength once more, is the task for the time that lies yet open to me.

And there, you have my two stories. There is power in story. There is also nakedness and shame. I write even so, believing these stories need to be heard. The system that took the most fervent believers and tricked them into sacrificing their sons and daughters is still alive and well. If I accept there is a God, then it seems likely that He may be saying to our world: "Enough!" Do we worship and know God, or do we know a system of theology and rules that has led us astray?

* * *

John attended Chefoo 1959–64, with grade three in Brisbane

Linda

I THOUGHT I WAS NORMAL until someone kindly pointed out that I wasn't. My husband, less kindly, to tell the truth.

It's no good asking a child if they mind being sent to boarding school and away from Mum and Dad. I didn't know. I was excited. I could put my left arm over my head and touch my right ear. My arms were long enough. A missionary uncle praised me, encouragingly, with the little game. That was all the proof needed that I was ready for the four- or five-months absence from my parents. I was a big girl now. I was six.

Yes, I sobbed convulsively when I got there. And yes, the next time, at six and a half I was not excited, I was crying at night for the weeks before the end of the holiday. I felt dread about the sight of the Bangkok railway, or the seaside, Hua Hin station, where we might start the journey from. But if you asked me, yes it was okay.

It was okay because I was told it was. The convulsive tears into a wet pillow and the tight lump in the throat were just how it was. And apart from the tears, and hard goodbyes, for me life at Chefoo was quite fun. We were proud. Our parents were telling people about Jesus.

But going to England aged eleven was a different matter. I already had misgivings. It felt like a portal. I had a vision of an open and ominous door, a bit like the one in CS Lewis' *The Last Battle*, which led from the sunshine, bright flowers, heat and green of the world where I lived, to another world that was dark, cold, grey and unknown and I knew, absolutely, that I did not want to pass through.

On planning the goodbye my parents, credit to them, decided on a well-intentioned ritual. At the end of the holiday, the evening before we left for school, there was a family picnic, which was meant to be a good leave-taking, but which for me had the awful feeling of a kind of Last Supper. We drove to the local golf course near Hua Hin in Thailand. I had the sense of an impending disaster. I hated the fateful sandwiches and tears were ready to spring in my eyes as we hunted for a good spot on the grass. I looked at my parents as they walked ahead with their different postures, dad with his, determined, bouncing step and swinging arms, which I thought he had got from his time marching in the army. Mum, dutifully trying to keep things peaceful. Sometimes they bickered. It felt awful looking at them. I loved them both very much despite all the complex feelings. In a few hours I wouldn't be able to see them anymore. It would be a year. I would not speak to them, apart from a minute or two, on Christmas Day. It was like a death.

The last evening at bedtime was a family Bible reading and prayer for us before we said family goodbyes. Typically the Psalm was read about a young man and "the way that he should go". I listened carefully and I sincerely hoped that I would stay on the path. There were lots of dreadful things in England to be avoided. But it was the Home Country. That's what it was called. Frankly, it had not impressed me much during a brief stint in South Wales for our furlough 18 months before that. It seemed cold, dirty and stupid. Nothing in my heart wanted to go. But I wanted to please and I wanted to do the Lord's will.

No one who gave up lands or Brother or Sister for my sake will be unrewarded, said the Bible verse[46]. I thought of my younger brother that I was giving up. He would be a long way away. I would miss him. We had some funny running jokes together which we both appreciated. But he might be loved more than me by mum and dad. They might find his quiet intellect more peaceful than my persistent questioning, over-emotional reactions, constant demands for approval, unnecessarily wanting physical contact, or hugs, and paper to draw on. I suspected it might be so. But I wanted to please the Lord. If I pleased

46 Mk 10:29 and parallels

the Lord enough, I might also start to please my parents.

So at the end of the holiday, I said my goodbye to mum and my brother. Dad accompanied me to Bangkok. It was a short stay before my flight and, one afternoon, we went to a large department store to choose a watch, and then to an engraver to get it marked with my name. "Try not to let it get stolen in England", dad reminded me. I felt very sad about the whole thing. Buying the watch felt so important, and very expensive for my parents, who seemed to have so little money and I promised to be careful. The next evening, with no fuss, I said goodbye to dad. I got on the plane, which took off in the black evening in Bangkok, and arrived eighteen hours later in a grey England.

Mum and dad, I knew sickeningly, were 10,000 miles and at least two- or three-days' journey away. There was no phone connection. A phone call to us, in those days, meant for my parents a three-hour journey to the nearest large town. Letters would take a week. Asking and answering a question could take nearly a month. I cried a little bit. I would be fortunate to see mum and dad next summer. A few years ago, the term of separation for families had been four years, my new Aunty told me when I arrived. I accepted that good fortune thankfully, and miles away from them, grieved for my parents with their fragilities. I knew mum would sometimes cry in the bathroom after an argument with dad. Dad himself was constantly uncertain about his ability to speak Thai and felt pressured by the other doctor he worked with. Even at that age, I was distressed by his sense of inferiority, and his feeling that he lacked enough spirituality. So far away, I felt my inability to protect my parents emotionally and theirs to protect me.

And then in England, which was, as I remembered, cold and stupid and often dirty, I tried to find how to please my new carers. I could not be talkative and bossy like I was, a bit, at home. I could not be demanding and ask questions. I became quiet and very, very, very good. I became as good as I could be. And as earnest as I could be. I went to every Bible study. I went to children's Bible studies and I went to adult Bible studies. At school I went to the Christian Union. I dove in as deep as I could, and tried to find the closest thing I could to my parents. I tried and tried.

Most of the world stopped making sense. I was trying to find my parents every day and trying to find my home. I looked up at the damp, leafy elms and sprawling oak trees, and tried to find the heat and the white sun and the palm trees of Thailand. The small English hills and hedges were nothing like the flat green paddy fields. When I finally reached my new bedroom on my first day in England, I opened my suitcase and tried to breathe the air from Bangkok. I kept a scrap of sand and dirt, from my school in Malaysia, in a bottle. One homesick afternoon, when the English winter had pressed cold and endless dark onto everything, and home and everyone from my family felt so far away, I opened the lid and tried to breathe the air. I had saved it up and I knew after that it had gone.

I bitterly missed and longed for my friends. Friendship had been one of the things that had made sense. Life at Chefoo was bright and full of conspiratorial whispers and imaginary games which could last for days. I felt their absence and treasured the little gift and messages we had exchanged before we said goodbye, and yet there was nothing I could do to find them. Scattered around the world, I had no idea where they were.

At school in England I was lost. It was cold, it was redbrick and tall. There were long corridors of splintery wood and girls who barged about. I suppose I was familiar with some of that, but it was not Christian! So on Saturday night I huddled in with the others at the Junior Christian Union. A kindly teacher opened the door of their house and let us all squeeze onto their living space, scores of us, pressed in rows on the living room floor and in the hallway and stairs and scoffing toast. Even the most heathen of us went, because it was warm, it was a home I think, and there was an endless supply of buttered toast and sweet lemon squash in plastic mugs. We watched slides and sang lots of choruses. Afterwards we were tipped back into the dark again and ran across the school grounds to the dorms.

Every exam time I did my best writing. It was one thing, apart from drawing, which I could do quite well. It was an opportunity to witness for the Lord, to make an impact. The story had a good ending and a Christian one and I hoped the teacher would come closer to the Lord.

Despite all this I had no clear way of describing my unhappiness, apart from homesickness, which was a word and feeling I knew. But this was something much more complex, much more far-reaching in scope, and the time it played out in. I was living it, but had you asked me I would have had no way to describe it. I would have told you I was okay.

In my late teens something started to go wrong. I mean, I started to notice it. I went home and found I disagreed with my parents. I found it hard in England and I began to feel that they did not get it, that they did not understand. I also began to think that the way of evangelising was also a way of getting people to be more Western, not just Christian. I started to question what my parents were doing albeit in a half-informed way. My parents were hurt and confused and didn't seem to understand. The life and missionary choices they had made were, almost literally, still black and white. The known world was Christian and the unknown world, the rest of it, was the un-Christian one. I wanted to feel safe.

And then in the sixth form I chose RE as one of my A Levels. A benign choice and I hoped I could do well as I knew lots of the Bible. But I was not prepared for the series of shocks that came my way. We studied the Bible from a historical perspective, as a document written in time, by real people with real human foibles, and not simply breathed by the Holy Spirit. I read that the birth of Jesus was not a divine miracle, that Mary was not actually or technically a virgin, and it dawned on me that it could not possibly be so. Later we studied the death and resurrection of Jesus. It became possible suddenly that Jesus had not physically died and risen. Something remarkable and intense had happened to kick-start the early church, but I was suddenly and dreadfully much less sure of my facts about Jesus rising from the dead.

I was deeply shaken. I ran to the house of the School Chaplain and asked him for some way to help. It was unthinkable. The stakes were so high. If all this was not true then why were my parents so far away giving their lives for it and more importantly, why was our family separated for the sake of something that might not be true?

My by now twice-yearly visits to see my parents became more fraught. I disagreed with them and yet was also trying to continue my faith and come back to the Lord. I often returned to England beset with guilt and distress that I had disagreed with my mum, and determined to follow the Lord even more. My doubts would make me stronger, people assured me.

At eighteen I went to teacher training college near Oxford. My institution of choice was a vague, soft egg of a place, Methodist in origin and also a kind of preparatory theological college. I thought it would be good to study there, principally because it was Christian. Quickly I realised that I would have been better served in the rigour of a proper university, with real un-Christian people around me, but it was too late. I had chosen a sort of continuation of boarding school. The study of religion continued, and I continued to suffer theological shocks and profound depression. I began to discover that many of the hoary bespectacled middle-aged male theology lecturers, some quite well known in the evangelical and academic world, often visited the rooms of female students, quite openly, for hours, with the curtains closed. It was troubling and shocking. My escape was working with the homeless people in Oxford. I slept in the homeless shelter on my on-duty night and came back in the early morning with all my clothes stinking. I had to throw everything in the washing machine, and scrub myself from head to toe to get rid of the smell, before hurrying to a lecture. But it helped to try to help. I was with lost people and they at least were more lost than I was.

I was not ready for life in the UK. The teacher training college soon sent us out to schools to practice educating real children in classrooms. It became apparent I knew nothing about living in England in the real every day of the country. I had no handle on social mores in the real world, and nothing of the subtleties of culture in the UK, apart from the Christian Union and the boarding school set up. The confusion and sense of being utterly lost overwhelmed me. I began to flounder emotionally. I went along to church with an eager heart and hoping for connection and to after-church student lunches, Christian Missions, children's missions, Sunday Schools. I did as much of these as I could because it seemed as close as I could get to what I felt was familiar. I had no way to describe this disorientation at the time. I looked white and I was British. Yet everything was so odd, so unfamiliar, in thousands of ways and I felt so unhappy.

I started to walk alone around Oxford on a Sunday afternoon, feeling bleak and utterly alone. I recognised nothing. It seemed hard, unwelcoming, snobby, distant. Even the people at church could sometimes be kind but they did not know Thailand. They did not know my family or my brother. At that time I began to see, in my mind's eye, a frightening picture of a sort of vast, desolate and apocalyptic landscape. It was a mental picture that stuck around for years. But in the world outside my head I made some friendships at the college, and I wondered quite often and hopefully, if I could ever get a boyfriend. It seemed a remote possibility. I felt very unsure about how you went about these things.

The guys I met seemed a million miles away from me in terms of life experience. They seemed small-minded in perspective, and only knew one or two places in England or Wales. And the Oxford students, even the Christian ones, whom I felt should have been kind, spoke and behaved strangely and seemed full of a sort of remote and complicated disdain. I didn't understand what mattered to them. I could not comprehend what it was that the girls they did choose as girlfriends had. But I knew that I did not have it.

My marriage some years later, occurred like a bad dream. I met my husband when I had no real understanding of what I really needed in a relationship. There was no sense of maturity, or of steady accompanying friendship, between us. I had assumed that because I was attracted to this man, and he was attracted to me, and because we were both Christians, which was the principal decisive factor for consideration as I thought, it was okay for us to marry. The Lord's will could be as arbitrary as you like, and of course it defied emotion and common sense, but that seemed not to matter in the way things were done. If we were not altogether well suited, I trusted that the Lord would help us, with prayer and persistence. My parent's advice on such matters seemed arbitrary, impractical and over-spiritual. The main thing was that we should not have sex before we got married. The second thing was that the person should be a Christian. Hopefully, the right kind of Christian and hopefully not foreign. I fulfilled the conditions but nevertheless I had kept my relationship mostly secret from them until I was engaged.

Shortly before the wedding day my fiancé and I went to the priest who was preparing us for the marriage ceremony. I hoped desperately that afternoon he would notice that I didn't really want to marry the person I was sitting next to. I hoped he would glance up from the Book of Common Prayer and The Solemnisation of Marriage in his hand, and see in my face the truth of the situation. I hoped he would give me spiritual guidance that it was not okay. I waited for his advice passively, because submitting to the guidance of the Lord was the safe way forward, whatever your feelings told you. But he did not. And shortly thereafter I married unwisely and very unhappily, and I had no clear sense that that was not a problem. Every other important decision in my life had been subject to the same "override" principle: emotions and feelings don't matter if it is the Lord's will.

There is a process of preparation of an empty-mind state which leaves members of church congregations, perhaps especially those with low self-esteem, to find a sense of worth in doing the unthinkable. It happens in Church and Home Groups and Bible studies even today. I have wondered if this was part of the process that led to my parents making such unnecessary sacrifices. I hear it when I pop back into church from time to time. Sermons and hymns urged us "Not my way but yours", or the preacher would recount how "I tried to do it in my own strength and I failed," and "I need you Lord," and "Perfect submission", or "Perfect surrender to the will of the Lord", sung over and over, with great feeling. So much of my experience was a day-by-day training not to listen to your own feelings. Self-actualisation was the opposite of what we were groomed for, I submitted and submitted and submitted again. I listened and listened. Unfortunately, the will of the Lord often turned out to be the will of somebody very human, who wanted to be in charge. Usually, but not always, it was a man. It wasn't my will. But it really wasn't the Lord either.

Yes, some Church and mission work is good and extraordinary even, but good deeds mix in with the truly wicked, the wheat and the tares. Jesus wisely said that it would be so.

I grew confused early about what I really thought and felt. As I mentioned before, I told my parents aged six I was so excited to go to school and it was probably true in the moment. They were amused and relieved. But there was little wisdom around to question what was really happening, or any perception that my words were yet untested by the years of separation that were to follow. Utterances from the mouth of one so young, from the mouths of babes and sucklings, was taken as good proof that I was happy, as I should be, and a vindication of what was being allowed to happen to children of missionaries. So many serious choices were made with apparently no real knowledge of the likely outcomes.

There was a sense, I think, that it was not good to love your child too much, or to become too attached to them. Too much love was perhaps seen as being weak or over-emotional. A weepy goodbye from parents was not approved of. I once witnessed a parent struggling with a goodbye at an airport. I remember the negative comments that followed. Perhaps not surprisingly, my adult relationships have often been characterised by distance, both geographical and emotional, which I really felt it was my part to endure. It is not until recently that I have begun to feel confident enough to show vulnerability, and be met by kindness and understanding. I know now that it is important that I too can be me, the energetic, opinionated, strong person as well as the uncertain, emotional and frightened person, and it will be okay. But even today that sense is fragile.

Today, I practise meditation that draws from Christian and Buddhist traditions. I am often still confused. I am often still lost, disoriented, and full of grief. I have applied my intellect and emotions to try and adapt to life in the UK, to nuance of language, the rhythm of the seasons, the need for different clothes and shoes at different times of year. I have learned to cook, absorbing British food and recreating dishes from other cultures which I enjoy. I have listened carefully to British culture and tried to learn about its different forms. But I still feel unconnected to British people in general, many days. From time to time, I still find myself wandering in the town where I now live, feeling utterly lost, disorientated and looking for something or someone that reminds me of home. I am a mix of things, but becoming surer sometimes of my heritage as a person who lived far away, and who also lives here in the UK. I understand I am not Eurocentric, although I have tried to educate myself about this culture and history. I am sometimes an over-thinker, with an intense dislike of people who don't let you make your own mind up about things. But I have deep friendships. I have a profound and loving relationship with my now adult son who is highly critical of the missionary set-up. He has, in turn, suffered directly as a consequence, not least because of the depression I have suffered; the third and fourth generation. We talk about it all often. Perhaps not surprisingly I work with refugees. I hope that one day I will feel that I don't have to.

I have tense and fragile relationships with my parents, who I still desperately want to protect, and who in turn desperately worry about me. My father attends church regularly but he is open that he has doubts about his faith, and he has apologised for "sending us away." That admission was a relief and I respect him enormously for it. He also challenged the mission organisation on several points, including the way they dropped responsibility for housing missionary children once they reached eighteen and finished school. Dad has asked me recently to accompany him on some of his early morning walks. A very elderly man, he presses forward now with two sticks, and still with a trace of the military march. It has been a time of telling me things he has never said before. He breaks his lifetime habit of frugality, and buys me a cup of tea and a slice of cake, which we share. He recently told me that he found life on the missionary field difficult emotionally and some of the pressures he experienced. When I pressed him, he said that when they joined the mission, they had actually agreed to not seeing their children for four years. That never happened. It was only a year at a time. But what a thing. And what a cost.

The final thing I want to say is for those who have responsibility as spiritual leaders and influencers, ordained or not. And it is by way of a one last story. In early 2018, a cold and snowy Sunday morning, I went to a church service in an affluent rural parish in an evangelical Church of England church in the Cotswolds, not far from Oxford. Fairtrade coffee was available at the back for after the service. The congregation were kind, educated people. They supported persecuted Christians in Iraq. All good. The priest was similarly well mannered and educated. He preached from the verse in the Gospel of Mark 10:29 which I quoted above and which I turned to for comfort, when I was eleven or twelve years old, and first arrived in England. "No one who gives up lands or brother or sister... for my sake will not receive a hundred-fold in return."

He concluded the reading and turned to the lectern and to the congregation. "No one," he said, with a confident assurance. "I know of no-one who has given up all they have for the Lord *and has ever regretted it*". I sat quietly on the chair and heard him. I breathed deeply. I think finally I was glad to know that I had clarity. I knew I would go and question him in a few minutes, after the sermon had ended and the rousing song had been sung about a "task unfinished", and that he would actually refuse to really hear me, because he preached as a well-respected and trusted priest. He was telling the gentle and serious congregation what they hoped to hear. And I knew that whether he knew it or not, he spoke a lie.

* * *

Originally from Wales, Linda's parents joined OMF when she was four years old. She was at Chefoo School from 1971–76, then lived at Donnington Hurst, the OMF hostel near Newbury and attended King Edward's School, Witley. She trained as a teacher and eventually retrained to teach English as an additional language to adults. She has one son from her marriage and lives in Bristol.

Carol

I HAD FORGOTTEN ABOUT this writing that you asked me to do. At the time that you asked me, I thought well, it was fine, no negative outcomes, beautiful scenery, what am I going to write about? It's all in the past. So I wasn't really inspired.

But this morning I do have something to say about it. Firstly I want to say that I have the awareness now that we all, including me, are creating our own lives through our own thoughts in the mind, so that I really and truly know that there is never anyone else to point the finger at about anything, but it is only through understanding that you can become aware of the consequences of your own thoughts, words and actions.

Something happened this week that caused me to see the similarity in going off to boarding school at a young age and how I felt about it. I understood with my head why I needed to go off to boarding school, and later why I needed to stay in Canada, at the home for missionary kids, but my heart (my feelings) didn't really accept it. I did feel rejected. Although my mom and dad communicated with me through letters and came to visit me at the bungalow, I still felt rejected. But since they did all that I couldn't really feel rejected by them, so instead I felt kind of abandoned and angry at Christianity. I didn't feel totally abandoned by God, because I knew that God wasn't a physical being, but a spiritual being, but I couldn't stand all the confusion in Christianity of mistaking Jesus for God. Even as a small kid I would only talk to God but didn't care for Jesus at all. Today I can look back on this desire to connect with God, and not a human being, and see it as a very good thing and something that brought me to God, through Raja yoga meditation.

The only person at Chefoo school who played a mothering role for me was the nurse, Betty S. I seemed to get non-stop attacks of tonsillitis and spent weeks in the infirmary being pampered by this nurse. She was wonderful to me, and every day I would hope to have a fever again so that I could keep staying there. When I was there, I got to stay in bed and play and read and be read to. It was very comforting and non-threatening.

Although I loved many things about Chefoo, the walks, the scenery and monkeys in the trees, the cool air, the short cut to the bungalow, Boh Tea, etc., I was quite a loner, and spent a lot of time singing and talking to myself. Today I look back on this and I think part of it was just my own personality (I have no regrets or anyone else to blame), but I was also fearful of being around other people too, and preferred to be alone quite a lot, due to fear. I just felt more at ease when I was alone, and with nature, and doing art. It made me become the artist that I am today. I notice that, even today, when I am crowded in a small space with other people, I really don't like it, and want to get out of there fast.

I think my experience at Chefoo shaped my life to be one who hides my true self quite a bit, due to the fear of the opinions of others. I used to have dreams at Chefoo of being trapped in a jail. I would be sleeping and then I would wake up, but my body would still be asleep, and I couldn't move it at all for quite a while. The tears would be rolling down my cheeks, and I would see bars in front of my eyes, like being in a jail and looking out. This was a recurring dream and I never told anybody about it. It may have been a real past life experience, the experience of being in jail.

I also used to save my bread and butter at break time, because I wanted to have it in case I wanted to eat it later. I had the fear of running out of food and not being able to get more. I saved it in my underwear drawer, and one day some teacher found it and pulled out all this mouldy bread and said, "What's this?" I was so embarrassed.

I was also very humiliated at age six when I wet the bed due to really believing that there were snakes under my bed and I couldn't get up to use the washroom, and then seeing my sheets hanging on the line for all to see the next day. I hadn't wet the bed since I was a baby, and I was so ashamed for that to happen to me. The cooler air, that I wasn't used to, also seemed to cause me to wet the bed. I also remember bigger girls shaming little girls, to tell who plugged the toilet with the toilet roll. I think we were told that we couldn't leave the dorm until someone confessed who had plugged the toilet. Of course, the bigger girls took on the responsibility of figuring out who that was. In the end, just to get us out, Libby H always confessed. She always seemed to play that part whether or not she had done it.

There are many good and bad memories from Chefoo, but I also seldom think about them. I'm very good at suppression. This week is the week leading up to Diwali, the Festival of Lights, a celebration of God's light coming into the world. We celebrate it quite differently from Hindus, but more meaningfully, since everything that they celebrate is symbolic, but they don't know the symbolism (most of them don't). One of the things we are doing is settling the accounts of karma from the past, tolerating everything with love, and forgiving everyone for everything, giving all the burdens to God, because Diwali is really the celebration of a new year.

Because God is really an incorporeal Being, a Being of Light, just as I am too when I leave this body, I can have all relationships with Him, so God is not only my Father, as in Christianity, but also my Mother and my Teacher and my Friend and Beloved. Right now I'm working through meditation on the relationship of God as my Mother, the one who loves me unconditionally, who never abandons me, who nurtures, feeds and clothes me, who always understands me, but who guides me in the right direction. I missed out on having a mom like that, not just because of Chefoo, but because my own mom had severe low self-esteem. But she was also lacking due to her own childhood, so there is no blame involved.

We just all have to turn our minds to God who fills in all the missing pieces and makes us full. No one in your life can be your everything, and people always expect someone to be their everything. Only God can be your everything and that is how it's meant to be, especially at this time when the play, the drama, is coming to an end. If you don't believe me, just take a look at the state of the world. Unless you are an ostrich it's pretty evident that human beings are about to destroy this world. It's time to tie up the loose ends, forgive everyone and go back home now. We all have to pay off our debts and connect to that Supreme Light.

I am so grateful to Chefoo for not being my everything, so that I could keep on searching and finally, at age forty-seven, find God. Chefoo was the best thing that could have ever happened to me, because it pushed me into God's arms, finally. Chefoo made me reject Christianity, but still love God.

* * *

Carol attended Chefoo 1960–65

Richard A

NOTHING BAD EVER happened to me.

Ok, sure I went off to boarding school aged six. But everyone did that. What I mean was, I wasn't bullied, abused, beaten up, tortured – so nothing bad happened.

More than that I actually had a privileged upbringing. I grew up seeing, from an early age, parts of the world that most people from my country never get to visit. I was educated at English public school and university. And better than that, from a very early age I was saturated in the Gospel of our Lord Jesus Christ; the Bible flowed through my veins. It says in the Bible, "From him to whom much is given much is expected." I was a privileged one – much was given to me. No Christian could have a better start to life than I did.

Fast forward forty-six years, and one night my wife found me curled up on the floor of our shower room crying my eyes out like a child. We had been arguing a bit as is the wont of married couples, and I had suggested we sleep in different rooms for one night, just to get some sleep. It was no big deal, a minor marital tiff, no more. But here I was crying uncontrollably, muttering the words, "Don't make me sleep on my own." She held me until the shaking subsided, she comforted the little child in me, she was there, she stayed with me. But what was that all about? How does that correlate with nothing bad ever happened? Where did the pain come from?

How to tell this story, how to tell a story that only half makes sense? I think we'll have to give flashbacks from that date, as we move forwards into the present.

Let's just set the scene with some basic facts. I was born in Aomori, Japan in January 1962. If you google Aomori, you will find its claim to fame is that it has the most snowfall of any city on earth. My parents were Christian missionaries. My older sister and brother each went to the missionary boarding school, when I was about one and three, respectively. I went to that school when I was six, at which point my brother and sister were at boarding school in England. I followed them four years later. My parents would return to England, after every four years in Japan, for a year's furlough (as it is called in missionary circles) so, every so often, we were in England as a family. I overlapped with my brother for a year or so at school when I was thirteen. In the holidays, the mission had a hostel (I call it "the orphanage") where a bunch of missionary kids would fake being "a family" while all away from our parents. Summers typically everybody got away to see their parents, either for two months out east, or if parents came back to England then one month. The scene is set allowing the all-important work of preaching the gospel to the millions of lost and dying souls of East Asia to continue unimpeded by children getting in the way.

So here I am fifty-two years old crying like a small child. I'm not what our society would term a failure. I've got a good job, my career, at least to the external eyes, looks pretty good. I'm not a high-flyer but I'm pretty comfortable. I get Caribbean holidays quite often, I had a 1964 Corvette Stingray for a while, and am currently driving a Mini Cooper Convertible JCW, 215 hp in a go-cart! This thing hugs the road like nothing on earth. I have a house in Greenwich, Connecticut (OK, it's a townhouse, not a back-country celebrity mansion, but still like I say, I'm pretty comfortable..., I mean it's only the two of us and we have four loos, so I'd call that at least moderate luxury). I have been married to the same gorgeous Chinese princess ("princess" meaning daughter of the King of Kings, not daughter of a human emperor, but to me she is princess!), I've been married to her for nearly 30 years. Two wonderful children who both have their acts together – at least on the outside. In my thirty years of working I have worked for only

four different companies, and one of them was a takeover of one by
another, so hardly counts ... I don't flit around. I've even had my Mini
for six years at this stage. I don't even church hop much, once I've
moved house, I settle into a church pretty quick and stay put. I'm
loyal, steady, balanced, in control and a general success, so don't try
and tell me that my weird upbringing caused me any trouble. No! This
is my strength, I'm independent and can stand on my own two feet.

So why is this small child inside me crying?

Around this time I was seeing a therapist. I am living in a posh part
of the USA – having a therapist is not a sign of weakness, it means
you've made it, so don't judge me for being "in therapy". On top of
that I only started seeing the therapist by accident. My wife was taking a Masters in Marriage and Family Therapy, and part of her course
required that she go with her husband to experience receiving therapy.
I joined her very reluctantly, I was most upset that her course could
somehow require me to attend anything. But then I found I really
liked the guy; he had worked most of his life in business management
and only began as a therapist after retirement. So I found him dead
useful to talk to about work issues. Bit by bit though, I was opening up
more. At some point he felt I needed to look into what was wrong in
my childhood, something my wife had been telling me for some time.
Well there was nothing wrong in my childhood, idyllic upbringing in
the wonders of northern Japan with childhood holidays on the beach
of the Pacific Ocean. Even just the words "Pacific Ocean" still bring
a soft cheerful joy to my soul. But my teenage years? Hey – I can tell
you about them, "the orphanage", I hated it so much, there is this dark
cloud that sits over those years, a time of loneliness, failure, despair.
You can't even see past it into my childhood – the cloud is so black.
So I explored those years with my therapist and got a whole new angle
on it..., those weren't failure years, they were just growth. They were
success years: feeling lack of friendship in one place, I reached out and
found it in other places; somebody doesn't laugh at my jokes, I find
somebody who does; feeling trapped in this place, I went out to others.
These were success years. I still hate the place though.

So still, why is the small child crying?

Around this time there was this letter written by the mission apologizing for the unnecessary pain of sending children to boarding school. With the benefit of hindsight they have concluded the gospel could have reached the East Asia millions even without abandoning the children. I now know that there was a lot of background and context to this, but for me it came out of the blue. It hit me like Thor's hammer hurtled out of the heavens. No! It hit me like, like, I had this beautiful manicured lawn, white picket fence, lovely vegetable and fruit garden, summer sun shining down, children playing happily, and out of the deep, from way down below the earth's crust this deep sound of rumbling begins to rise, the peaceful scene starts being disturbed by the sound, then the ground starts to shake, G&T glasses fall off the garden table, tea cups are rattling, the Sancerre bottle falls over, and the shake strengthens into a deep powerful rumble, until the ground finally bursts open and fifty year old pain explodes up out of the depths, the flood waters pounding and pounding, destroying everything in sight, years of manicuring the lawns gone and wasted in an instant. Everything is lost.

The sound of the flood waters deep down took a few months to rise as one storm after another pounded into that tiny hidden child soul way down inside me. Poor little boy. The man has got his act together, the man has figured how to make it through life, which emotions to numb and how much to trust and feel, but the poor little boy had never received the comfort he needed. And now at fifty-two my princess wife is comforting the poor little boy. These tears continued for quite a few months (or was it years?) as I would drive up the I95, from Greenwich to the office in Stamford. As I passed Exit 6, I would switch off the tears, my eyes needed to be dry before I arrived at the office.

We returned to London, we rented a flat in the centre of London, like about as central as you could get, right next to Tottenham Court Road. There is no better place on earth to live, it is the most brilliant experience anyone could ever have, and we lived there two years. But I was still regularly crying, the flood waters were still destroying my land. One sunny day I was walking across St. James's Park, possibly the most beautiful park on earth, and it hit me that I was not going to cry my way through two years in central London. We would have to move back to the suburbs soon, and I can cry my way through the suburbs for another thirty years for all I care, the suburbs are so rubbish anyway! But I was not going to miss out on living in central London. So I constructed a dam. You see you don't want to bury this stuff; it causes trouble even if you can't see it. And it had all been buried for forty or fifty years. Now that it had erupted and destroyed my world, I wasn't going to bury it and let it explode all over again. So I built a dam. Gradually drained the flood waters out into the resulting reservoir where I let them out, a little bit at a time, to analyse them and drain them off. Meanwhile, the ground is dry again and I am planting lawns and gardens and I have new G&T glasses and tea cups. And my two years in central London was ludicrously awesome and, at the same time, I began to be at peace in myself so that when we returned to the suburbs, which would have been the worst experience of my adult life, it actually turned out to be the best move ever because this was a move where I was more at peace with myself than ever before.

I have found out, since then, some explanations about what was going on. Research has shown that repeated separations in childhood can be traumatic leading to symptoms of PTSD. As an adult I have learned to hide behind a mask, I have numbed emotions, can't cry. "Everybody leaves me," is one of my mantras. So I'm not easily going to connect with anyone at any depth. Looking back, I can even see how my leaving and moving to the USA, when my kids were at university in England, was partly to protect myself from them leaving me. By the way, fifteen years later they haven't left and I'm back! I'm generally quite closed – actually it's a bit cleverer than that – what you do is you make an appearance of opening up – you have a layer that you allow people to see into, and then keep a firm barrier so they can't get beyond that. That way you're not quite so obviously closed up and people don't pry too much. The perfect hiding place in plain sight.

You don't have to be a TCK (Third Culture Kid) to have these kind of characteristics but, as a TCK, you get the benefit of understanding something of where it all comes from, and as a member of the CR movement, you meet another 100 people with overlapping experiences and characteristics.

One thing I realise is that my identity as a human is inextricably intertwined with my identity as a Christian. I'm not talking about what some Christians call "identity in Christ". If such a thing existed that would indeed be groovy, that would mean having an identity based on a relationship with a person, a relationship with the universe and a relationship with "the source" all in one. No, I am referring to identity in belonging to the Christian team, the organization and all the rules, regulations and beliefs that go with it. So when the letter from the mission arrived, I fell apart as a person, because my identity collapsed. Actually, it kind of came in waves over a period of time. Initially it was just, "So what? I went to boarding school and have done well with my life out of it – what difference does it make whether I needed to go or not?" But bit by bit, it began to emerge that it was extremely important to me that I needed to go. Try to get into the mind of a six-year-old trying to make sense of the world without an adult to process for him. He doesn't argue out well-structured explanations in writing, but rather builds up a world view that takes root deep in the psyche. My parents and my brother and sister all love me, but they leave me, they abandon me, they toss me aside, for one purpose: to reach the lost souls with the gospel; it is evangelism. There is, therefore, this thing that is more important, more significant, than even loving your own children, and that is evangelism. Every child knows they are "meant" to be loved by their parents, and every failure in that love (which, of course, there always is with every human parent – even the good ones) leaves a negative impact. Parents not there definitely fits that category.

So evangelism is everything, it's the defining factor of value and purpose. Now I was never very good at evangelism, so I always felt a bit of a failure. It was kind of pyramid selling, I think. As the number one important thing in life was evangelism, my "message" to people was, "You should evangelise too." This isn't entirely fair on me, my conscious mind has always believed you have to share something better than that, it's just that, with the benefit of hindsight, I look back over my life critically and conclude that, on balance, it was pyramid selling. My point is, I wasn't good at it, I didn't reach many (any?) lost souls in my entire life. However, one thing I did, my sacrifice as a child contributed to this great cause. My parents were only able to reach the lost souls of Japan because of my sacrifice. Had I not gone to boarding school, the mission would have been thwarted. And along comes this letter saying, "You didn't need to go, we could have done the evangelism without it." Oops! Sorry! It was almost like I could see my body crumbling into ashes, somehow this was more of a foundation than I'd ever imagined, this was a massive significant truth I had always held onto. That my sacrifice had value, my pain had value, I was martyr for a purpose, I had value, I had purpose. And somehow now, I didn't. Everything collapsed.

If you think I'm being melodramatic, if you think it doesn't sound a big enough deal to collapse over, then, well... I would have said the same. But I did collapse and now, looking into the mind and emotions of a six-year-old, making sense of abandonment, now I can see how your early experiences shape you more than you could imagine.

There's a couple of phrases that have haunted me since the awakening: "again" and "in God's name". Something hadn't gelled right, there was a contradiction. I had communicated to my wife, even from when we first met aged twenty-two, that I was a person who couldn't cry. This is no great shock: I am male, English and had been to boarding school, of course I can't cry. However, another defining moment in my self-awareness was that at age fourteen, when I went back to school without my brother for the first time in four years, I burst into tears in front of everyone. Now I had always interpreted that event as evidence that I was particularly mature, that I was so emotionally balanced that I was able to cry. And to cry over something only moderately serious, I mean going back to school without my brother was upsetting, he meant a lot to me, but I would see him at the next holiday, so sure it was "a deal", but not "a big deal". So how does this tie up? What's going on – am I an emotionally balanced crier or an emotionally stunted stoic?

Only after the awakening did it start to make sense. There is no contradiction here. The question is: what happened that was so bad that it would cause a male, public-school teenager to burst into tears in front of his peers? It was not that I am emotionally balanced, it was that something ludicrously bad had happened. That my brother was leaving? No, that's not bad enough. That my brother was leaving again! That is it. "Again". This is the big enemy of the TCK. My brother had left me when I was 3½, 4, 4½, 5, 6, 7, 9, but from 10-14, he was there, and then he leaves again at 14. And this is what happens, you go off to boarding school and leave your parents over and over again, every term. You make a best friend, his parents return on furlough, so six months later you make another best friend, his parents leave the mission, time after time, again and again, you are wrenched away your home, your friends, people you love, places you love, food, smells, sights and sounds that you love. Everybody leaves me, everything leaves me. Sure, you learn to be numb, you belong nowhere, roots are shallow, but then sometimes, there's a break in the clouds of numbness, and for a moment you feel the pain. You oscillate between super-controlled, cool, independent, strong person and a blithering wreck. Sometimes I am so cold and strong, but on the other hand I can put down shallow roots so fast that one night in a hotel will set me on the verge of tears, as I am leaving "home" again. I love holidays, but the night before returning home I am always an emotional wreck. And be really careful before you call anyone a "friend", because they are going to leave you "again". Everybody leaves.

As I said, my faith and my identity are closely tied. Actually, I should say "were" – there's been a ton of healing in the last five years, and being a Christian no longer defines me. But at least they were closely tied. What messes up my faith, messes me up. It's not a hobby, it's central. So when things are done "in God's name", this is a big deal, and if they are bad things, then it makes God look bad, which messes me up. If you want to take a job moving around overseas, and you feel that your kids are best off with the continuity of boarding school, instead of uprooting them all the time, or if you just don't care about your kids, and love your job better, then go ahead and do it, just don't do it in God's name. Take responsibility and admit you chose to do that, and your kids face the consequences of your choices. How much, over the years, have I ridden roughshod over other people's emotions in God's name? How often do I use God's name to determine that their immortal souls are more important than whatever is happening to them now? How many people do I write off in God's name? How often have I neglected my own children, wife or my own responsibilities in God's name?

But here's a little happy part of my story. About a year before my dad died, I got a chance to talk to him and open up a bit. Why hadn't I opened up before? Well partly, I'd learned long back to be closed, but partly, he would shut me down; I'm guessing he found it hard to take the damage done to his kids, but he's gone now, so I can't ask him that. You must understand, my dad was not from a wealthy or classy background, and left school at fourteen, so my world of public school and university was a little bit of a move up one might say. What he told me on this occasion was, "I was so happy that my children had been able to do what I never did, that they had made it through high school and university and had opportunities in life that I never had, I never saw the emotional cost!" Wow! Wow! Wow! My missionary father... no mention of God's name, no mention that my price was worth paying because it's for God, or for a greater cause. Just the simple reality of a father, who wants to make a better world for his children than he had himself, and makes some mistakes along the way getting there. This is a story I can handle! This was a major healing moment – it's not all in God's name. I am not now an atheist or agnostic, I am probably still Christian, but that does not define me anymore. I don't really know what this Christianity looks like, where not everything is in God's name. Where I am a grown up, where I take on my own responsibilities, where I am even allowed to pat myself on the back for my own successes. It feels really good ... being a human.

* * *

Richard was born in Aomori Japan in the early 60s.
Schools: Day school London age five for one year, then boarding at Chefoo School Nanae for 4 years, and in England 7 years.
Gap year Sapporo Japan (which he still considers home)
University: Birmingham, England.
Married at 24, still married with two grown-up children, son and daughter, both married living in London.

George

I WANT TO THANK the Chefoo book committee for allowing me to share some thoughts on life as a missionary kid for inclusion in this book. I want to state at the outset that the majority of my experiences at the China Inland Mission schools in Shanghai and Kuling were positive and helped shape me into the adult that I became. Thank you, Chefoo. However, when selecting my subject for this article, I chose a darker side of the MK experience, one that was not constructive either in my childhood or in my adult life. The words of Jean Valjean, in Victor Hugo's novel *Les Misérables*, so succinctly capture the moment in his life, and mine, that I quote them at the outset: "If I speak, I am condemned; if I stay silent, I am damned."

It was a day like most days in the Chefoo school in Kuling – rising bell, devotions, breakfast, classes, games on the athletic field, dinner followed by singing from *Golden Bells*[47] and then the inevitable lights out. What followed was not. The boys in my bedroom would often play a version of dare and double-dare as we would sneak onto the girls' third floor, race through their rooms and back into bed, without getting caught. But on this evening my activity was different. I snuck into Frank A's locker and stole about a dozen of his Australian stamps. Stamp collecting was a big deal in the mission school and most children had a stamp collection. I gave mine to my son a few years

47   Hymnbook that was widely used in the mid-years of the 20th century. Succeeded by *Hymns of Faith*.

ago. In it were over 1500 stamps from over 100 countries. We loved collecting most anything – butterflies, dragonflies, insects, leaves, even manufacturer's labels from our clothes – remember *Fruit of the Loom*? My younger brother Dick and I had an Aunt Helen in the US, who had no children of her own and so "adopted" us, and sent us many items including stamps. As a result, I had quite an extensive collection; but mine lacked many Australian stamps. Frank was Australian, and I stole a dozen of Australia's finest.

Frank reported the theft and the nightly interrogations began immediately. Should I confess and bear the condemnation of the adults in my life, including my parents, or remain silent and magnify my sin against God? I recalled references to the literal lake of fire (*Gehenna*) that was the inevitable destiny for anyone failing to confess sin. Scripture memory was important in Kuling, and I had memorized hundreds of Scripture passages, many on the theme of sin and the inevitable guilt that resulted from failure to address it. But night after night I remained silent. Finally, the interrogations ended, and I breathed a sigh of relief.

But the relief was temporary. In my mind I had committed an unpardonable sin and was therefore damned to an eternity in hell. I chose to remain silent; Jean Valjean chose to speak. A sense of spiritual gloom and doom surrounded me. I saw all of life through a spiritual prism. You never made errors in judgment, you *sinned*. In *Pigtails, Petticoats and the Old School Tie* by Sheila Miller, two boys in Chefoo share this story. "I remember on one occasion when about 12, being involved with two senior boys who raided a tuck shop and took a bar of chocolate each – which we thought a huge joke, just like you read about in school stories. We got a caning which was richly deserved but the episode was blown out of all proportion and we were held up before the school as 'thieves' and '*sinners*' (emphasis mine). We were made to sit down and write letters confessing our sins to our parents which, of course, worried them and made us feel lower than a snake's tummy. I was expected to say I had sinned grievously. This episode was held against me all my school career."

I struggled on in silence and alone, not knowing where to turn. I couldn't share my unpardonable sin with the boys in my dorm room and certainly not with any adult. I seldom visited my parents since they were missionaries on the border of Tibet – a three-week journey, one way. My nightly prayer became, "Now I lay me down to sleep; I ask the Lord my soul to keep. If I should die before I wake, I ask the Lord, my soul to take." But no assurance of salvation ever came, my heart was never "strangely warmed" (John Wesley). Any spiritual growth was impossible.

Looking back on my childhood days in the CIM Schools, I wonder why I memorised hundreds of the gospel songs and so much Scripture. One reason was that, although I was not a good student, memorisation came quite readily to me. But I also believe, in hindsight, it was an effort on my part to assuage this wrathful God that had been created in my mind.

The technique used to get us to memorise Scripture was the bamboo sheath. I distinctly remember the one I carried in my pocket. A long strip of parchment paper four inches wide was folded every two inches, accordion style, until there were 100 panels each four inches by two inches. We were assigned 100 verses on a Biblical theme: scripture, salvation, hell, heaven, sin etc. In perfect English longhand, we wrote out the 100 verses on one side of each panel and the King James reference on the reverse side. They were then placed inside a bamboo sheath and carried in our shirt pocket.

It reminds me of the phylactery that some devout Jewish men place on their foreheads. The sheath was in your pocket most of the time and in spare moments we were encouraged to memorise verses. After we had memorised 100 verses, we could request a sitting for a proctored exam. Ten verses, or so, would be selected at random and we had to write them out in perfect English longhand, without any spelling or punctuation errors. If successful, we were given another bamboo sheath, and the process was repeated with 100 new verses. I don't recall how many sheaths I piled up on my nightstand. I do remember flunking one sitting because of incorrect penmanship.

I have always enjoyed singing. In Kuling, every child had a copy of *Golden Bells* (words only) on their nightstand and every night before lights out we selected a couple songs to sing. We always chose songs based on length since it would delay the inevitable. It amazes me how many of the songs I can still sing, word for word, after not singing them for years. In the spring of 2010, I organized a quartet and we made a CD of thirty favourites. In the introduction to the booklet that accompanies the CD I wrote: "I have many memories (school in Shanghai and Kuling, separation from parents, sports and games, Bible memorisation), but my most vivid memory was singing at bedtime, songs from *Golden Bells*.

In retrospect, I learned more theology from these songs than from the Bible memorisation. Unfortunately, more of the words, as I recall, dealt with sin and its dire consequences than with grace. I was reflecting on the words to one gospel song recently. The words are:

> "I was sinking deep in sin,
>   far from the peaceful shore,
> very deeply stained within,
>   sinking to rise no more.
> But the master of the sea
>   heard my despairing cry,
> from the waters lifted me,
>   now safe am I.
>
> Safe am I (four times)
>   in the hollow of His hand.
> Sheltered o'er (four times)
>   in the hollow of His hand.
> No fears can harm me,
>   no foes alarm me,
> For He keeps both day and night.
>   Safe am I (four times)
> in the hollow of His hand".

Nothing could have been farther from the truth. I didn't feel safe in the hollow of His hand. I knew I was a sinner in the hands of an angry God. I certainly knew I was sinking deep in sin far from any peaceful shore.

When our now family of five returned to the United States in 1951, my brother Dick and I went to live in the mission home in Wheaton, Illinois, and our sister Lois returned with mom and dad to Taiwan. In the summers, all the kids in the mission home went to church camps and Camp Awana. At these camps I would repeatedly "accept Jesus Christ as my personal Saviour." But I kept it a secret from my peers and adults. What would they think if they knew I had never accepted Christ for all these years? Finally, when I was about twelve years old Mr L., the Director of Camp Awana, asked if any campers would be willing to share their conversion story at a camp rally. I raised my hand. One of the most traumatic moments in my entire life occurred at that rally. I had memorised the verse that states: "If you believe in your heart the Lord Jesus and *confess with your mouth* that God has raised Him from the dead, thou shalt be saved." I had never dared to share publicly with my mouth that I hadn't been saved. Utter terror encompassed my entire being as I waited my turn to go to the podium. God must have felt my terror and Mr L. never called on me.

I remained in this perplexed, frantic spiritual state for some years. Shortly after this terrifying ordeal, I finally gathered the courage to ask my younger brother how he knew he was "saved". I could tell from his reaction that he hardly knew what I was talking about. How can you explain that one child can carry so much sin and guilt, and another, growing up in the same environment, carry so little? But that cloud of spiritual gloom and doom did begin to lift.

Our childhood experiences do impact our adult lives. I've often said that guilt is my middle name. I can feel guilty over most anything. There are hundreds of examples, but I'll only share one. The incident that sparked this confrontation is not important to the story. How I dealt with it and my reaction to it is. I became incensed over what I considered to be insensitive treatment of a close professional friend by our School Chaplain. Since I was Department Chair and the productivity of my colleague was being negatively impacted, I shot off a furious email to the Chaplain. He responded, requesting a meeting. What followed was a "boxing match" with me on one side of the table and the Chaplain and his assistant on the other. I had good reasons to be upset, but the "match ended with a knockout in the first round." Guilt can render you powerless and, in the hands of a skilful manipulator, I was no match. I could say it was two against one, but it would have made no difference. A sense of guilt that I in no way deserved washed over me, and I was asking forgiveness for questioning his motives in the incident. After praying together, they left. I was left alone filled with rage and guilt. Reflecting on the incident years later in an article, I wrote: "I realized that day I will never overcome the scars of my childhood; that I will always be chasing grace; but the sweet sound of amazing grace will remain elusive."

That was then. I am now 79 and life goes on. Guilt is a terrible burden for anyone to bear. Many years ago, I became an avowed universalist. All creation will be gathered together forever in the arms of a loving God. No God of love can assign his, or her, children to an eternity of agony in "hell." That would be a total contradiction and denial of God's very self. As William Barclay said so eloquently in *A Spiritual Autobiography*:

> "I believe implicitly in the ultimate triumph of God, the time when all things will be subject to him, and when God will be everything to everyone (I Cor. 15:24-28)"

For me this has certain consequences. If one man remains outside the love of God at the end of time, it means that that one man has defeated the love of God – and that is impossible. Further, there is only one way in which we can think of the triumph of God. If God was no more than a King or Judge, then it would be possible to speak of his triumph, if his enemies were agonising in hell or were totally and completely obliterated and wiped out. But God is not only King and Judge, God is *Father* – he is indeed Father more than anything else. No father could be happy while there were members of his family forever in agony. No father would count it a triumph to obliterate the disobedient members of his family. The only triumph a father can know is to have all his family back home. The only victory love can enjoy is the day when the offer of love is answered by the return of love. The only possible final triumph is a universe loved by and in love with God. [48]

And what about "sin"? Is there such a thing, or is it a theological construct that has imprisoned humankind since we first appeared on the face of the earth? In the evolutionary process when did man emerge and when and how did sin? Rev. Leslie Weatherhead offered this rationale as a British pastor in London during World War II in his little book, *The Will of God*. It was God's intentional will that we live in harmony with self, nature, humankind and God. We "sinned" and as a result now live in an extended period of God's circumstantial will. This was not God's intention. However, God's will ultimately will prevail in the new heaven and the new earth. It's a neat theological package, but I'm not sure I believe it anymore.

I remember reading this quote years ago: "Free to be who I am with the hope of becoming what I was intended to be." I wish I had been given the freedom to question and explore the spiritual world as a child. I was not, and resorted to massive memorisation of Biblical passages and gospel songs, with little assistance from any adult in making sense of it all.

Is there a heaven and a hell? Is there life after this life? And what of sin? Is *Amazing Grace* more than the most popular hymn ever written? I don't have answers to any of these questions, but I'm free to explore them without fear and guilt.

* * *

George was born in Chengdu, China on November 14, 1939. His parents served in the China Inland Mission in Kanding, now called Dardo, the crossroads between China and Tibet. His family returned to the United States for two years during World War II. Upon their return to China, he attended the CIM boarding school in Shanghai (1946–47) and in Kuling (1947–51). After a year of deputation work in the USA, his parents along with his kid sister returned to Taiwan and his brother Dick and George went to live in the mission home in Wheaton, IL.

---

48 William Barclay, *A Spiritual Autobiography*, 1975, pp 65–67.

Jane

I FIND IT HELPFUL to think of life as a series of dots. These dots are things like family, school, friends, relationships, pains, joys, achievements, talents, work and hobbies. Over recent years I've seen many of the dots in my life join up, like a "join the dots" picture we enjoyed as children. I do not yet see the full picture; it is still a work in progress. Here are a few of these dots...

A group of children – one who is not yet five years old – walk across a gangplank onto a large ship called the *Chusan*, sailing from the Philippines to Singapore. They are on their way to school and waved off by parents, who stand on the quayside. All know it will be many months before they can gather together again because the parents are missionaries. All of the children are Americans, except for one English girl. When they go to the ship's restaurant, they choose meals from the menu. The Americans want hamburgers, but the English girl asks for a lightly boiled egg.

An imposing, austere building stands in Newington Green, London. It was once HQ for the China Inland Mission, and later the Overseas Missionary Fellowship. In a room stands a bookcase with glass doors; full of Chinese artefacts collected from the years the mission worked in China. To a four-year-old, it's a treasure trove of musty old books, pictures of faraway lands, and an exotic fan. But most intriguing is a long, thin, gold tube. Many years ago, the wealthy Chinese rulers would fix the end over their small fingers, so it hung twelve inches down, or more. Nails could grow long inside without breaking, as a sign of wealth and status – not having to do menial work.

A Mercedes taxi full of young children and luggage is driven from Kuala Lumpur to the Cameron Highlands. There are three hours of winding roads, up and up and round and around the mountains, before arrival at Chefoo. At least one of the children feels very car sick.

A 55-year-old is prayed for by three Chinese Church leaders (or "Fathers" as they were known), in Hong Kong, finding freedom from an "orphan spirit" and from her own difficulties growing up as a missionary kid. The Chinese Fathers express deep gratitude for the missionaries who came to China many years ago to bring the gospel, and for the sacrifices they made.

An Englishwoman hugs a weeping Chinese woman in Hong Kong and has an overwhelming realisation of why many missionaries loved the Chinese so much – enough to leave home to bring them the gospel.

I sit in a care home in Birmingham with two ex-missionaries: my parents. Both have many wonderful memories of their friends and work in Asia, but also hold some very painful memories which came from family separation during those missionary days. We are watching "Songs of Praise" as the programme follows a group of Chinese, on pilgrimage to Nottingham to visit the home town of Hudson Taylor, founder of China Inland Mission (now OMF), and to express appreciation for his life's work to bring the gospel to China. They wouldn't have met Jesus had he and many other missionaries not come. It feels like a joining up of the dots, as my family sits together fifty years later, watching a video showing Chinese Christians who have come all the way to England to express their heartfelt thanks.

In 2013, I was invited by a close friend to a "Gathering" in Hong Kong. I was very excited about the trip; I hadn't been back to Asia since I was eight years old. As a missionary kid, I'd always loved to travel and go on adventures, so I eagerly joined the team.

Once I stepped off the plane and arrived at the hotel, I had a strong sense of arriving "home". The Gathering was called "Homecoming", and this so aptly described how I felt that moment. The hills, vegetation and smells were so familiar. To my surprise many memories stirred; Asia, I found, was deeply woven into my DNA.

As a team we had been invited to bring an apology to the Chinese Christians for the way the Imperial nations – Britain included – had behaved oppressively towards the Chinese during the Opium Wars, and to ask forgiveness as a representative group. The Chinese had requested this gesture as they felt it would enable the Chinese Church to get free from the effects of our Imperialistic past. They responded in kind by asking forgiveness for the missionaries who had been killed during the Boxer uprisings.

There were over 25,000 people in the arena. It was humbling to be on the platform with this team, bringing our apology to a group of Chinese Church leaders. It felt like more dots of my life were joining up – having once been a child in a mission that had originated in China, and now sharing in what was an historic moment of reconciliation.

If this was the reason I had come to Hong Kong, and if my life up to now had only been leading to this moment, it was more than enough for me. It made sense of my past.

But amazingly our apology opened the door to far more than I could have ever imagined. After hearing the Chinese Church Fathers talk about the reality of experiencing God as their Father, I found myself very moved and emotional. Through an extraordinary chain of events I was prayed for by three of the Chinese Fathers through an interpreter.

As I mentioned before, they felt I had this "orphan spirit". I think it dated from my years at Chefoo which, although wonderful in many ways – who wouldn't love being at school in the jungle – also came with the pain of separation from family, loneliness, bullying, silent tears and paralyzing fears.

After they prayed for me in Mandarin, it was as if a glass bubble around me shattered. I felt a deep connection to God as my Father, and to those on the team, in a way I'd never been able to feel before. I felt God's love for me as his child in a new and beautiful way. It reminded me of the scene in Narnia when Aslan breathes on the statues, after the white witch had turned everything to winter and to stone. Everything comes back to life again, turning frosty greyness into colour and warmth.

As if that wasn't enough, a few months later I heard of an event called Chefoo Reconsidered (CR). What had come to light was how many of the children, now adults, had, like me, struggled all their lives with issues from their experiences of boarding school in Malaysia. Separated families, where children had been sent away for the sake of mission work, had caused deep pain and heartache. Many of us, including myself, were still struggling as adults.

The time had come to address this issue, and the mission wrote a letter of apology for the way things had been done in those days. They recognised the damage caused, and wanted to do what they could to help both children and parents.

I had a strong sense God was saying, "This wasn't how I meant it to be." Seeing the struggles of children and parents, both on the mission field and afterwards, had made his heart heavy, and the time had come to put things right. In October 2014, I was off to Asia again. It felt like more dots were joining up. As Hong Kong had been a time for healing, I hoped CR Malaysia would be a time of restoration.

It was a great week back at Chefoo, now a Conference Centre, rather than the school it once was. I enjoyed climbs in the forest, eating Asian food, singing, walking to the waterfall, enjoying the stunning flowers and wildlife including the butterfly farm, visiting our old church for a service, and drinking wine smuggled into our dorms. Most of all, it was a special time, reconnecting with long lost friends and making new ones.

There were two Third-Culture-Kids counsellors to help us process our time. During the week, we had opportunity to do something to symbolize how we felt. We each lit a candle from a central flame, to represent our painful memories, and then let it extinguish, before choosing a piece of ribbon from a colourful pile to take away as a tangible memory of the good times.

On the last day I wanted a personal memory from Chefoo to take home so took an early morning walk by the stream at the back of the school, hoping to find a stone or pebble to pop in my suitcase. It was misty, beautifully lush and green, peaceful, and quiet, and as I walked I thought of Psalm 23. I had an almost tangible sense of Jesus walking with me in the misty stillness of the morning.

Then I felt "little Jane" close by, in the shadows watching from behind a tree, shy and hiding. I spoke with this little girl and asked her to come back with me to England, but she wanted to stay. Her friends were here, and she liked being with them. This was her home.

As I walked to breakfast brushing tears away, mascara running down my cheeks, I met Ruth, one of the counsellors. She walked me back to the stream, as she felt it was the moment for "little Jane" to come home. I gently spoke with "little Jane" saying I wanted her to meet my family and be with us now. Eventually, I sensed "little Jane" slowly walking towards me, and as she drew closer I found myself crying out from the depths of my being: "I let go, I let go, I let go; this place no longer defines me."

It was a release. I was no longer held inside a child at boarding school in Malaysia. I was a free and complete adult. "Little Jane" was coming home with me, another "Homecoming" – more dots joining up. I'd gone to find something to take home and found the best gift of all – little Jane and a new freedom.

Now, the dots are still being joined up. It takes a lifetime to see the beauty of the whole picture but I'm deeply thankful for what I can see so far.

* * *

Jane's parents worked in Manila, Philippines and Jane went to Chefoo Malaysia from 1965–68. The family left the OMF and returned to the United Kingdom where she continued her education. Jane trained as a nurse and has three wonderful children and a granddaughter.

Interlude 7:
Sacrificial Hymns

'These are words from the soundtrack to our parents' lives and decision-making and the soundtrack that reinforced every aspect of our lives. Every culture has its rhythms and codes – these were ours.'

> "Take my soul and body's powers
> Take my mem'ry, mind and will;
> All my goods and all my hours,
> All I know and all I feel;
> All I think, or speak or do,
> Take my heart, and make it new."

Charles Wesley

> "Forbid it, Lord, that I should boast,
> Save in the Death of Christ my God:
> All the vain things that charm me most,
> I sacrifice them to his blood.
>
> 'Were the whole realm of nature mine
> That were a present far too small;
> Love so amazing, so divine,
> Demands my soul, my life, my all"

Isaac Watts

"The way of the cross means sacrifice,
    As to God you yield your all,
To be laid on the altar, the place of death,
    Where fire will surely fall."

M.E. Maxwell

"All to Jesus I surrender
    Humbly at his feet I bow
Worldly pleasures all forsaken,
    Take me Jesus, take me now."

W.S. Weedon

"My goal is God Himself, not joy nor peace,
    Nor even blessing but Himself, my God;
'Tis His to lead me there – not mine, but His –
    At any cost, dear Lord, by any road."

F Brook

"I suffered much for thee,
    More than thy tongue can tell
Of bitt'rest agony,
    To rescue thee from hell;
I've borne it all for thee,
    What hast thou borne for me?"

Frances Havergal

"Is your all on the altar of sacrifice laid?
    Your heart, does the Spirit control?
You can only be blest and have peace and sweet rest,
    As you yield him your body and soul."

Elisha Hoffman

"Take my life and let it be
    consecrated, Lord, to thee.
Take my moments and my days;
    let them flow in endless praise,

Take my silver and my gold;
    not a mite would I withhold.
Take my intellect and use
    every power as thou shalt choose,

Take my will and make it thine;
    it shall be no longer mine.
    Take my heart it is thine own;
it shall be thy royal throne"

                            Frances Havergal

"But we never can prove
    the delights of his love
until all on the altar we lay;
    for the favour he shows,
for the joy he bestows,
    are for them who will trust and obey.

Trust and obey, for there's no other way
    to be happy in Jesus, but to trust and obey."

                            John Sammis

8

Reflecting on the Past

At last, we come to the chapter in which reflective remembrance occurs. Here, Andrew L, who was one of the key architects of the Chefoo Reconsidered Movement, leads off with his deeply honest and intelligent review of his life. We all owe him a debt for his keen sight that allowed him, even as he processed his own wounds, to open the way for us all to join in with him. David H is another involved in organising CR-1.

Then others interrogate their lives to see underlying patterns and themes.

Andrew L.

IF I AM TO REFLECT on my life to any purpose, I must understand not only what happened but why it happened, what were the consequences and how I am to understand those consequences today. In other words, I must see my life not just as a set of experiences and consequences, but as the journey it continues to be. I must understand that my life, as I must live it today, is not defined by my past, but by what I have learnt from my past and how I am able to apply that learning to my present. Either I am the victim of the failures, and sometimes the wickedness, of myself and others, or I am being transformed by my suffering and mistakes, having looked them in the face, walked into the fire with them and allowed them to be burnt away, emerging wounded and scarred, but healed, refined and led from out of the furnace by the one who walked through it with me.

Two points, made by wiser minds than mine, are worth stating as I begin this reflection.

> *Every time we remember something, the memory itself changes. Our memories are not static things that sit inertly in the safe deposit box of our minds. They are changed by the very circumstantial information in which we both encode and recall the events in question*[49].

49 Curt Thompson, *Anatomy of the Soul*, Tyndale House Publishers, 2010

Remembering is not mere nostalgia; it is an act of survival, our way of watching over our hearts with all diligence.[50]

So, understanding that remembrance is both an unreliable and a necessary exercise, let me tell you briefly what happened, why it happened and what were the consequences.

Called to evangelise Chinese-speaking communities in Asia in the late 50s, my parents applied to join the Overseas Missionary Fellowship in 1958. They had some concerns over the mission's policy regarding children being educated away from their families but, five years into their marriage and still childless, they laid these aside and my mother took the letter of application to the post box on her way to the doctor's one morning. Whereupon the doctor told her she was pregnant. But they went ahead with their decision, were accepted and sailed for Singapore in March 1960, now with a one-year-old son.

Four years later, having spent the whole of my conscious life thus far in various villages in what was then North Malaya, I was sent to board at Chefoo School. I was a happy, bright five-year-old. After one term, a year of furlough in England followed, and then it was back to Chefoo for the next four years, with its 20-week terms and interminable separation from family. The beauty of the situation, the privilege of an exciting childhood spent in the jungle, playing around streams and waterfalls and hiking up mountains notwithstanding, I was heartbroken. Sent from loving, affectionate parents and a safe, secure home in which music, beauty and reassurance were highly valued, into a playground and dormitory environment where privacy was non-existent; affection rarely, if ever, given; and danger lurked around every corner; I began to live in fear. By the time I left secondary school twelve years later, that happy, bright five-year-old had become a broken, suicidal, desperately needy young adult, cast adrift on a sea of rejection and abandonment.

The inability of a child that young to rationalise meant that I became the victim of an unavoidable set of default childish responses.

50   Brent Curtis and John Eldredge, *The Sacred Romance*, Thomas Nelson, Nashville, 1997

I was not rejected by my family, but it felt like it, and I could not see past that rejection. I had not been abandoned by my parents, but it felt like it, and I could not see past that sense of abandonment. I was neither unloved nor unlovable, but it felt like it, and I could not see past my unlovability. And so, my childish mind resorted to coping strategies that were extreme, inappropriate and all the more dangerous for being largely subconscious.

Abandonment by the mother is the greatest of all a child's fears, tantamount even to death[51].

I would not love again, because all those I loved were taken away from me. So I simultaneously craved and rejected relationship with anyone.

I would not reveal my true feelings because to do so was not safe. So I sobbed into my pillow at night, my tears silent and hidden for fear of being teased by the other children or, worse, my parents would be told and I would be discovered to be weak, a cry-baby, and unable to fulfil the task that God, the mission, my parents and the school needed me to accomplish; to cope alone while my parents served Jesus. Not revealing our emotional vulnerability became a habit for Chefusians, initially because our letters home were "censored", and any hint of unhappiness resulted in the letter being torn up and the child being instructed to start again, but later because we simply didn't want to be responsible for our parents feeling they had to return from the mission field because we were unhappy. It was a crushing burden to carry.

I would not ever express a need for help of any kind. I had been left to cope on my own, and cope I would. Any indication that I could not cope would be a sign of weakness, of somehow having failed my parents, and I could not allow that to happen. And so, even at five, I took on an adult responsibility for my well-being, carrying hugely inappropriate burdens for myself and others and frightened of making even the smallest mistake.

In other words, I became ruthlessly independent, terrified of failure, insular to the point of paranoia and veering wildly between a desperate

---

51 Joseph Chilton Pearce, *The Biology of Transcendence*, Simon & Schuster, 2004

need to know love and relationship in my life, and a complete inability to form appropriate relationships due to my certainty that I was not lovable, and any friendship I might form was destined to end in further rejection and abandonment.

In 1969, my parents returned to England for another furlough. This time, I was to be left behind in boarding school while they returned to Asia. There was just the year of leave in which we had the opportunity to be a family together, for the first and last time; for me to go to a local school, and know the safety and reassurance of coming home every evening, of weekends with parents and siblings, building the relationships that would need to be strong for another upcoming separation. But it didn't work out that way. My father decided that I would go to boarding school straight away – for the duration of the furlough. I was ten – a year too young and academically unprepared. And so, the year, as I saw it, was wasted, as I spent it away from the family, only to be held down a year upon their return to Asia, a humiliation from which I never recovered during my school years.

But worse was yet to come. The school – barbaric, violent and abusive – arranged *exeat* ("going home") Sundays twice a term. It was a chance for a child to escape the terror and boredom and be taken out by their family; a day free from fear and with the consolation of time with loved ones and maybe a decent meal. On one of these *exeats*, I gathered, after chapel, on the front drive of the school and waited expectantly for my parents to arrive, eagerly scanning the cars as they pulled up, desperate to get away and know some love and security for a few precious hours. But they never came. And when, seven hours later, I finally tore myself away to find a phone box and make a reverse charge call home, I discovered that, not only had they forgotten it was an *exeat*, but they had spent it entertaining new missionaries in their home.

Thus was the camel's back broken. I had always known that I was less important than Asia's heathen lost. Now I knew that I didn't even come second, but some way down their list of priorities, behind even a group of new missionaries they scarcely knew.

My teenage years were a miserable and lonely time. Bullied, sexually abused, exiled from the country I loved, truly "a stranger in a strange land", I adapted, compromised and finally left school, with such an ability to blend into any group in order not to be side-lined by them, that I had no clue who I really was. It was at this point that the mission informed me I was no longer welcome at the hostel they had provided for my school holidays, and so I left for university, effectively homeless, and with no formal support structure of any kind. I was eighteen and had spent a grand total of four terms of my education living at home. The rest had been spent in boarding schools, the holidays in children's homes. Yet I was the child of loving, godly parents who had dedicated their lives to the service of God.

We have put the Great Commission before the Great Commandment[52].

Why? Many reasons, some complex, some understandable, others born of corrupt systems, bad theology and the perennial habit amongst many Christians of creating God in our own image, and using the Bible to justify what we want to believe. Perhaps I will just list some of these reasons and you can judge their merits for yourself.

In the 60s, OMF were newly out of China, where many missionaries had seen colleagues martyred and an ethos of sacrifice coloured the thinking of those who had survived. There was a cost to Christian service, and those who served should expect to make major sacrifices. So should their families.

There were logistical issues that made travel expensive and rendered local schools impractical, meaning children could not be educated near the family home and Chefoo terms were necessarily long.

There was little or no understanding of child psychology and the damage that a child experienced in being separated from their parents at so young an age.

Scripture was everything. Had not Abraham been prepared to sacrifice Isaac? Had not Hannah given Samuel into the service of the temple "after he was weaned?" Had not Jesus said that anyone who left

52 Jack Frost, *Experiencing Father's Embrace*, Destiny Image Publishers, Shippensbury, PA, 2002

family for His sake would receive a hundred-fold in this life? Was God not to be trusted to care for the children of those who were giving their lives in service for Him?

The legendary, saint-like example of the mission's founder, Hudson Taylor, was held up as something to be followed, worshipped almost. Returning to mission HQ in my fifties, I found Taylor's life and words to hold no less sway, often seemingly carrying more weight even than those of Jesus, as had been exampled by the mission's actions over the years. The accounts ledger of OMF holds the names of many Asians brought to Christ through the dedication of its members. Sadly, the debit column holds the names of many of its children, victims of a closed system and its confused priorities.

The organisation's stated aim as a faith mission was to hold fast to Taylor's maxim that "God's work done in God's way never lacks God's resources." So, without advertising their needs, they would budget for the next quarter and then pray in the money to meet that need. Unfortunately, it seems the need for children to be reunited with their parents, even once a year, was not considered anything God cared enough about for them to ask Him to provide for it, thus revealing the mission's priorities; in stark contrast to Jesus's own clear prioritising of the needs of children and New Testament teaching on family life and nurture. As recently as 2015, I was aware of some children of OMF missionaries who were left to spend Christmas at their boarding school so that their parents would not be distracted from their calling – a decision made by parents, but one which the mission, at the very least, continued to enable.

Pastoral care, even of its own members, was never any kind of priority for the mission. One leader from another mission, brought in to investigate a serious failure of care within OMF, confided that the mission had little or no idea when it came to the pastoral care of its own members. This, in the twenty-first century. How much less did they care for their missionaries' children fifty years earlier?

And so to the consequences of these failures. I touched on these earlier, but let me lay them out here.

For those who know the pain of... permanent loss of support from
a parent, that sense of abandonment easily casts a shadow on
their impressions of God. It makes them feel like orphans[53].

You cannot remove a young child from the family home without
damaging them. Early childhood separation leaves deep and lasting
wounds. Sending me away to boarding school removed love from my
life, however godly, sensitive and well-meaning the staff were. A five-
year-old – some of us were only four – needs their mother. There is no
substitute for her. Nothing and no-one else will do. Testimonies from
Chefoo children recall that, instead of playing Mummies and Daddies,
some played Orphans and Children's Homes.

Homesickness is a bit like seasickness. You don't know how awful
it is till you get it, and when you do, it hits you right in the top
of the stomach and you want to die[54].

To take me away from the safety and nurture of my family home was
to bereave me and introduce an inexpressible loneliness and fear into
my life. Children of the age at which most began attending Chefoo
were significantly short of the age at which we might have been able
to rationalise our separation. Grief and fear, raw and visceral, were my
companions. I sucked my thumb until I was forty-three and remain
homesick to this day.

In all cases, early rejection or perceived rejection leads to
distorted, unrealistic thinking[55].

I resorted to extreme and inappropriate ways of coping, employing
survival techniques that got me through the next hour, the next lesson,
the rest of the day, but which ultimately left me with an unsustainable
lifestyle. And, because these were subconscious responses to a situation
which was impossibly unbearable for a child to manage, I grew up
largely unaware of the decisions I had made about my life, and so
continued in my extreme and inappropriate ways into adulthood.

53   Bradley Jersak, *A More Christlike God*, Plain Truth Ministries, Pasadena, CA, 2015
54   Roald Dahl, *Boy: Tales of Childhood*, Jonathan Cape, London 1984
55   John White, *Changing on the Inside*, Servant Publications, 1991

When we do not feel loved by those who gave us life, we often suffer our whole life long from a low self-esteem that can easily lead to depression, despair and even suicide[56].

Not being loved is perhaps not the same as not feeling loved. But the effects are the same. I was unquestionably loved. But for a young child to feel that love when a twenty-week term had blurred the face of my parents, when illness, injury or abuse had to be endured without their comfort, when the safety and reassurance of the bedtime hug and goodnight kiss was just a distant memory too painful to recall, to still feel that love was too much for me. Low self-esteem, depression and despair would shadow me for the rest of my life. For others, that pain became too much, and they determined that the rest of their lives was an unendurable prospect and they could no longer go on.

And there, but for the grace of God, went I.

I was a child who was forced to confront an adult. I had to take the power position before I should have needed to and before I was ready. I paid for it in fear[57].

A child forced to cope alone and without the security and nurture of parents assumes aspects of adult responsibility and independence before they are ready. This leads to a toxic combination of unfounded overconfidence, allied to a huge fear of making mistakes, and an associated inability to acknowledge failure. I grew up with an impressive layer of capability and competence that was paper-thin, and which was only the cover to a deep and churning well of fear and self-doubt. I became incredibly needy, arrogant, possessive and patronisingly pious, thus reinforcing to myself my perception that I was unlovable.

When one has been traumatised or deeply conditioned through fear while young and impressionable...later in life...conclusions are drawn based on meanings born out of past trauma or early conditioning[58].

56 Henri Nouwen, *Life of the Beloved*, Better Yourself Books, 2002
57 Brené Brown, *Braving the Wilderness*, Random House Publishing, 2017
58 Peter Levine, *In an Unspoken Voice*, North Atlantic Books, 2012

A career psychologist once confirmed to me what I had been unwilling
to believe – that what I was suffering from was post-traumatic stress.
I was responding to events taking place in front of me with the emotions of my immature inner child when he first experienced such a situation. So, if my wife announced that she must go away for a while, my
response was that of the five-year-old who was told he must go away
to school. My reaction, being that of the child in me, was then fearful,
resentful, angry and inappropriate, because I had never acknowledged,
understood or dealt with, the pain and grief I experienced aged five.
To my wife, my response was inexplicable and hugely inappropriate. To
me, unaware that my emotional responses were still that of the child,
who was never able to grow up in this area, I just experienced untold
grief and abandonment. Again! The consequences of living with
our immature inner child, still grieving, still abandoned, still feeling
unloved and unlovable, are behind many divorces and other relationship tragedies amongst those who suffered early childhood separation.

> *The way people learn to manage emotional states as children
> will follow them into their adult friendships, marriages and
> work relationships*[59].

The way I learned to manage my emotional states, as a child, was to
suppress the difficult ones and indulge the joyful ones. So I refused
to acknowledge, and especially to show, my grief. I never spoke of my
loneliness. I never revealed my sense of abandonment. I threw myself
into the joys of hiking and jungle-bashing and sausage sizzles. I still do.
I still hide from my pain and console myself with happy trifles, some
of which, over the years, have become addictions. My need to be loved
became so desperate, my way of assuaging it so inappropriate, I lost all
sense of reality and ended up in prison.

> *If the parents in each generation... knew what really goes on
> at their sons' schools, the history of education would be very
> different*[60].

59 Curt Thompson, *Anatomy of the Soul*
60 CS Lewis, *Surprised by Joy*, 1955

Acceptance of our lot was a major factor. At Chefoo, as already mentioned, we were not allowed to speak of any unhappiness in our letters home. And as I progressed to secondary school in my "home" country, the sheer pointlessness of relating how I had been bullied, or abused, or beaten, turned me into a protector of my parents' peace. On the one hand, to complain about how I might be being treated would be to admit that I was not coping, a weakness I was not prepared to admit. On the other hand, the prospect that my parents might be panicked into coming home and abandoning their calling, invited the ire of God, the mission and the school, never mind my parents, and pressed my shame buttons so comprehensively that I never even considered such a course of action.

Children who never find a place where they feel they belong carry an incapacity for attachment into their adult lives[61].

Missionary Kids generally face one of two problems with the issue of belonging. For some, the feeling that where we belong is not the homeland of our parents but the land in which we were raised, means we live in a constant state of emotional exile and resentment when we are sent "home" to school, or denied the chance to live in the place we understand as home. For these, being sent back to school in their sending country piled an additional bereavement on top of the loss of parents and siblings. For others, multiple moves, added to repeated injunctions from parents that where *they* are from is where they belong, however alien and unfamiliar it may be, results in a permanent sense that we don't actually belong anywhere. The "where are you from?" question confuses and embarrasses us, reminding us that we have no roots and no safe place to return to. For me, the unrecognised, and so unacknowledged bereavement of exile was an open wound well into my fifties.

At some level, I never got back home again, and always felt a stranger in my family's house[62].

61   Tim Keller, *The Prodigal God*, 2008
62   Nick Duffell, *The Making of Them*, 2001

Being sent to boarding school so young, even if it was only for a couple of terms, had a permanent effect. The betrayal of abandonment in the mind of a child is so traumatic that many are completely unable to trust again. And the effect of having to cope alone, to manage one's own safety and become independent at so young an age, meant that moving back under the umbrella of parental discipline and authority was all but impossible. This was particularly the case for me as a teenager. By then, I had been separated from family, and coping alone, for more than half my life. The idea that a furlough meant my parents suddenly coming back into my life, like nothing had changed, and assuming once more a role from which they had defaulted, was fiercely resisted by me. My reaction is best summed up in the question, "Who do you think you are to leave me to cope all these years and then suddenly expect to come back into my life and pick up where you left off?"

For good or ill, it is after our likeness that our children fashion their image of God[63].

Is this perhaps the direst consequence of all? That in teaching us that God is our father and then sending us away from the family home, our earthly fathers presented to us a false, damaging and wholly inappropriate picture of the very God they sought to reveal? I once asked an Asian church leader how the mission's policy of sending their children away to school had gone down with local people. "It was a rank bad witness," he replied. "In a culture where family is paramount, to preach a God of love and then abandon your children kept many from committing to the faith for a long time." And so it was for me. The child of godly, dedicated, much-admired missionaries, I was completely unable to accept God as my father since He was modelled to me as distant, uncaring and largely uninterested in my life.

The "bad theology" of my childhood left me believing that winning souls for Christ trumped everything else; that preaching, Bible studies and prayer meetings took priority over my needs; that I was less important than those my parents had gone to serve; that God was

63   John Pridmore, *Playing with Icons*, 2017

more interested in judging me than loving me; that His promises that He would never leave me were lies; that the sacrificial examples of Isaac and Samuel were proof that He was complicit in my sacrifice; that having children carried no implicit responsibilities before God, as long as there was another Christian to step in; that even though I had been taught that God was good, His treatment of His own Son in requiring Jesus's agonising death and then abandoning him to it smacked rather too readily of my own experience – which was not good! And so on.

But that's not the end of my story. It took me until I was almost into my fifties to realise how very unhappy I was, and the extent to which that unhappiness lay deeply rooted in my childhood. And so began a journey of return, recognition, reimaging and relinquishment which continues to this day.

The way of peace is not without pain. The way of peace comes only by walking through pain[64].

I returned to Chefoo to face my demons, for demons they were. I faced up to the grief and sense of abandonment I had carried for so many years, and began to allow myself to be walked through that place of all-encompassing darkness; to cry the tears of my grief-stricken self; to scream the anger of my abandoned five-year-old; to hurl out the questions of my rejected inner child.

I began to recognise what had damaged me, how it had broken me, how I had dealt with my brokenness in so many desperate and inappropriate ways and what was necessary for me, as a midlife adult, to mature my inner child and journey through the process of healing my brokenness. I am immeasurably indebted to the love and work of fellow MKs – TCK guru Ruth van Reken, family therapist Ulrika Ernvik and writer William Paul Young – for their work with the Chefoo community in giving us a language to express our pain, showing us the extent of our damage, and offering us tools with which to journey away from our brokenness towards a place of healing.

Paul Young, in particular, led me through the process of reimaging

64 Erwin McManus, *The Way of the Warrior*, 2019

– wiping the face of my earthly father off the face of Father God, and coming to a place of sufficient peace to accept that the image of God presented and modelled to me throughout my childhood, both personally and institutionally, was not a true or healthy one. Behind the misrepresentations stood a God who had never requested, nor required, that I be sacrificed in His name and was not pleased for me to be so offered. Here at last was a God who was good, who was loving, who was present and looking for relationship with me. Not the distant, angry, vengeful God of my childhood who was more interested in judging and punishing me than in loving and nurturing me. But a God who had wept with me and for me in my loneliness, grief and abandonment, and wept still as I cried away the well of tears He now took me to almost daily, as He bled the poison of anger, resentment and fear from me.

Here, too, were the answers to my questions as to where God had been, why He had not stepped in to comfort or rescue me, and why He had appeared to be so disinterested in my pain and grief. I began to understand how I had been complicit in my brokenness, by accepting so many inconsistencies and contradictions in the theology passed down to me, and in failing to challenge doctrines which suggested one thing about God when my experiences seemed to prove the opposite. I even saw how my behaviour had sometimes dared Him to destroy me, as I rebelled against the crushing burden of my need to be good in the face of His apparent absence and disinterest, and threw in His face the worst that I could be and do. Even those times when I had resolved to take the number of my days into my own hands I now saw as brazen challenges for Him to prove He could be good to me.

I began to see how the evidence I had received, whether by teaching or experience, that contradicted the nature and character of God as revealed in Jesus had to be addressed from a position of, "If it's not true of Jesus, then it's not true of God," which required significant interpretation of the Old Testament in that light[65].

I saw that the theology I had received, through my parents, the

---

65 Jesus is the complete manifestation of the Father, Hebrews 1.3

mission, my schools and churches, had been flawed – at times, down-right wrong – and often used Scripture to self-justify. (I began to see you could "prove" any theological position you wished to take from the Bible, as long as you were prepared to quote verses out of context and weren't challenged.) But my own worked-out theology had been lazy, overly respectful of both the out-of-context source, and its manipulated presentation. As a result, I had grown up "believing" all kinds of things that, when it came to it, I didn't actually believe at all.

My parents' mission, moved by the thought that "unnumbered souls are dying and pass into the night", had so devoted themselves to saving those souls that they had unwittingly cast aside the souls of its own children, sacrificed them on the altar of evangelism, and left us as infants, virtually orphaned, to walk alone through our childhood and teenage years. I was not unloved, but I was loveless; not abandoned, but hopelessly alone; not rejected, but without visible means of support.

But the story continues. Today, my scars are healing, my faith is restored, and my journey is one of hope. I am no-one's victim.

"I am who He says I am."
"There is another in the fire, standing next to me."

* * *

Andrew is a musician and writer who attended Chefoo School in Malaysia in the 60s before going on to study music at Manchester University and the Royal Northern College of Music. A variety of roles followed in schools and church work, but his life fell apart in his thirties and a personal crisis in his fifties precipitated an examination of his life and faith which identified for him the deeply rooted damage of his childhood experiences. Out of this came the Chefoo Reconsidered movement, which sought to assist generations of MKs in realising the impact of early childhood separation upon them in midlife. For Andrew himself, the consequences were huge, sometimes devastating, but always transforming, and his journey towards wholeness continues.

David

I AM SIXTY-SIX.

Mom and Dad are dead. Some years now.

Do I miss them? No, not really.

I ask myself why. I guess there's a gradually increasing emotional distancing that develops from one's parents as they and you grow older. It starts when one begins school and others outside the family become a new source of bonding.

Chefoo. I was so excited as the train to Kuala Lumpur was about to leave Singapore station. My Dad was on the other side of the carriage window, his heart heavy at the thought of losing me. But for me it was a new adventure.

We lost each other. At boarding school, my heart broke in the night as I thought of him and my mother far away in Singkawang, Indonesia; as I lay in my bed, listening to the cicadas and the heavy footsteps of Uncle Bill, or another member of staff, on the gravel in the quad outside.

My father's heart knew something which I wouldn't realise until later. I was an orphan. Something has been lost forever.

～

Dear Mom and Dad

Suddenly you were gone. I was still reeling from the news that Victor and I were going to live with the Es. I can't remember you saying goodbye. As you sailed half-way across the world to Singapore with Libby and baby Andy, Victor and I have landed on a different planet.

When Mr E. started bossing me around, I reminded him that he was not my dad. He replied that you had given him "guardianship" over us. I was dumbstruck. I have no idea what this "guardian" thing means, but it sounds like Mr E. is now my dad for all intents and purposes. Or at least that's how he put it.

I was flabbergasted that you would agree to such a thing. Have you given me away? Mr E. does not know me. It's not the same as the teachers and staff at Chefoo. They bossed us around, said nasty heartless things and even hit us but, at least, I knew that they were not my mom and dad, and that my real mom and dad would stand up for me in the final showdown.

Mr E. is a lawyer. He seems to make quite a lot of money. The E.'s have a nice house and car. I don't like riding in the car as I am terrified of being involved in a fatal accident.

They have two children – Mary and Mark. They have the same name except for the last letter! Mary is older than us, has sexy legs and seems to hate us.

They have given us each a small booklet to read. It's about sex. I wouldn't have believed an adult would give me such a book as I thought they viewed sex as dirty. The book says it isn't, but I can't imagine Mr and Mrs E. getting up to what it says in the book.

We have been signed up to judo class and the scouts. Oh, and we have to go to a new high school even though I was only six months at the last one.

Love from David

Dear Mom and Dad

We had just come back from camp during the school holidays. I don't know why we always have to go to camp. I would much rather stay in Cape Town and go to the beach.

Anyway, we were picked up at the station by Grandpa in his old

Daimler. Strange. Some of our stuff was in boxes on the floor of the car. Grandpa told us that Mrs E. had had a "nervous breakdown" and from now on we were going to stay at the mission home.

I know I did have some bitter arguments with Mrs E., but I must have been really horrible to have caused her to have a "nervous breakdown". Am I worthless? Is that why I have to stay in South Africa? Have I been thrown away?

The downstairs public telephone rang. It was Mrs E. She wanted to know if we were okay and whether we wanted her to arrange for the desks she had bought for us to be brought over. I said, "No, thank you." I'm not sure why. Perhaps I didn't want to have something which would remind me of my stay at the E's.

Victor and I share a large bedroom. We have arranged the wardrobes in the middle of the room so that we both have our own space. I usually get home before him as he is more involved in sport and goes to visit his friends.

As you probably know, the couple running the home, Mr and Mrs C., are now looking after us. We sit with them at mealtimes but, apart from that, they leave us pretty much alone. Which is nice. Mr C. likes filling up my glass to the brim and then giving me a scare when I start to drink it. He thinks he's very funny. I said I wanted to become a pilot. He joked, "Is that the nearest you're likely to get to heaven?"

Love from David

⁓

Dear Mom and Dad

There's a question I want to ask you. Why did you send me to boarding school, knowing that you would only see me for holidays twice a year? Did you have to do that? Could we not have been taught at home? Like Mom used to teach us Afrikaans in the holidays?

I'm missing you all so much. I wish I was there in West Kalimantan with the flowing rivers, the green hills, the coconut palms and the warm, friendly people. I so loved returning to Pemangkat during the holidays from Chefoo. Mom would send me to the market with a shopping list. You took us to the beach. Mom made us a midnight feast! I made a raft to float along the dirty canal next to our house. And endless games of Monopoly with Victor.

Here in Cape Town it's so dry. The rivers are dried up or they are no bigger than drains. Everything is brown and the kids at school are mean. Victor no longer wants to play Monopoly.

After school, all the other pupils go back home to their moms and dads. It doesn't take them long to get home, whereas we have to catch a train and wait for a bus – which takes an hour and a half. Well I used to do that. I did a deal with Mrs C. that I could keep the money for the train and bus fare if I cycled to school. It's a long way and the south-easterly wind along the main road makes it tough going. Coming home there's that long trek walking my bike up the slopes of Table Mountain in a hot blazer.

On the bus we sometimes encounter some real orphans who like to bully us. Another reason for using the bike!

I miss the friends I had at Chefoo. Keith and Dave and John and Paul. I don't really have any friends now. I hang around with some other boys from my class at break time and one of them walks with me to the station after school. Back at the mission home I busy myself with electronics and taping pop songs from the radio on Mr M.'s tape recorder. I know you don't agree with me listening to pop music but it's very meaningful to me.

I have a huge crush on a girl who sits behind me in class. Her name is Charlotte. She is new to the school. She is German. I am so in love and I daydream about her all the time. She doesn't know. One day she was going from desk to desk with a list. I looked up and suddenly she was right in front of me, smiling. I think that must have been the best moment in my life so far!

Just above the mission home tower the granite walls of Table Mountain. It's becoming very familiar. Sometimes I feel it is my mother. Or my friend?

When I was at Cape Town High, there was once a white-cladded figure atop nearby Devil's Peak. He stayed up there for some days, thinking himself a prophet shouting out his prophecies down to the city. They said he was mad. I was intrigued. Did he have something to tell me, perhaps?

Love from David

———

Dear Mom and Dad

There's an old organ in the mission home dining room. I found a hymn book and have been trying to play some of the hymns in it that I know. I especially like "Guide me O thou great Jehovah". At Chefoo, Miss S. was kind and wonderful, and taught me piano for about a year. Now I am very much "a pilgrim in this foreign land".

Miss D. was my class teacher at Chefoo. She was also kind but firm. She once asked us to head up our page with "Grammar". She laughed when she saw what I had written. "I wondered why David looked so puzzled!" she exclaimed, "he wrote "Grandma" at the top!"

Do I wish I was back at Chefoo? No, not really. Do I wish I was back in West Kalimantan? Yes, of course! But I guess I will never be there again.

Those years I was at Chefoo, I was so proud to have come from South Africa and, I guess, I hesitantly looked forward to coming here. At the Singapore mission home I read a book which justified the apartheid policy, which I then passionately defended. I didn't know any better. I had a big argument with Victor about it and ended up crying.

You remarked that I was a bit old to be crying. I felt ashamed and made up my mind never to cry again.

No, I don't like apartheid now. Some of the kids at school say they would never sit next to a black person on the bus. That's not how we thought when we were children in Indonesia. Funny though, how come there were only white kids at Chefoo? And we never spoke anything except English?

You tell me Andy has been making friends with some of the neighbours in Gang Haji Saman. Uncle Bill arranged for us to play soccer against kids from a local Malayan school. They were bigger than us, so they had to play with one hand behind their backs!

Talking about Uncle Bill – he told wonderful stories and taught us to sing "I zig a zuma" and how to play softball.

He also likes his cane. I was sent to him to be caned because I shouted out in class without putting my hand up. I decided never to contribute in class again. Maybe I am just stubborn.

If someone didn't own up, he would cane everyone.

Love, David

Dear Dad,

I wish you were here. I remember how during the holidays from Chefoo you would take me and Victor on your evangelistic trips with you. I clearly remember the ride on the small launch across the wide Sambas river and up a narrow creek to an isolated area on the far side. After landing, we rode on bicycles along white sanded paths through the coconut groves to a small village where we spent the night. I remember the kerosene pressure lamps, the small crowd as you preached, and sleeping upstairs above a shop, on the floor on a sleeping mat.

You introduced me to the world. The world of buses, roads, towns, boats, the Indonesian way of life, the politics of the country. You travelled with us children to Singapore aboard a small coastal ferry. I was amazed when you cooked us a basic meal of rice, eggs and tinned peas in our cabin.

Do you remember what happened towards the end of my time at Chefoo? What you called an "escapade"? Unlike the British pupils, who were forced to enter the UK schooling system when they were only ten, the four of us "older boys", being from the US, Australia and South Africa were already, or going on, twelve. We were tired of being babied and started to sabotage the system a bit. One of us was involved in pantry raids, egged on by the younger boys. The others of us weren't involved in that, but we decided the staff were overly strict. One of the teachers let us head off into the jungle from a clearing above the school. We soon became lost, but did find our way back, via the stream to the north of the school.

I noticed that the younger children who had been with us were lining up at the headmaster's office to receive a beating with a shoe. They had to bring one of their own to be beaten with. So they would remember? I thought we might be next. John went to the office before me and came back in tears. I was indignant. He will make you cry, said John. We have to write a letter to our parents.

I was also summoned. I protested that I did not take part in the pantry raids, and that we had found our way back from the jungle safely. Uncle Fred said, no, you are guilty by association. He had a large Bible set out on the table. He pointed out the passage in Isaiah "though your sins are as scarlet you shall be white as snow".

Then came the killer blow:

"You have let your parents down".

I was devastated. I so missed you and mom. But I felt you were on my side against the inhumanity of this mission school regime. I so longed to please you. I saw myself as the good boy whom you so loved.

My world was broken. My tears followed in a flood.

As John predicted I was sent off to write a letter to you. To tell you about my scarlet sins. Did you ever get it? In it I said that Auntie Ann had let us go into the jungle and that my only involvement in the pantry raid was to sleepily accept a piece of stolen bread.

You must not have received the letter as the only time when you later mentioned the "escapade" you thought I was the only one involved! I think I can guess why – my letter was never sent to you.

I never told you this, but a week or so later I got an envelope with letters from you to Victor, Libby and me, and also one for Uncle Fred. I told the other boys. They said, "Let's see what it says." I was too scared to touch it so one of the other boys opened it and read it out loud. In it you talked about a "rebellious attitude" and that it needed to be stamped out.

I felt I had betrayed you. That you would disown me as a son. I dreaded seeing you again. But when I did, you didn't mention it.

Love from David

After nearly three years my mom returned from the East with Libby and Andrew. This was about a year before my dad returned. It was the best time of my teenage years! Victor and I now had our own separate rooms, and the large bedroom became our family room. What great times we had together! I wrote an essay about the church's stuffy attitude to youth and music. On my birthday I got loads of little presents from Mom, Victor, Libby and Andy. It was the best birthday I ever had!

I looked forward to my dad returning and the family being all together. Sadly, things went downhill for me after he got back. He didn't like my long hair, or my music. He criticised me often. I was heartbroken that the father whom I had loved more than anyone else in the world could now be so cold.

I never actually confronted my parents about Chefoo, although I did write a letter to my father asking him to treat me as a friend, rather than a cold and critical parent. He responded positively and our relationship was a lot better after that.

I also wrote to Uncle Fred who told me he was sorry for having hurt me. I met up with him for lunch at a pub one day, near his home in St Albans.

I did go back to West Kalimantan. Three times in fact – the last time in 2018 with my daughter, which was very special.

My mom had a number of mini strokes some years before she died. I was devastated to discover that she had "lost it" and hardly recognised me anymore. To me, she had already died in an emotional sense.

My dad died suddenly of a heart attack about nine months after my mom. He had planned to come to the UK where I was now living. It seems he would have had time to visit me during his busy schedule touring the country.

That's how it always was.

* * *

David attended Chefoo, initially when sited at The Bungalow, from 1958–64. High school in Cape Town. Short term worker with OMF for six months in Thailand in 1972. Was married, with two children. Now living in the UK and working as a computer programmer.

Hilary

I LOVED CHEFOO. Compared to the other schools I went to. But maybe that's just in hindsight. I didn't like being separated from my parents at age almost six. I was the first child in my family to go. Nothing prepared me for it. I would cry after "lights out" and write sad letters home. And I wet my bed. For years.

I went to the smallest Chefoo School, in the north of Japan. There were two teachers, one for grades 1–3, one for grades 4–6, one nurse and a married couple who were house parents. And the house parents changed every year. Not that I ever thought that was significant at the time. But missionaries couldn't be expected to leave their work to care for us for long, could they? When there was the "real" work of the gospel to get on with.

My parents were missionaries on the northern island of Japan and so we had a four-hour train journey from home to school. I can't really remember anything about that. Did the parents take it in turns to accompany us on the train or did the teachers come and escort us? I was a quiet child and spent a lot of time reading at Chefoo. I didn't really like the outdoors to the extent some of my friends did. But we had great times playing Kick the Can, climbing the huge gingko tree and taking our turns on the tyre swing, riding our bikes up and down the driveway, and immense fun in the snow. We had backwards meals sometimes, when we dressed back to front, had our meal in reverse order finishing with saying the grace. I used the backwards idea once when my son was thirteen. We organised a backwards party, with the invitations written back to front and encouraging dressing back to front. His friends didn't all do it. I'm surprised my son went along with it, to be honest.

I cried myself to sleep many times at Chefoo. And five was far too young to be sent there. At least we went home every six weeks for half-term or holiday. Although I believe that was stopped later, so my brother and sister had three terms a year but no half-term holidays because the travel was too expensive, or something. Our parents were allowed to visit us there once a year, I think. They stayed at the school for two nights and generally joined in whatever we were doing. I can't remember those visits, but my mum has said since that she wondered if they'd been a good idea as she heard we were upset afterwards. Huh! What?

The girls I shared a room with I never saw again. When I returned to the UK, my parents were on furlough for a year, so I lived with my family and attended school daily. I remember a time that year, when I was twelve, I'd gone to bed and started crying loudly and angrily, because I wanted to be heard. But when my mum came and said that I'd wake one of the others, I couldn't tell her why I was crying. In fact, I couldn't talk to her at all. I don't think I knew why I was crying to be honest.

Apparently, the brother down from me wasn't as meek as me and didn't always conform to expectations, so he was one that was seen as needing special prayer. And my sister too, made more of a fuss. Was it assumed that the other brother and I were fine because we were good and got on ok? But as adults, it's possible that people would say that we are doing less well than the other two. I don't know and I won't go into details. But maybe there is an argument that children need to be heard, and their feelings validated and valued. I wish I'd been braver to say how I felt or what I found difficult.

Then my brother and I were left in single-sex boarding schools in England, only meeting at the hostel in the holidays, while the rest of the family returned to Japan. There was another family from Chefoo Japan that we knew, two of whom were starting at schools in England as well, but guess what? We weren't placed in the same hostel as them during the holidays so we could maintain contact, but in separate OMF hostels (there were two at the time). Maybe it was just what space was available but really, where's the thought and care in it? All the other youngsters at Maxwell House, where I was, had been to Chefoo Malaysia. The hostel was even harder than boarding school. At least I was busy and made some friends at school. What did we do at the hostel? Played a bit of football (I was rubbish at it), table tennis and snooker (a bit better). There was an incident one Christmastime, when the mistletoe came out and I (amongst others, I guess) was chased around the house for a kiss. I felt so uncomfortable and hated it. Aged fourteen I didn't know what to do with boys! I was just a desperately sad teenager wanting to be with my family and wanting to matter to someone. I used to write long letters home detailing the minutiae of my life.

I can't remember at what stage I said I didn't want to go back to Maxwell House. Aged 16–17 I lived with my parents in the holidays, as they were on furlough. At that time I did normal things like learning to drive, though I was only taught by my parents, and our car wasn't great (first gear wasn't good, so the cry was, "Quick, go to second gear.") Also my parents' driving was questionable, in hindsight, so I probably didn't learn the best habits and only passed my driving test at the fourth attempt.

So, while on furlough, my parents asked, at the church we attended, if anyone would be willing to put me up for my last year at school! One brave couple did and have become lifelong friends. I am so grateful to them for their open home, and a room to call my own, and for being my surrogate family. I stayed with them during the holidays for longer than a year. At the time I didn't think it was anything special, probably because I was still so mixed up. They gave me advice about part-time and holiday jobs, when I was at university, since I hadn't had one before. But we have kept in touch over the years, the mother and daughter and I, which is lovely.

One brother spent time in Japan after finishing his schooling; another brother had his first job in Japan, through a contact to whom my parents taught English; my sister left boarding school in the

UK after GCSEs and returned to Japan to do her last two years of schooling at an American school in Japan. (My father must have been worn down by then because, when we were younger, he was always correcting our American accent: "It's not twenny four. It's TWENTY-four." (Apologies to our friends in the US) So I was the only one who made it through to work, without returning to our parents in Japan. Does that mean I was stronger? No, definitely not! Probably just more acquiescent. However, we all have good relationships with our parents still, and visit them (or they us) regularly. One brother lives with them, the other brother has bought a holiday flat in the town they live in, and my sister spends quite a bit of her annual leave there. And I think my parents recognise that it is to do with our prolonged early separations, but don't feel guilty, and instead just welcome it. And I'm so thankful for the time we have had together since they've retired.

But there's an anomaly. Only one grandparent was still alive by the time my parents married. She was Scottish and retired to southern Scotland, although she had lived in France and England too. My parents bought the house next door to her and we visited her every furlough; though once we were in boarding school in England, we spent most of the furlough year at various locations in England, convenient to one school or another. So what happened when they retired? We'd spread out around England by then, as all of our boarding and university education was in southern England. But my parents decided to go to their house in Scotland, to be near Granny, and in the only place where they've had some continuity of contact over the years. Well, good for them but not so close to most of us.

I have no friends from pre-university days. I lived amongst people and then moved on. Probably didn't even say goodbye. Who knew whether you would see them again or not? And so I found it quite hard making friends. I still do. I have friends but, sometimes, it's up to them more than it is up to me. If they like me, I'll like them, but it doesn't always work the other way around. Often, I don't know what to say to maintain the relationship. And I don't like talking excessively about myself. I prefer to talk about other people. When I was quite depressed earlier this year, I did try to tell some people how I felt, and why, but it wasn't easy, and I couldn't sustain it. I think there are some things I genuinely haven't told anyone. It feels too exposing. And I'm not sure if I know what I'm feeling anyway, and so it's hard to articulate it. I know when I don't react well to things, and I know people are genuinely concerned and want to help, but I've learned to rely on myself and that's a habit that's difficult to break. But I can bounce up to virtually any new person to welcome them into a group (when I'm not depressed). That doesn't faze me at all. Isn't that because we were constantly having to adapt and present ourselves to new audiences? Or maybe because we remember what it was like to always be the new one?

I wanted a boyfriend but knew he had to be a Christian as I was (more about that later). But I was so naïve and unnatural with boys, even though I have two brothers. So my first boyfriend became my husband. And it's been difficult. Did I know what I was getting into? No. I'm not even sure I loved him. I just wanted to get married. Poor guy. And no one was around when we were getting to know each other, and so see us together, or hear of developments as they happened. He has Asperger's (or High Functioning Autism – undiagnosed, as yet, but of which I'm convinced) which I'd never heard of and probably didn't realise until about ten years into the marriage. It did make sense of a number of his behaviours, but he doesn't like the label.

Children kept me busy for years, but as they started secondary school, I began to see a future I wasn't looking forward to. And I bottled it all up because I thought I could cope. It's only in the last few years that I've been more open about it. And amongst Christians especially, it's difficult, because you're supposed to respect and obey your husband and well, I don't always, or maybe even often. And couples do things together and we often don't from choice, well, my choice anyway. He's very quiet and doesn't volunteer much, so it's hard to sustain a conversation. I've had to rely on my children and others for conversation, and to remind myself of what is normal, and that what I say is interesting to others. So although that is not down to boarding school life, I feel it may have come about partly as a result of it. Why are we still together? I'm not sure. A combination of reasons, I guess, including fear, shame, finance, love for my children, loyalty and acceptance of that's the way it is, as well as quite a good life in other ways. Not much to do with obeying God because I think God's kinder to us than we were brought up to believe.

I first got involved with the Chefoo Reconsidered movement in April 2015. And I thought it was odd. Why now? I'm in my fifties. I'm ok, aren't I? I went to a day conference first and it was interesting, but I wasn't convinced. I hadn't kept in touch with anyone from the mission and my growing up in it. Well maybe Gill and Randall, who were hostel parents at Maxwell House for a few years. I send them Christmas cards. So then I joined the Facebook group and started reading people's thoughts and contributions. And it raised things I'd never considered before. Like goodbyes. What is a good goodbye?

We experienced too many to process, I guess. I remember one when my brother and I were at Narita Airport, Tokyo, ready to return to the UK after our summer holiday, and I was in floods of tears. My brother said, "What are you crying for? We'll see them next year." How were we so brainwashed?

Then there was the question of separation, not just from our parents, but our siblings too. We did an exercise, at an autumn Chefoo Reconsidered get together, of where we were in relation to our siblings at different ages in our lives. On the same side of the world, or on the opposite side of the world? (For those of us who came back to the UK). And it revealed to me very starkly that I hadn't spent much time with my siblings, so it was hardly surprising that I didn't know them very well. Our formative years were largely spent apart. That took some of the guilt away that I had, of thinking that I didn't know them. Obviously, there are other factors which might account for not having so much to do with them as adults e.g. faith, partners, children.

It's been a privilege to meet so many other Chefusians and hear their stories. And I think some of them have been harder than mine. I can't imagine four-month terms at Chefoo from age five, and maybe only seeing your parents once every two years as teenagers. And communications with parents that were too spiritual, and fobbed children off with "Just trust Jesus for that," or "You don't want to worry your parents with that as they're busy with the Lord's work." All very shocking!

I don't feel I know how to celebrate special occasions very well. I only had one birthday at home after age five, and two (or three?) Christmases after age twelve. I don't really like being the centre of attention, although I like giving and receiving presents. For my fortieth and fiftieth birthdays I organised a meal out and invited all my girlfriends (and some from church whom I wouldn't see individually outside church, and therefore not sure if they're friends) and they all seemed to want to come. Which isn't a foregone conclusion to me.

When my children were young, I liked doing parties for them although I'm fairly cheapskate. Was that due to not being able to be frivolous with money or just a lack of it at the time? But when they wanted to celebrate at eighteen and twenty-one, I wasn't sure what to do. Fortunately, they mostly organised their own, and they were sensible, so I didn't mind what they chose to do. It just seemed smaller than what everyone else was doing. And Christmases are an issue too. My husband takes little interest in it, so it falls to me, and I feel caught between what I want to do (not much) and what is expected. So I usually do some decorating, and it feels a bit pathetic. It's an effort and I run out of steam.

My faith journey has been bumpy. I always believed what I was taught at Chefoo and in Sunday School. Our motto at Chefoo Nanae was: "Remember Jesus Christ". We were encouraged to read the Bible every day, but I struggled for ages to make sense of it. Maybe partly because of deep personal trauma. And was it just what you did because your parents had done it? A friend at Chefoo got baptised aged ten, or so, and I didn't really understand why. I struggled at secondary boarding school and didn't want to go to the Christian Union, or whatever else my father suggested, even Greenbelt[66]. I did join the Christian Union at university through which I made friends, but it was a bit of a mixed blessing. While teacher-training in Leicester, I got introduced to Young Life and United Beach Missions and they have been a huge blessing to me, in teaching, as an example and in fellowship. And I have enjoyed doing beach missions, more post-children, because I find it easier to

---

66 Greenbelt is a well-known annual Christian music festival in the UK.

talk to the parents and I can have other responsibilities, like playing the accordion, and cooking for the team. The church I'm in now is the best. Praise the Lord! The preaching is excellent, it's very caring and a real family atmosphere, a great emphasis on prayer is modelled, and there is lots with which to be involved. I'm so thankful.

I'd always said I'd never send my own children to boarding school. Thankfully, that has never been necessary. But I did show my children round Monkton Combe School where I went aged 16–18. They commented that it was in a very scenic spot with great views and countryside round about. (Actually they never said that, teenagers wouldn't! But they did say it was very different to what they had experienced.) And the buildings, mostly in Bath stone, are so very olde worlde compared to the concrete jungle of a school that they went to.

I love being a mum and all that entails – the walking to, and picking up from school, having friends round to play or for tea, seeing them on sports day, or in plays or concerts; also being there when they're ill, just chatting over meals, reading to them at bedtime. Just think what we and our parents missed out on. And it all passes relatively quickly. Now two of mine have flown the nest, first to university and then work, and one son is at home working.

I've found it quite helpful writing this, but it is very personal. Thank you to everyone in the Chefoo Reconsidered group and those that I have met at events. It has been a useful journey to travel together.

* * *

Hilary attended Chefoo Japan 1970–76, with furlough in UK, Dec 1970 to Jan 1972. Furlough in UK September 1976 till Sept 1977, and attended day school.
Clarendon School, near Bedford September 1977 to July 1981. Holidays spent at Maxwell House, Warlingham, Surrey.
Monkton Combe School, Bath 1981–83. Her parents were on furlough 1981–82 and lived close by, but she was still expected to board at school. 1982–83 She spent the holidays with a family with younger children (not related) so didn't have to go back to the hostel.
Three children.

Philip

I WAS AT CHEFOO from grade two through grade four. Chefoo, a boarding school for missionary kids in the Cameron Highlands, the central hills of Malaysia, was about four hours' drive from where mom and dad worked. At an elevation of about 5,000 feet, the average temperature was a salubrious 70 degrees. Sometimes, misty clouds would sweep through the school. We felt none of the heat and humidity of the plains, where my parents toiled in the vineyards of the Lord.

Four-fifths of Malaysia, about the size of Florida, are covered by tropical forest covering mountains up to 7,000 feet high. This jungle is inhabited by tigers, elephants, bison, monkeys, gibbons, deer and bear, and is alive with all manner of insects, including malaria-bearing mosquitoes (we would always sleep under nets); bloodsucking leeches, pythons, and multi-coloured birds, where orchids and rhododendron flourish. As a boy, I liked nothing better than to "jungle bash" – hike through these sometimes treacherous, always beautiful jungles.

While visiting my parents in Malaysia, with my sister Anne, in the summer of 1972, I described the mountain jungle to my Grandmother. "What I enjoyed most about the Highlands is the landscape and the atmosphere," I wrote. "Thick, indolent sunshine, a heavy gold light balancing the green and black jungle shadows—great lazy, black butterflies, and the scent of unseen flowers, and a sweet afternoon languor."

Chefoo exists now only in fond memories: our little gardens where we cultivated mainly mud; our go-cart, the Silver Streak; King, the Alsatian, who was eaten by a tiger ("Does anybody remember the tiger at the *padang* in Tanah Rata that a park ranger had shot?", Bill Hanna writes. "Its head was propped up on a chair, and all of us kids were admiring it. Suddenly it rolled off the chair, but looked like it was rolling over to get up. Scared the wits out of us!"); the bamboo strands and the Rajah Brooke butterflies; the jungle gym and sandpit; allowance day; marmite[67] sandwiches and milk at tea time; building dams in the stream that wended through the property; Sports Day on the ridge (Leo[68] forever!), and looking for bullets in the Gurkha military base nearby.

And so the memories that bless and burn keep tumbling out.

Diesel yellow-roofed Mercedes Benz taxis would take us to the school but not before negotiating countless fantastic, hairpin curves. The verse "I shall lift up my eyes until the hills" had a special poignancy to me, as mom and dad would give me a final hug, and then leave around the playing field under the Ridge, to vanish. There was loneliness and home-sickness. My years at Chefoo have cast long shadows over my life and my values, as they have on all those who went to school with me.

As I write this in 2019, agents are ripping babies, toddlers and teenagers from their parents on the southern border of the United States and putting them in cages. It's hard for me to comprehend this. I recoil at this making of orphans. It reminds me of my orphan-hood. The time I was with my mum and dad amounted to no more than eight years of my life. In the eyes of the law, I was an orphan. In my case, a mission organisation chose to sacrifice me, and my siblings, on the altar of expediency to achieve what it saw as higher goals. The Great Commission was used to justify child abandonment.

Children are resilient. Most can tolerate isolation, and abuse, to rebound and live normal lives. But some don't make it. They succumb to neglect, anxiety, drug abuse, alcoholism, crime, poverty, mental ill-ness and sometimes suicide. And the predicate to some of that damage, is damage from damaged people. In my case the "Aunt" – the mission's

---

67 A savoury yeast extract spread

68 For many years, children at Chefoo were organised into three teams, named Leo, Orion and Taurus. Sometime around 1973–4 they were renamed after local mountains, Jasar, Beremban, and Erau, respectively, to avoid giving a "bad witness" to locals, who might wonder why a Christian school had teams named after signs of the zodiac!

term for the woman who became my foster mother – as well as her daughter, put a bullet through their heads.

If a child lives with insecurity, then what? For the first two decades of my life I did not feel safe. Kids are often spoiled, not only by their toys, but also by parents who are too busy to pay attention to them. They're spoiled by being ignored too much, or by harshness, not by kindness. Alone, they cry for their mother who is not there, and for their father who is not there. Such children learn, as surely as night follows day, nothing but the fragility and insecurity of their existence.

Most of my teachers were kind but others were brutal. I don't remember the same kind of nastiness from other kids at Chefoo, perhaps because we were all of the same tribe. It was different in America. Academic excellence was the last thing on my mind. I just wanted to survive the day and avoid the terror those thugs delighted in inflicting on me.

I was ten and had an accent. That, and my background, provoked sadistic glee from some at middle and high school, a house of horrors that made the Stephen King book and the movie, *Carrie,* look wholesome. Four decades haven't dimmed the misery of that shark pool. One kid was teasing and pushing me in a bathroom when finally I had enough: I swung my fist and delivered a haymaker to his nose. The blossom of blood shocked me and shocked him, and he left me alone from then on. Another hood threw me against the lockers. He was killed three days later, during a road rally, with a knife in his ribs. So I then adopted the strategy of excelling and achieving. The succession of failures and successes increased my self-confidence. From my parents all I got were thoughts and prayers – when they knew what was really going on a half-world away.

Were mum and dad failures as parents? Not at all. My premise is that they were not failures as parents. Nor did I suggest to them that they were failures as parents. Rather, they fervently believed they were acting as people of faith in alignment with the will of God. Furthermore, they must have done something right as their children live happy and fulfilling lives today.

That said, I'm not going to walk away from my conviction that their model of parenting was built on sand. My parents' model of parenting was an anti-model to how I should raise children. I was determined not to pass along the broken baton to another generation, well before I had children. I wouldn't travel on business for more than a few days, or take a promotion, or take on service projects, if it impacted my relationship with my family. This conviction brought blessings to our family beyond measure.

My MK years were, in the main, positive and privileged. My childhood was one of happy days, of birthday parties, trips to the beach, parks or hills, interesting travel, and contact with relatives, in Australia and from across the United States. Mum and dad would occasionally send us packages of toys and books. When we left for the United States, we could always expect a weekly letter and, after my parents retired, frequent telephone calls and, in recent years, emails.

My overall impression is that MKs go to extremes in how they turn out in life. Either they do exceptionally well, or they fail abysmally. I had to work through the implications of the pain of abandonment. Most MKs can take it, because circumstances have conditioned us to be self-reliant and resourceful. Others were devastated. The struggle between hope and hopelessness is always under the surface of life, as I suggest in my poem "Hope"

> The waves are pulling me under
>   From sorrow and grief asunder.
> Sorry Mum. Sorry Dad.
>   My heart bleeds. I am sad.
> The pounding surf whispers: Rest. Sleep.
>   The soaring gulls whisper: Wait. Hope.
> And so I wait amid the whispers.
>   And so I hope amid the waves.

My parents were acutely aware of the human cost of separation. Dad wrote:

> It is just not easy to be separated from one's own children. This is especially true for the mother. The heart pangs of separation are

accentuated when special problems arise in the life of the children as when (Philip) fell through the ice. There are problems arising from inadequate communication. The children's letters mainly relate factual happenings, but provide us with few insights into their inner thought life and personal problems and conflicts... The shift from Chefoo school to life in Ivyland in North America and attendance at a public school[69] involved quite a bit of cultural shock and adaptation on the part of the child.

Knowing the alternatives that were available to my parents in the early 60s, I might have made the same decisions that they made on Chefoo and Ivyland. But it does stretch the parental bond – to the point of snapping in some cases. Trans-cultural kids like myself, with shallow roots in multiple cultures, have unique opportunities but also unique challenges.

I spent the first decades of my life as an MK in an Islamic country, but living mainly among Hindus, Tamils and Buddhists. I adored my parents, but I struggled to understand their beliefs and values. Not wanting to put my parents in the dock, I put God in the dock, as I deconstructed Christianity to the studs. I tossed out everything and started with nothing, except my own intuitions and the Bible. I took a broom and swept the house of dogma clean. I whisked away the rubbish of two thousand years of councils, creeds and sermons. The Council of Nicaea and the Council of Constantinople – whisk! The Apostles Creed and the Augsburg Confession – gone. Luther, Calvin and Wycliffe – gone. Edwards, Moody, Billy Graham and Hudson Taylor – whisk, whisk, whisk! And all those words that aren't in the Bible but have caused schisms: trinity, pope, purgatory, evolution, and rapture. Out they went. I adopted a radical scepticism of all theisms, and all atheisms, and all knowledge as I deconstructed the foundations of knowledge itself. Accepting nothing unless I could firstly convince myself, without respect to appeals to tradition, or to what my father believed, or his father believed, or what any authority dead or alive believed.

---

69 In British parlance, a state school.

I saw this as a radical but necessary step to take responsibility for the only life I have, not just for my actions, but also for my beliefs. Trust was a luxury in my threatening and fragile world. With doubt, we kindle the tiny flame of hope and vision for something better. That is why doubt is faith. It's another kind of belief, and it's a positive affirmation. Certitude is apostasy.

I started with some basic questions. What is belief? What is truth? What is reality? What is good? What is God? Where did God come from? Can we be good without God? Is God necessary? Are the soul, spirit and will real? Did Jesus exist? Why is there pain? What is evil? What is freedom? Does it matter that I am a Christian? Do we need the church? What is our purpose? What is my purpose? How do we know what we think on any of this is true, or matters? For much of my life the sceptic in me has battled the mystic in me. My life's journey is like rowing a boat. Sometimes, the waters are calm and sometimes they are choppy. At times, I row against the wind and not always in a straight line. I've tried to avoid the reefs of credulity and fanaticism, on one hand, and smug cynicism and hyper-intellectualism on the other. My parents remain the measure against which I measure all others, and remain, even years after their deaths, my North Star.

Today, I am what I was as a child: a Presbyterian in good standing. I love the old hymns, and religious holidays, and I thrill to a well-crafted sermon. They are a backdrop to our life. But I spend a lot less time than my dad fretting about unsolvable theological problems, such as how the world was made, and how it will end, and trying to understand inscrutable doctrines. When it comes to my relationship with God, I can say it is well with my soul, and I alone get to define that relationship. I must agree with Voltaire, the great eighteenth century iconoclast, who never attacked the simple faith of my parents, but had boundless scorn for credulity and cruelty:

> 'O God unrecognised, whom all thy works proclaim,
>   O God, hear these my final words:
> If ever I have erred, 'twas searching for Thy Law;
>   My heart may go astray, but it is full of thee.'

I feel that I've lived a childhood of incredible adventure and privilege. But in these sunlit gardens of youth, there were snakes and shadows and sadness. There was, in my view, an excess of collective punishment, and sometimes cruel teachers. One such incident occurred perhaps around 1963. David, who is several grades ahead of me, picks up the story. "About that time, we visited the ridge with a lady teacher. We asked if we could go and explore – which we did. Only problem was that we got lost! I suggested we follow the sun and strike out due east – as that would bring us back down to the school. Which it did. Once back, there was a big hoo-hah. The smaller kids were queued up outside the headmaster's door and whacked with a sneaker. We older boys were not beaten – this is where the psychological stuff comes in. We had to wait to be called to go to Fred Collard's office. The first victim reported back that we would be reduced to tears – there was no possibility of holding out. Sure enough, we were shown in the Bible about how much God hates sin and that we should repent. We were then ordered to write 'confessions' that would be sent to our parents (they never were) – which we did in our now blubbery state."

I was one of the little boys in that party. With my over-active imagination, I wondered who would get us first – the tigers, or the head-hunters. I was duly thrashed. I was also spanked for not eating rhubarb – and to this day I will not eat rhubarb. The punishment generally, for talking after lights out, was to stand outside the dorm memorising a times table. Needless to say, I had mastered the entire times tables by fourth grade.

In April 2001, Dave and Fred again met in England, and this reunion perhaps is a fitting coda to our Chefoo experience.

The reason for our meeting is that I had written him a letter telling him about the hurt I felt he had caused me by wrongly punishing me at Chefoo School when I was twelve years old. I received a Zooty cartoon postcard from him saying that he apologised if he had misjudged me in the past and suggested we meet. He drives me to his house and after a cup of tea, Fred and I set off for the pub for a lunch and a chat. Over the superb meal, we talk about Chefoo, about our families, and every now and then we touch on the more emotional issues that I had brought up in my letter. It is obviously not that easy for either of us – we both feel a bit nervous about it but at the same time don't want to avoid it. He doesn't remember the particular incident I was referring to although he does remember some of the incidents that happened around the same time. He says he's glad I was open enough to write to him and was only sorry it had taken so long for us to come to talk about it. I begin to feel as if it was I who had misjudged. I also realise that he had not been at Chefoo very long when this happened. So what really happened to me emotionally when I was twelve years old? Time shifts things and makes a mystery of things.

Strangely, I'm not surprised that Fred is so open to hearing the way I feel. That's why I felt OK about writing to him. This is the intuition that I remember I had back in 1963. So the 12-year-old me was right in that respect.

Well, three cheers for Uncle Fred! Who else would have been so gracious? And three cheers for the 12-year-old me! You did just great, kid!

I have no way of knowing if I would have lived a better life, or a worse life, if my parents were not missionaries and if I had not gone to Chefoo, or to Ivyland. But now, as I move into my mid-sixties and as I look back over the broad vistas of my life, I cannot help but be grateful for the goodness and wisdom of all those who were part of my life's journey.

* * *

Philip's parents served in mainland China and Malaysia for the OMF for a combined total of seventy years. He was in Chefoo from 1962–64. Philip continued his education in the United States with a career in information technology. He lives in Arizona with his wife Nancy and has two adult children.

John G.

The Four Movements

I WOULD BREAK the journey into adulthood, for missionary children, into four separate movements which, when coming together, make a perfect storm. In doing so, all I am doing is using a way of reasoning I developed as a teenager, as a defence, to manage myself and the world around me. I am not saying it makes the problems go away but it offers a measure of control and understanding. I am writing this to explain to those who haven't been through this, those for whom a missionary childhood may seem odd, or even horrifying. To get some perspective we need to relate the missionary children's experience to that of other children and not to consider that it is unique, or substantially worse, than the experience of other children growing up. Many have experienced one or more of the movements, but few have experienced all of these together.

Here are the four movements. The movement from one country to another, raising the issue of where home really is. Though this is an experience for every migrant. The movement from institutional life, in boarding schools and hostels, to something like normality. As well as from the mission as an institution in its own right. This is the experience of all boarding school children, and also those whose parents belong to institutions like the army, the diplomatic office or the clergy, whose identity is unduly shaped by what their parents do, and the institutions their parents inhabit. The third journey is from emotional dependence to emotional maturity, something all children have to do more or less successfully. Lastly, the movement from a child's simple, often literal, faith to the more nuanced faith of an adult. And this last is the icing on the cake – the negotiation with a God whom it may be hard for the child to encounter directly, but frequently resents.

Let us take each of these movements in turn and I will use them to reflect on my own experience of a childhood in Japan; going to Chefoo in Nanae; boarding school first in Derbyshire, then in Surrey. Going to Donnington Hurst, the OMF hostel in Newbury, in the holiday time, and spending some summers in Singapore and Malaysia, where my parents worked, and where my siblings went to school at Chefoo in the Cameron Highlands.

Another country

Missionary children aren't unique. Like army children, or those working in international business, or the diplomatic corps, missionary children move around the world with their parents, often to more than one country. On the whole, they adjust to it, unless they fail to anchor anywhere and forget where they belong. Then that feeling of displacement becomes a wound, and they keep flitting backwards and forwards, unable to settle.

I was told by my parents, as soon as I could understand, that England was my country and that one day I would go back to school there, and that I would eventually go to university and settle down in that country. Staying in the Far East was out of the question. The reason for going to Chefoo to board, rather than Japanese schools, was because I needed to start a Western education which a mission school could provide, until I was old enough to leave my parents and return to my mother country. I was always grateful for this clear direction, since I also saw missionary children who had gone "native" (to use that politically incorrect phrase), who spoke Japanese rather than English and (as I saw it) were destined to be marooned in limbo between the two cultures, not acceptable to either.

I have accepted my lot – I have never regretted being pushed to be

English, or British, as I prefer to think of myself. Britain is the country I settled in after having moved here for my education, so that is my nationality. However I have learned to treasure that instinct to make every new place home. Travelling on business, I make friends easily – and try to experience as much about the country I am visiting as possible. In short, I start burrowing. I worry that others may find my behaviour weird, but nationals usually treat it as a compliment. I had a strange moment, visiting Tokyo, when I was making advertising for Honda and gave a short address in fluent Japanese – the accent was developed in a Japanese kindergarten. But I was under no illusions. I was a Westerner performing a clever party trick. I couldn't belong.

Boarding school and the Mission as a Colonial Institution

Missionary children aren't the only ones who go to boarding schools. Boarding was the default for British civil service administrators across the empire. The upper classes in the UK still use boarding schools as the default way to bring up children. That for me was always an issue: that what was supposed to be a good education – compensation for the family being abroad – was a ladder for social climbing. I once had an argument about it with Oz G., also an MK. He, with his Oxford education, couldn't see the problem. If you got a better education, and a better job, because your parents were missionaries, then it was the same deal offered to many sons of the clergy; privileged status their parents' income couldn't afford. I also have a problem with the priority given by my family to education. Having a missionary background didn't give me the automatic right to a university education, and a better education than if my family had not left the UK. And if the price of a good education was giving up family life, then it is hard to justify why education should always take priority. My American friends at Chefoo had the option for international schools or home schooling. We didn't. I didn't have a particularly difficult time at boarding schools in the UK, but it was a culture shock and a strange transition. My parents had the connections to send me to a farm in New Zealand, in a year between school and university, to blow out the cobwebs that boarding school produces. It meant that I was given the chance to burrow into a whole new culture for a year. And that served me well for going to Edinburgh to study at university the following year.

Boarding schools are supposed to be tough places – that is the model of child development. When I went to the school library, *Tom Brown's School Days* was on the shelves, a story about Rugby public school, where small boys are terrorised by Flashman, the bully who roasts them over a fire. Nobody runs off and "sneaks" to the staff. If you were a sneak, you were ostracised by the other pupils; but interestingly, also rebuked by the staff, who supported the "no grassing" code. We weren't protected from bullying, but the system was supposed to help us find ways around it. The contrast, from Chefoo as a nine-year old, was absolute. It is hard though to be critical because the boarding school system knew exactly what it was. At my secondary school, the school headmaster had been the head prefect at the school my father went to. I think my father had even been beaten by him! So we had family stories about how the prefects would look at the marks of the cane, on the ten-year old boys they had beaten, and would compliment each other on the evenness of the distribution of the marks of the cane. Violence, despite the protestations of public schools, was normalised there. Missionary children weren't particularly disadvantaged, but still came to these places totally unprepared. My first year in secondary school was particularly bad where, after lights out, the senior boys would come in and get the most vocal thirteen-year olds to run the gauntlet under the beds around the dormitory. If you didn't hit the victim hard enough you would be the next one made to run the gauntlet – and all to the soundtrack of *Riders on the Storm* by the Doors. It went on for weeks. And the staff of the house never stopped it.

The upside of this highly structured and regimented life is that it creates huge confidence in those who survive it. The system creates non-conformity and downright eccentricity. But it can be the case that children get traumatised by boarding school, and years of trying not to be noticed in the margins.

Boarding school was one thing, but I should also mention the role of the mission as a colonial-style institution in its own right. There is always a confusion of identities between the organisation your parents work for and your experience as a child. We were presented with the central dilemma as if it was ours too. The China Inland Mission had been thrown out of China. How had God allowed godless communists to take over? I was told the story of how the teachers and children marched out of Chefoo singing *God is Still on the Throne*, with Chinese Christians standing at the roadside in solidarity but not able to acknowledge them. This was presented as my continuing struggle as the mission reconstituted itself outside China, as the Overseas Missionary Fellowship, and frantically evangelised before the communists took over. Relatives of my Chefoo friends were busy bombing and napalming Vietnam, and the countries around it. I can't say that the mission was neutral.

We were warned about crucifixes and lighting candles to saints. But not the visits to look at Hudson Taylor's pigtails in the glass cabinet in Newington Green – the fortress structure in East London with *"The Lord will provide"* and *"Hitherto hath the Lord helped us"*, inscribed in Chinese characters, either side of the entrance. When Taylor returned from China, he would cut them off, and turn them into watch chains. This was presented to us as the sign of the mission's authenticity over other missionary societies. Our missionaries identified with the Chinese in ways the others didn't. We sang missionary hymns like *Praise God for These 85 Years*, incrementing every year. *The Lammermuir* – the CIM Mayflower – was the ship in which the first missionaries travelled with Hudson Taylor to China. There is even a church in the Borders of Scotland whose roof is made from the timbers of the very same ship. It was a strange cult, which condemned the idolatry of Roman Catholicism, but fetishised Hudson Taylor and the mission he started.

Travelling back to Asia on summer holidays from Britain we were used as couriers, to take all sorts of articles to and from mission homes, to save on postage. Strangers would turn up at the airport to give us packages. There were times when security asked me about objects in my luggage, I knew nothing about. Fortunately, they were usually treats, like crumpets, not available in the Far East. But once there was even a whole slide projector that needed to be declared. The mission couldn't afford for children to receive phone calls or telegrams – that would cost the mission money. But travelling on air tickets bought with mission money we were treated as if we were part of the mission. This didn't seem odd to me until, on holiday in Toronto aged thirty, I came off the phone having agreed to attend an OMF meeting, as a kind of proxy for my parents. If I couldn't make the Toronto meeting, I might be able to make Edmonton the following week. "What are you doing?", my wife demanded, "You have never worked for the mission, you're on holiday. You don't owe these people anything." And no, I suppose I really didn't.

I can't complain of any abuse committed by the mission, or by teachers they employed. But there was still an issue over governance. Now I know that others were not so fortunate. There was no way that abuses which broke the law could ever be properly policed and punished. There was no system of inspection or reporting. If abuse happened then, with the children from one sending country and offenders from another country, and with all having left the country in which offences were committed, there was no prospect of prosecution, or any real calling to account. So missionary children were unprotectable. The institution's primary mission was saving souls, not protecting the children of its workers. I write this not having a beef with the mission's ethos, I just wish the risks were made clearer to prospective parents. Some friends of mine are distressed because their children are taking grandchildren off to the mission field. "It's selfish," they say. "It's life," say I. Children, for better or for worse, stand with their parents. If the parents are in an institution, the children are affected by that institution. There is nothing unique about this. But missionary organisations could be more aware of the consequences of institutional behaviour on those who never signed-up to join in the first place.

Faux Independence

The third movement is the move from dependence to emotional maturity. Something every child with a healthy upbringing needs to learn, but may not receive if family life is not nourishing, or if they are removed from that family very young. The consequence is to find emotional connection by overinvesting in friendships, whether romantic or not. Destroying relationships by putting all our weight on them, placing burdens on partners they should not be expected to carry.

It took years for me to get over the desperate latching onto romantic relationships which inevitably sank them. And there were few adult figures to explain why it kept happening. Put it down to adolescence. And that really is why most of us, given the invitation, would never repeat adolescence. It isn't much fun. And arguably, missionary children have a level of awareness, and emotional independence, that leaves them better equipped than average for adolescence. I was fortunate. I married a wonderful woman without obsessing over her (as I had in every previous relationship). The marital troubles of missionary children should be monitored. I suspect they are above the level of the adult population in our home countries. But I don't know. I am happy to be proven wrong.

Adult Faith in the Face of Toxic Theology

The fourth and final movement is from a child's grasp of faith to an adult one. This is the kicker. Much of the anger at missionary institutions, at mission of any kind, at God, comes from arrested development – a view of God which has not really moved on from the child's perspective. There is/was a lot of toxic theology about – or, at the very least, sloppy theology that we picked up from the missionaries themselves. If you don't explicitly assure a child that they matter, and that they matter to God, the child will conclude that their parents' work matters more to God than they do. God is an activist, looking for more foot soldiers. Only activists and achievers need apply.

As recently as 2016, I heard a Bible reading from a former general director of the OMF. The reading he spoke from was Hebrews 11, including the attempted sacrifice of the child Isaac by his father Abraham, in response to a divine command. I was not surprised to hear the speaker explain the higher calling, where parents have to put their call, to prioritise the lost, over their own families. Children are collateral damage in the face of a higher call. In all my time as a youngster on the mission field, I never heard any speaker challenge this toxic theology. The sacrifice of children by fire to the god Moloch, and the Corban rule which was used to justify giving to God and neglecting one's own family, are both condemned in scripture, but ignored in a missionary context, which was using scarce resources as effectively as it knew how; and considered the levels of care of missionary children to be at least as good as those of other missionary societies. But we knew how to read the Bible for ourselves, and we discovered for ourselves the texts that speak of the priority of family responsibilities. At the very least this should have been presented as a tension, but it wasn't ever presented as such within my hearing. Where there were issues, at the hostel we went to in holiday times, we were informed that this was the devil trying to attack our parents and undermine their missionary effectiveness through us. "Sign an admission statement – say you'll agree, and we won't have to inform your parents and the mission can go on." Half a century away, I can see such emotional pressure for the spiritual abuse it was. Though I think our house parents were naïve, thrown in at the deep end, woefully underprepared to deal with the competence, self-awareness, and theological abilities of children who had been through a mission system.

I mentioned the trip to Japan for Honda. While there, I found my way out to the suburbs, and found the house I used to live in at age seven. And I found my way to the Japanese church I had gone to every week with my parents. I was given a meal. An extraordinary conversation followed. The pastor and the elders asked after my family, but particularly what had happened to the children. I explained that I was all right – I had kept my faith and my wellbeing, but the dropout rate was close to 50%. The Japanese have a beautiful understated way of communicating that I, brought up in a Japanese culture, recognised and was moved by. They explained that they knew how much our family life had been affected by the children being sent away. They wanted to say thank you, in a way that implied a subtle apology, that it had been necessary at all. These were the only people in my lifetime who expressed regret for what had happened. Japanese have a strong culture of family. It was news to me that the Japanese might be quietly appalled that Westerners would prioritise education over family. Ayako Miura, a Christian poet of national renown in Japan, writes a poem where she watches weeping parents put their children on a train off to boarding school. The poem finishes with the phrase: "For the sake of the gospel."

Isn't it time to do a review of what constitutes toxic theology, about mission and families, and ensure that missionaries and those in training are taught what is wholesome, and what is frankly abusive and unworthy of Christ? It matters because children are left to process these issues alone from five years old. We don't need a new apologetic, but a new way of articulating the missionary call that a child, left unattended, won't turn into a toxic narrative. What is the point of winning the world and losing the souls of your children? Well, there's a trade-off we should be talking about.

I am aware how many of those, who grew up with me, struggled with a notion of God which was stuck, and who seemed distant or oppressive. But that was not my experience. I dropped out of faith in my last year of school, irritated by the banality of the Christian Union. But once outside an institutional understanding of faith, I returned to it, and have been with it ever since. But that is because my understanding of God evolves all the time. And I don't blame God for flawed human decision making, even if it was done in his name.

Putting it together

The existence of the four movements is evidence enough of my ability to make sense of experience by analysing and abstracting it. When faced by a troubling aspect of the past, I consider to which of the four movements it belongs. The four journeys will never combine to become the perfect storm that overwhelms me.

So how do I score on the four journeys?

I love travelling overseas for work, but was told to treat the UK as home, so I have been educated here and lived here ever since, and have never quite taken an international job. I still have the strange tendency to burrow into new cultures, and to treat new acquaintances as if I have known them for years.

I have kept away from institutions and made my own way, working for myself these last nineteen years. After being made redundant from my five first jobs, I am probably unemployable now – I can't bear institutional life. And I don't trust large organisations which never have you as a priority. But having said that, I am a lay minister in that grand institution, the Church of England – though we are usually contrarians, not under the career pressures of the clergy.

After a series of disastrous relationships which all collapsed arguably because of the weight I put upon them and the way I would obsess over the other party, I met and married a wonderful woman, Karen. Her influence is best described by a backward compliment from a friend I met after an interval of some twenty years: "You've grown up a lot – your wife has done an amazing job with you!"

After a period at the end of teenage years when I rejected Christianity for its shallowness, and the judgementalism of so many Christians, I went back to it and felt my faith had grown up. I have still not lost my faith, but it keeps evolving and changing. And it isn't what it was when I was ten or twenty. Or even sixty.

* * *

John attended Chefoo Nanae Japan between 1964–67, then he returned to the UK to attend a Derbyshire prep school, Brocksford Hall. He went to King Edward's School in Surrey for secondary education. During holidays, he was at the Donnington Hurst hostel until he finished sixth form. Summer holidays, he joined the family, who were then in Singapore, and also stayed at the mission's holiday home in the Cameron Highlands – he is one of the few to visit more than one Chefoo. After a year of sheep farming in New Zealand he went to Edinburgh University. He studied philosophy and English but played a lot more guitar.

A chance invitation set him on a path to working in advertising. This came full circle when, as the lead strategist on Honda's UK account, he was flown to Tokyo business class, to visit Honda's head office and Dentsu, the Japanese ad agency. During that trip he managed to find his way back to the house he lived in when he was seven and visit the Koganei church which his family had attended.

Despite a few bumps and wobbles, he did not lose his faith. He became a trustee of the Bible Society, in which capacity he was flown to Singapore (upgraded to business class) to join a gathering of Asian Bible societies. While there he visited the Japanese expatriate church in Singapore that his parents planted. He has attended several Chefoo reunions but has basically survived the traumas others have experienced – for which he credits his wife Karen. He has three children and one grandson. He has never been remotely tempted to send his children to boarding school. He regards his upbringing as a blessing and a gift. But that doesn't mean that parts of it weren't totally awful.

Interlude 8:
Upon Returning
Andrew

From the valley rises up the sound
Of children playing quietly by the stream...
And I am home!

By the eucalyptus tree along the drive
I watch the sunlight stripe the banks...
Above the stones.

Round the buildings with the child who once I was
I walk and talk and laugh and mourn...
The years have flown.

And the family once taken, now restored
To me at last in this fair place...
I will take home.

9

Chefoo Reconsidered

"For many of us, in adulthood, the Chefoo community has become our surrogate family, our 'tribe'. With each other, we feel an instinctive sense of belonging: no effort required. No need to try to blend in. We can be our colourful selves with a freedom of abandonment that most of us have not experienced in our adult lives. We can share the deepest and darkest recesses of ourselves and still receive comfort from each other."

Rosie Longley

In this concluding chapter we have collected Kirsten Leed's story of how Chefoo Reconsidered occurred – a fascinating tale; and two accounts of the CR conferences themselves, written by the counsellors who became so very important to many of us. Their essays leave us with a powerful summary of the remarkable journey we have travelled together.

Have you been able to see some of the factors that influenced the outcome for each person? Age at first separation, individual vulnerability, place in family, family dynamics, place of birth, age of moving to Asia first, unshielded traumatic experiences, effects of growing up in a strongly religious culture, and whether separation continued into secondary education – the influence of these can be seen through the stories you have just read. Did you read the Biographies as well? Note that our writers, who survived, have lived "normal" lives. Maybe you sensed the contrast between the Bio's and the emotion and effects that we have documented.

Is boarding school an answer for the educational needs of missionary children?

Why did our parents send us away? We hope church leaders read our stories with great care. And humility.

What about kids who have been through horrible traumas today – as refugees, survivors of war and family dysfunction, and so many others? Can we build care structures for them as they reach their own days of reckoning? They will come.

Have you seen your own childhood in a new light? What shaping moulded you?

Now, enjoy our last chapter. We think we may have saved our best till now.

Kirsten Leed: Traces of Childhood

It's late in the evening in the last days of summer 2013. Kirsten Leed sits at her open computer with a list of 400 names and has just put in a call to/phoned someone on the other side of the world. When the call is answered, she begins:

"I'm looking for people who were students at Chefoo school in Malaysia. Did you go there in the late 60's?"

A long pause. Kirsten hears the other person take a deep breath. She knows she's got it right. She has just found one of her old school mates.

Third Culture Kid

AS WITH SO MANY other missionary kids, Kirsten Leed had a childhood some would think was colourful, while others would call it chaotic: born in Denmark; living with her parents at the age of two, at a Bible School in England; at three, travelling to Thailand where the family lived in at least three different places, before returning to Denmark, for their first furlough, four years later.

Furlough meant leaving her best friend, Janet, and travelling far, far north in a Douglas airplane, a trip that took two days with many stopovers. She now spoke Danish, Thai and English. Or a mix of them.

– When we arrived in Denmark, I discovered I had grandparents! Four of them! And cousins. An amazing invention! Kirsten declares with a grin.

– I got on especially well with one of my cousins. But I couldn't tell her of the world I had come from: that, for example, it took a month for a letter to arrive, and that for the last part of the journey the letter was carried by a postman on an elephant.

Her cousin, on the other hand, couldn't understand how Kirsten had never learnt to ride a bike, in Denmark, there's no other way to get to school! So she ran around in the sunshine, teaching Kirsten how to keep her balance on her bike, for it was only a short time before school started.

One of the Flock

The missionary family, now consisting of Kirsten, her parents, and a little brother and sister, rented a house in the village of Hou. Kirsten would start her first year of school here. She was given her first school bag and pencil case. She was six and a half and felt very grown up.

– It was fantastic starting school. I made friends immediately. In Thailand, I'd been the one who stood out with my light hair and blue eyes, but here, I was just like the others, she remembers.

– And then it was my birthday. All my friends came home for buns and cocoa and it was just so cosy. Shortly after/a couple of months later, it was Christmas. My grandparents and my aunt, uncle and their children came over and celebrated Christmas together with us. I especially remember the Christmas Tree with all its candles lit up. It snowed and my father and uncle played with us, building snowmen. There was a real family atmosphere.

On the Road Again

The year in Denmark flew by and Kirsten worked hard at her Danish – and forgot all her Thai and English. Before she knew it, the family flew back to the East in a propeller plane, and it wasn't long until holidays were over and school began again.

Now she had not just her schoolbag, but also a big suitcase, and there were long lists of all she would need: sheets, towels, underwear, blouses... her mother spent a long time sewing labels with her name into everything. She also had a little case to take with her, for when she would travel back to her parents in the school holidays. Her parents were to live in Thailand, but the school was in Malaysia, and Kirsten had no idea where Malaysia was. The school was a boarding school and she didn't understand what a boarding school was either. She was seven and a half and she felt very small.

– We landed early in the morning in Kuala Lumpur. It was hot and we were tired, and we had to haul all our luggage ourselves, Kirsten recalls.

– My father found a taxi that would take us on the long drive up to the school. The journey took us on poor roads through vast rubber and oil palm plantations. By afternoon, we had driven up into the highlands and now, there was jungle on both sides of the road that twisted its way round hairpin bends, so I was thoroughly carsick.

And at long last, the family reached the mission guesthouse, where they spent the night. It was an utterly dark, tropical night, and jungle noises began outside the windows – birds, monkeys, and other animals that cried out. It was an unknown world and terrifying for Kirsten: there had been no jungle where the family had lived in Thailand.

The next day, they walked for half an hour along the narrow road to the school. The school lay in a clearing with a green wall of jungle all around it. An island in the middle of the jungle, with nowhere to go. Kirsten stood and gazed at it all and thought: "This must be the end of the world."

Alone in the World

– I trailed after my father and the headmaster, Mr C., who was showing us around the school. The headmaster spoke a language I didn't understand and, every so often, my father nodded and said something in the same unknown language. Afterwards, my father told me that this was where I would be going to school and that it would all be fine.

The family was there for a few days, staying at the guesthouse. The day before her parents were to travel on to Thailand, Kirsten suggested she could sleep at the school while the others stayed at the guesthouse. The seven-year-old had hatched a cunning plan: if her parents missed her, they might just change their minds and take her with them to Thailand instead.

That night she slept with the C. family, as the other students had not yet returned from their summer holiday. She was put to bed in the guest room and she can still remember Mrs C., standing silhouetted in the doorway, saying something that probably meant good night.

But of course Kirsten's parents didn't miss her after just one night. They turned up the next morning to say goodbye, and then they were gone, on their way to Thailand. This time, they would be living in a different place than their home before their furlough.

– I didn't know where they were going. It was in a different country, so it must be so far away, Kirsten explains, and relives the feeling of being completely alone in the jungle with all the strange noises, unable to imagine where "home" was.

– I was told I'd be home for Christmas. In five and a half months. That is an impossibly long time for a child. How many times would I sleep before then? Could I even count that high?

The idea was that she would play with the headmaster's children, David and Anne, until school term started, but David played with his dog and Anne with the kitchen ladies' children. So Kirsten wandered around by herself, looking at the roses and hibiscus bushes, sitting on the grassy playing field singing the rhyming games she'd learnt in Denmark, holding her invisible Danish friends by their hands. "I could get lost here," she thought, "If they can't see me, they will forget I'm here." So she made sure she was always in sight of the grownups, so she didn't disappear. But no one spoke to her because she couldn't speak a word of English.

When the children from Thailand arrived a week later, Kirsten couldn't wait to see her friend Janet again. But there was no Janet. She had gone home with her family for furlough in England.

Smallest and Biggest

Kirsten was put in the big girls' dorm because she was *almost* eight years old. But because she couldn't speak English, she was put in a class with those who were two years younger. So she didn't make friends in the dorm because there she was too little, nor in her class, because there she was the big girl who never talked.

– I often went over to a group of children and just stood and watched, while they played with marbles or skipped. I was the girl who never said a word. The first term at school was the loneliest time in my life. I used most of my energy to simply survive, she states today.

At one point she received a letter. It was from Denmark. She could tell by the stamp. But she hadn't learned to read in Denmark, and this letter was written in longhand, so she didn't know who it was from – one of her grandparents, she guessed. She tried to get the teacher who was her contact person, to read it for her, but the teacher shook her head – she couldn't speak Danish – and returned the thin airmail letter back to her. For some weeks, that letter was her most precious belonging. She slept with it at night, for it showed that somewhere out there in the world, there was someone who remembered her and cared for her. But at some point, it got mislaid and was gone...

– And then it was my birthday, and I remembered how cosy it had been the year before. But this was not the same. There was a little party with cake, and you could invite some friends. But she didn't know any of the others, so the teachers invited some of those who weren't invited to many birthday parties, Kirsten recounts.

– Finally, after what seemed like an eternity, it was Christmas and we would be going home for the holiday. We were woken in the middle of the night at 1 am and got ready to go with our little suitcases. All the local taxis were lined up outside the dorms waiting, and they drove us back through the night, round all the hairpin bends down to the train station in the valley. In the train, two carriages had been reserved for us. We would take the train all the way back to Thailand and there were three or four adults to accompany us. It was a long journey and we slept two nights on the train (in bunks). The others talked and laughed excitedly, while I simply sat and wondered: "Has anyone told my parents I'm coming? What if they're not at the station?"

But they were waiting for her. The Christmas holidays lasted five weeks and, in that time, Kirsten got to know some of the missionary children whose parents worked at the same hospital as her parents did. And she became good friends with them. When the long holiday was over, and she sat once again in the train back to school, it was now a very different experience for her. Now she knew where her home was, now she knew the school and its daily rhythm, now she had friends, and her English had become so good she was moved up a class.

Kirsten finishes the phone call. It has been a long one. When her old school mate got over the initial shock of being found, they had so much to talk about remembering their childhood at Chefoo: The strict discipline in the dorms. The Sunday service in the chapel far down in the village. Excursions to tin mines and rubber plantations. Treks in the jungle, where they stuffed themselves with passion fruit and threw them at each other. The gibbons that swung in the trees behind the school. The strong, confidential friendships. The many hellos and goodbyes with best friends who didn't turn up after the holidays, because they were on furlough with their parents.

She checks off another name on the list. It seems more and more likely that it will be possible to arrange a reunion. She begins to look forward to it.

Back to the Beginning

For four years Chefoo school was Kirsten's world, interrupted only by summer and Christmas holidays with her parents. Chefoo was a safe place for her; all the children came from the same Christian environment, and were separated from their parents, and many forged strong bonds with each other.

In 1971, the family returned home to Denmark for good, and Kirsten and her siblings started in Danish schools. She was now two months shy of twelve and felt so foreign.

– I knew no one in Denmark, and it was a massive culture shock being thrown into the liberated and free 70s, she remembers.

– I had to pretty well learn Danish all over again. On the other hand, I was better at English than my teacher in seventh grade, and was put in an English class two years above my own. But there I was *still* the irritating one who corrected the teacher, so I was taken out of those classes for a couple of years and when I started lessons again later, I'd forgotten most of my English.

– I missed all my friends. Even though I was Danish, I didn't feel Danish. The second-most lonely period of my life was my teens in the 70s. I made no close friends, just acquaintances.

She managed to keep in contact by letter for a while with Peigi and Janet, two of her closest Chefoo friends. She even managed to visit them in the UK a couple of times in the 70s and 80s, but this contact gradually petered out. She saw Janet, one time again, in the 90s.

Looking for Roots

One decade followed another. Kirsten graduated, started working and had a son, Andreas. When her son in turn went off to a Danish *efterskole*[70] at the age of 15–16, she noticed how much his new friends

70 An efterskole (literally "afterschool"), is a voluntary independent residential school for young people aged 14 to 17 unique to Denmark, where students can choose to spend one or more years finishing their primary education (9th or 10th year). An efterskole usually offers a variety of study options, focusing on specific themes, e.g., sports, the arts, Christianity.

meant to him and she began to think about her old boarding school friends. Would she be able to find them again? She found her friend Peigi in Scotland, and she and Andreas travelled over to see her in 2008, and there were a couple of others she had also made contact with again.

– It was an incredible experience. We could immediately feel how much we had in common, Kirsten remembers, and tells how surprised her son was to see adults, who hadn't seen each other in so many years, open their homes and say: "Of course you must come and stay with us!"

– It was then I realised how incredibly special it is to have friends spread all over the world, Kirsten declares. She intensified her search for old boarding school friends.

She was one of the first Danes with a Facebook profile and this meant that after two years she had already made contact with thirty former school friends. Many of them lived in the UK and, in 2012 she packed her backpack and criss-crossed England and Wales, visiting old friends. At one place, someone invited their old Chefoo friends to a barbecue – a little group who now met again for the first time in almost forty years.

– The same year, I invited those I had contacted to visit me a couple of weeks before Christmas. Twelve made the trip over to Denmark. "Some stayed with me, bedding down on sofas, mattresses and in the guest room; others stayed at a hotel and one couple were put up by my vicar," she explains.

– I'd prepared some activities, but they simply weren't necessary. It was the best weekend ever. Suddenly we were all nine years old again and had so much fun. We also had serious conversations, but more than anything it was fun.

Chefoo Reconsidered

One of those who was visiting Kirsten in Denmark told her about his plans to travel back to Singapore and Malaysia to confront old demons. He intended to visit the old school, which was now closed and had been converted to a church Camp and Conference Centre. While everyone sat together in Kirsten's living room, the idea formed of arranging a Chefoo reunion. At the beginning of 2013, OMF, the mission who had run the various Chefoo schools, was contacted and encouraged to do something for the students who had struggled in later life as a result of their childhood experiences at boarding school.

OMF understood the value of helping former students reconnect and reconsider their time at Chefoo and Kirsten was part of the planning committee. OMF searched their archives, and managed to dredge up incomplete lists of some 400 former Chefoo Malaysia students from the 60s and early 70s. They sent them to Kirsten, who grouped the names by classes. And so began the huge detective work necessary to track down the 400.

Kirsten used countless hours at her computer and on the phone. Tracing women was especially difficult, as many had married and changed their names. She trawled through the internet and when she did find someone, there were often connections to siblings and friends. In fact, there were even two old Chefoo students in Denmark, which she'd had no inkling of.

– I began simply by trying to find those friends I remembered. But it snowballed and I found more and more, Kirsten remembers.

– When I reconnected with old school friends, I could see that our friendships were cemented through our common history. We had all experienced the trauma of early separation, both from family and from each other. For some, this had caused problems tackling relationships later in life. We became a kind of extended family for each other.

– Our families left their homes, called by God, and it was our experience that our parents prioritised their work higher than their children. And when the work was God's work, how could one question it?

By 2014, Kirsten had tracked down 300 people on the list, and the planning group had come so far with their preparations that they could invite them – not to a Chefoo Reunion – but to a Chefoo Reconsidered, at their old boarding school in Malaysia. They knew it was important that this not simply be a glorified party, to celebrate the good old days, but that there also should be focus on the trauma and bad experiences, as well as the valuable experiences they had taken from there. They therefore had a programme including, among other things, what it means to be a Third Culture Kid. When summer came, she packed her suitcase and flew to Malaysia.

> *Kirsten stands at the entrance to the familiar old school building, welcoming the eighty participants, who have accepted the invitation. She knows many of them, but not all. But they all get a huge welcome hug as they arrive. For they have all experienced this place, this childhood; they have this in common. She feels she's back with her family again. She's fifty-five and feels overwhelmed.*

Later there are more Chefoo Reconsidered get-togethers, not just in Malaysia, but also at the Chefoo schools in the Philippines and Japan, as well as locally in the home countries, not to mention informal gatherings of Chefusians simply meeting up together. *Chefoo Reconsidered* is designed to be a safe place where all can share experiences, renew friendships, and form new ones. Kirsten Leed feels a great satisfaction in having been able to help fellow Chefusians from all over the world reunite, and she in turn, knows her own life has been enriched by all those she has met.

* * *

Kirsten Leed, Class of 1971, attended Chefoo School Malaysia from 1967–71. She lives in Denmark and works as a counsellor. She has two siblings. Kirsten's parents worked at Manorom Christian Hospital in Central Thailand from 1968 to 1971, her Mum as a midwife and her father with leprosy out-patients.

Article by Anette Broberg Knudsen
Translated by Rhona Li (née Cooling), Class of 1974, Chefoo School Malaysia

Used with permission

Ruth Van Reken:
Finding My Clan

I HAD BEEN TO CONFERENCES in Malaysia before, but this time was different. As I headed to CR-1[71], I realised that this time, instead of talking *about* third culture kids (TCKs) I was going to be talking *to* them. Even better, or worse, depending on how I looked at it, I would be talking to my particular group of TCKs... those who had grown up as fellow missionary kids (MKs). As I prepared to go, I felt both nervous and excited.

Why nervous? I had already watched and listened to the video *Tigers in the Grass* by Richard Lane[72] and cried my eyes out. Maybe I hadn't met those kids, but I knew them. I was them. I have several pictures in yellowing scrapbooks of my own leavings. But the kids on the video looked so tiny, so resigned, many with such sad eyes. Were we really that small, that young, as we took off to face a world on our own? How could that be? I wept for every child on the video. I wept for myself. But how could I go and do any sort of coherent presentation, to a group that so closely mirrored my story, if I was this emotionally tangled in the topic?

I saw the parents in the video trying to be brave. I was them too. Flashes of the day our thirteen-year-old daughter walked across the tarmac out to the airplane taking her to begin High School in the

---

71 The first Chefoo Reconsidered event, mid-October 2014
72 *Tigers in the Grass*. Words and music by Richard Lane. Niltava Music

USA, nine months ahead of when we left Liberia. It all made mental sense that she wouldn't have to change schools in a year, that she would live with her grandparents, who had invited her to come, but my heart felt pulled out of my chest, as if it were attached to her. With each step she took towards that plane, it ripped a little further out of my body. How could these parents have let their children go? How could I? I wept even more.

But then, even if I could manage to compose myself enough to speak at CR-1 about the world of TCKs as I had come to understand it, would my peers – the fellow attendees – be willing to listen, or consider what I might have to say? After all, each of them had their own story to tell. Why should they listen to mine? Maybe their stories in Asia were so different from mine in Africa that what I said wouldn't make sense to them.

Even more, would they hold it against me when they learned that I had "wimped out" and been home schooled after my first two years at boarding school? Growing up, I knew some fellow MKs called us "cry-babies" because we weren't "tough enough" for boarding school.

It is true that after *Letters Never Sent* came out in its original form, I received countless letters from fellow adult MKs who thanked me for the book. Before reading it, they told me, they thought they were the only ones who cried in bed after the lights went out each night at boarding school. Now they knew they weren't alone in those tears. Some parents bought copies for each of their MKs to read so they could discuss, as a family, how each had experienced their own MK story.

But I also heard (through the grapevine of course, and sadly what I easily remembered more than the affirming responses) of parents and other adult MKs who felt I was simply trying to make MKs feel sorry for themselves, by talking of my sadness. Some wondered if I had published this book because I had lost my faith or become bitter against my parents. Their defence of boarding school and all the positive aspects of it was very strong. Thus, my fears were many and growing between the time I was asked to speak at CR-1 and all the way up the winding, climbing road to the Cameron Highlands. How would I be received?

At the same time, I was incredibly grateful and excited for this opportunity to come back to "my people". Back to the world I knew with every fibre of my being. Back to the world of being a missionary kid. And, despite my fears, I wanted to come – yes, with all those same fibres of my being. Why?

Because, just in case our Asian/African MK stories were similar in their essence, if not in the external details, I wanted to explore matters together with CR attendees that related specifically to my life as an MK, in addition to the characteristics I shared with TCKs from other sectors, such as, corporate, military, or foreign service communities. For one thing, most in these other groups hadn't gone to boarding school, and surely there would be common ground to consider from that shared experience. I hoped in our conversations, we could all normalise our feelings and reactions to this experience and, if needed, together find increasing release from secret places of long-held shame, depression, or even anger we may have known.

I hoped we could look together at the amazingly paradoxical messages and experiences of our lives. Perhaps MKs in Asia had grown up, as I had, with either/or filters for considering such things as: pain vs faith, sorrow vs joy, or doubt vs hope. Without the option of paradox, we had to choose one or the other, rather than living in the richness of a both/and world. Could we reflect together on both?

And, just maybe, we could look specifically at how some of the messages from the systems in which we grew up had unintentionally added to some of the places of shame, as we struggled to look at these and other paradoxes in our story. Could we consider that some messages were not healthy, or true even, while holding on to the richness of upbringing, which we valued, and which taught us many positive things as well? I was eager to know.

So how did it come out? I can't speak for others, but I can for myself. It was far, far better than I could have imagined. For me, I did, in fact, have a strong sense of "coming home'" – even though I hadn't known anyone personally before coming. But somehow, I knew this world without any explanation needed.

When I arrived, I felt welcomed and cared for by all who met me.

The arrangements to transport, house, and feed me went flawlessly. Meeting and rooming with Ulrika Ernvik was a special privilege and joy as we, like the others in their rooms I'm sure, shared our own stories of boarding school days. I appreciated our partnership and learned much from her sessions applying theory into practical application each day.

And then, all the wonderful individual conversations I had with so many at meals, while walking around the campus, or in more scheduled moments, affirmed for me that I wasn't alone in what I had also felt, both as a child, and in the longer term of how it impacted me – not only in challenges but in the gifts. I so appreciated the openness and willingness of those I met to reflect on how what we talked about in our public sessions might apply to their personal stories. My heart was grateful and full. I felt I had found another part of my clan, who understood and accepted me as I am, rather than what it might seem I should be. Yes, it was a profoundly rich and life changing experience for me.

In later interactions with the CR community that feeling continued. Watching you establish a way to connect with each other long-term impressed me, particularly for a community more used to "out of sight, out of mind" relationships. But perhaps, in the end, one of the richest gifts of knowing the CR community is to see how, as you have stayed connected, you have cared for your own. In watching that I have seen the truth that adult MKs are not victims of the past but can make choices for the present that can change old messages into new. It is a powerful message indeed, particularly that your love and care transcend the differences of personality, occupations, and even faith among you. You have given me hope and joy that despite the real challenges I know you also face, there is a light that shines strong through it all. You are a remarkable and beautiful community. Thank you for sharing so much with me. I am definitely the better and richer for it.

* * *

Ruth Van Reken is a second generation Third Culture Kid (TCK) and Missionary Kid (MK); and mother of three now adult TCKs and MKs. She is co-author of Third Culture Kids: Growing Up Among Worlds,

3rd ed., and author of Letters Never Sent *(Van Reken, 2012), her personal journaling seeking to understand the long-term impact of her cross-cultural and missionary kid childhood. For more than thirty years, Ruth has travelled extensively speaking about issues related to the impact of global mobility on individuals, families, and societies. She is co-founder and past chairperson of Families in Global Transition. In addition to her two books and many articles, she has written a chapter in other books including:* Strangers at Home, Unrooted Childhoods, *and* Writing Out of Limbo. *In 2019 she received an Hon. Litt.D from Wheaton College for her life's work. She now lives in Indianapolis, IN with her husband, David.*

Ulrika Ernvik:
Chefoo in my Heart

As soon as I heard that there was a need for a counsellor and facilitator to the first Chefoo Reconsidered (CR-1), I knew I wanted to go. I felt an urge to go, like I had no choice. I knew, somewhere within me, that going there would be an important part of my own journey. Thirty-five years earlier I had left the Congo and my boarding school there at the age of thirteen. I had never been back, but I had, some years before CR-1 happened, organised a reunion in Sweden for all those who went to my boarding school in Semendua, Congo, and I had seen what a huge impact that had on me and everyone else that came. I had felt, in my whole body, the healing power of meeting people of all ages who had experienced the same kind of childhood, and I wanted to be part of that again.

I knew none of the Chefusians. I had talked over Skype and communicated over email with a few of those in the planning committee. I had briefly met with Ruth Van Reken once, and I looked forward to leading the sessions together with her. I was picked up at the airport and got to spend the first evening with Ruth and a few others, and the following day we started the winding journey up the hills to Chefoo.

The first thing I heard, as I got out of the car when we arrived, was the silence. I knew from the first minute that I would love this place, far up in the mountains surrounded by jungle. I got some warm hugs, and could feel the nervousness and expectations in the atmosphere, as people started to gather. Some knew each other, even though they hadn't met for decades, some found out after a while, when they started to recognise each other that they had been classmates and friends, and some didn't know anyone, having no one else there from their age group. It was amazing to see people getting out from the cars, and to observe their reactions as they took in that they were back, back to their childhood place, that many had not been back to since they left as children. It felt like the whole place was soon filled with the hustle and bustle of kids, who had just come back after a school break. Eager to see each other again, eager to continue the games and play that had had to stop because of the break. But also filled with the questions: "What will this school year/reunion be like? Will I get friends? Will I be able to sleep? Will they be kind to me? Will I be able to behave as they expect me to? Will I get some food I like? Will I be part of this group? Will anyone see how I am actually doing? Will anyone share my laughter and see my tears?"

My own strategy when I come to a new place is to look out for a few people that I can feel safe with. I soon spotted a few safe people, who became my anchor people during the week, without knowing it. People I searched up, and just hung around, when I needed some input of stability and safety in the rollercoaster of emotions that I very soon realised I was on – not only my own emotions, but the emotions of everyone that was there. As a highly sensitive person who easily takes on others' emotions, *and* the facilitator of the emotional journey, I was glad I had a good bed, beautiful surroundings, wonderful people around me, and a good and stable co-facilitator in Ruth Van Reken.

Even though my jungle had been the Congolese jungle, not the Malaysian jungle, and my boarding school had been much smaller, I at once felt a part of the group. This was my reunion too. Many of the participants were my age, and knew what it is like to lie awake alone in the darkness, and be scared of thunderstorms; to have loved the intense tropical rains; and knew how to play with nothing and anything in the jungle. I shared the joy with a group of "kids" who found their playground overgrown by the jungle at the outskirts of the campus. I ran out in the rain together with all the others, as Joy led us in a spontaneous, but well prepared, rain dance – Joy is like the rain! I sang from the depth of my heart "I've got joy, joy, joy, joy down in my heart," and the tears ran as I remembered sitting around the bonfire at the campus of my boarding school, singing that song and longing for my parents. I was moved to the core of my soul, again and again. Not only by observing and sharing others' emotions, but also by feeling the joy, the grief, the longing, and all the other named and unnamed emotions myself.

And so, together with Ruth, I led the group step by step, emotion by emotion, through the process we had prepared, that we hoped and knew would bring in understanding and healing. Understanding to ourselves, to how our childhood experiences had made us into the weird, broken, odd, wonderful, creative people we became. We started with "walking the globe". Year by year, everyone was invited to walk over the globe laid out in the large meeting hall. Back and forth, between passport countries and the countries where our parents served, back and forth between home and boarding schools. The walking filled our bodies with the memories of trains and planes, railway stations and airports, goodbyes and reunions, of feeling safe and feeling alone, of joy and grief.

It became clear that our lives had been a constant journey of transitions; with long times far away from those who loved us, and that we felt safe with. And it became clear how very lonely a child can be if she does not have a safe adult to go to when it hurts; when she feels misunderstood; when her friends do not want to play with her, or the adults expect far more from her than she can perform; when she cannot sleep, or when the jungle and thunderstorms feel too dark and scary. And it also became clear that some of the adults who had been there to offer safety, instead of our parents, were not actually safe at all. Without safe adults, children cannot process what they go through. And so they shut down. They focus on the here and now, the games and the fun, while inside there is a burning longing to be hugged, loved and protected.

We drew our timelines, where all our transitions again became so clear, and where we could remember the people, the houses, the pets and friends, vacations and furloughs, celebrations and accidents. We could see how much we lost in each transition. The silence in the room was palpable when the whole group was seated in groups around tables to draw their timelines. But what a surprise when Joy, in the midst of the silence, stood up and took off her clothes and ran out in the rain that had just started, followed by giggling room-mates and all of us, as the tropical rain shed its tears of joy and grief over us. And in the evening, among many other songs we sang, the song "Joy is Like the Rain" got a new and deeper meaning!

As the days moved on, many long-since-forgotten and buried memories started to wake up, memories of fun times and memories of scary times. We helped each other to name and grieve the losses, as well as to celebrate the good memories that more and more came to the surface, as we shared and drew our treasure chests. And the hard parts, those we now had processed and felt ready to leave behind, we left in the grounds of the Chefoo school, dug down in the soil close to the little creek.

As the week unfolded, more and more people shared their stories with me. And at the very last evening, a slip of paper was put in my hand, "I need to talk to you." And so, a very sad story was finding its way from the darkest corners of childhood memories, through lanes of body memories that had not been able to make their voice heard for decades. Memories of total vulnerability and helplessness.

And with that we needed to ask the burning questions: "Why did our parents leave us? How on earth can parents send away little kids of only five years old? What emotions did the parents shut down? Why did they not just say 'no'? Or did they? Why did the organisation set up a system that expected parents to send away their children? Was God part of this? Did God want the parents to send away their kids? Were the people our parents served more important than us? How could this go on for so long? Does it still go on?"

We shared our questions and listened to each other's stories. Some parents *did* say "no" – and then had to leave, and go back to their passport country. Some things changed over the years – staff became more trained, young children were home-schooled, so they did not have to go to boarding school so early. But there is still a lack of knowledge and understanding of children's needs. This is what has forced me to work with, and stand up for, the missionary kids – young and adults.

Then there is that story. The story that many use to support the idea that God expects his servants to give up their children. The story about God telling Abraham to sacrifice Isaac as an offering. But God is not letting it happen. God screams "NOOO". He does not want any child to be sacrificed. And over the week I could hear that "NOOO" build up within me, as a strong stable rhythmical "NO", "NO", "NO", then change to a "YES", to all the power I saw as the abandoned little children felt safe, and loved, and started to blossom. The lies we came to believe in because no one was there to remind us about who we truly were, and how loved we were, have no power over us any longer. We do belong. There are people who care for us. We are valued and loved. We have power over our lives.

During that week we started to see how the lack of loving adults in childhood made it hard for us to give and receive love in close relationships as adults. We saw how hard it had been to trust others, as our experience was that no one was there for us – and if someone was, they would soon leave, or we would have to leave them. We didn't get to see too much of what marriage could be like, with the beauty to enjoy, and the struggles to work through, and so we struggled to build up our own marriages as adults. And we could also see why it had been so hard for us to build up healthy relationships with our parents. They left us, instead of us leaving them. They made us independent long before we were ready for it, and so we never got to fight ourselves away – which made it harder to come back to them.

When the cars started to leave the campus on the foggy morning of the last day, and slowed down on the other side of the field for the last waves of hands, I couldn't stop the tears. It felt like my whole body was full of tears. All the tears that the small children cried as their parents and friends left, all the tears that we had cried, and not cried, during the week – as memories caught up with us. And my very own tears, as

I realised that I had found a tribe that had generously welcomed me, and that I now would have to say goodbye to... another of all of these goodbyes in my life. Tears ran for a couple of hours as the car took me and others down the hills.

But there was a big difference from my childhood goodbyes and this one: I was now an adult, and I could myself make it possible to be in touch with those I left behind. And another difference that makes a huge difference is the possibility to be in touch on social media. Through Facebook I could follow how the tribe continued to support and encourage each other, trying to understand and move on. Over Skype, I could continue to support and guide those who felt stuck in the process. I felt humbled and honoured to be invited to continue to walk alongside a few of the Chefusians for some more time. Over Facebook, Skype and Messenger I could also continue to build bonds that made it easier for me to continue to walk my own journey.

The word that stayed with me after that week was "beauty". I found myself, again and again during the week, looking out over the meeting room, dining room or courtyard, and thinking: "These people are incredibly beautiful." Maybe it was because everyone made themselves so vulnerable. Maybe because buried parts of lives and personalities could start to blossom. Maybe because of the deep connections in between people, who had shared childhood experiences and emotions. Maybe because of all the healing and freedom that was going on. Maybe because of the pain that could finally find its way up to the air, and be shone on, with love and understanding. During that week, the now grown-up kids could be the attachment persons to each other, the attachment persons they never had when they lived there as children, and as children never could be to each other.

I was later invited to one of the reunions in the UK. It was wonderful to go there and meet up with some of those I had already met, and meet with new people who wanted to be part of this amazing and healing journey. I was also invited to come and facilitate CR-2[73], and I cried as I had to say no to that invitation because of studies, and

73 The second Chefoo Reconsidered conference, held at Chefoo Malaysia in February-March, 2016.

very, very blessed when I again was invited to CR-3[74] and that time was able to accept the invitation.

Coming to CR-3 was like coming home. Not that I knew everyone, but I knew some, and I came back to a place I had come to love, and a tribe that had become mine. In between CR-1 and CR-3 my own journey had continued, both my professional and my personal journey. I had come to experience even more the power of going back to memories, and bringing in safety to them, and already the first evening, I felt an urge to share my experience of this. My schedule then became full of counselling sessions, where we brought in safe people and animals to unsafe memories. Again and again, I could see the change in bodies and minds, as imagined safe people offered protection and support to vulnerable children, took them away from unsafe situations, and scolded the perpetrators and unsafe adults. Together we listened to our bodies' urge to do unfinished movements, and we ran, kicked and fought. Tears ran and faces started to smile – smiles that said: "I am safe now." "I am at home." At CR-3, we focused even more on the little child we all have within us. We realised that our little children within have been longing to be seen with glad eyes. And we started to understand that many of us got traumatised as children, as there was no one there that we could feel safe with, through the challenges of daily life. But as safety can be invited now into the traumatic memories of the past, healing can happen, the child within can feel safe again, and we can take the little child in the hand, look at her with glad eyes and say: "It is over."

The Chefoo Reconsidered movement has meant so much to me. Being invited to be the speaker and facilitator I have learned a lot. I am still amazed by the love I have received that has given me a tribe with sisters and brothers. I am glad I listened to my inner voice that literally shouted to me: "You are to be part of Chefoo Reconsidered!" To those of you I have met: Thank you! If you read this and are a Missionary Kid who has not been able to go to any kind of reunion – try to make it happen. If you read this and are one of those who care for MKs – try

74 The third Chefoo Reconsidered conference, held at Chefoo Malaysia in August, 2018.

to find out if there is any way you can support reunions to happen. Encourage MKs to share their life stories, listen to them, listen for the moments when they felt lonely and unsafe, and see if you can be part of bringing in safety into these memories. Basically just ask: "Who could have been there with you, and what is that person doing?"[75]

Once upon the time, there were tiny little children left on trains and planes, buses and cars, to go to the good school up in the beautiful mountains, surrounded by the dense jungle. They could not understand why they could not stay with mummy and daddy. But they understood that they should be happy to be able to go to a good school. Some of them had siblings who already had been there, and they also wanted to be big enough to go and play and learn. But it can be very lonely to be a little child in a big school. It can be very lonely in the bed in a big dorm, with other children, but no adult who comes and sits and holds hands and sings. It can be very lonely when no one wants to play. And it can be scary when adults scold you, or another child, when thunderstorms and lightning fill the night, and when you don't know when you will see mum and dad the next time.

But there is a tiger in the grass, who never leaves a child alone. Not to make any harm to the child, but to protect, love and enjoy the child. He walks around the campus and looks out, with glad and curious eyes full of love, for any child who might need him. He takes a swim in the pool to watch over the children playing, he walks up to the one who sits alone on the side, he pushes the swinging child so he gets more speed, and he stands beside the goal keeper at the soccer field, he lays under the tables in the dining hall and under the bed in the evening. He looks at the children with glad eyes and tells them: "You are a beautiful little one. I am here with you. I will do what I can to protect you. I will play with you. I will take care of you."

That tiger can be you and me. We can take care of our little child within. And we can look out for the children in our daily lives, who might need us, as we had needed someone long ago. No child should

75 If you want to know more about this, read Ulrika's book "Third Culture Kids: A Gift to Care For", look at her websites www.familjegladje.se or www.safetystories.se, or contact her.

have to feel lonely and unsafe. Every child should have someone that looks at them with glad eyes.

I think and hope that Chefoo Reconsidered became a place where we looked at each other with glad eyes. Let's continue to do that.

* * *

Ulrika is a Licensed Psychotherapist, a Missionary Kid and mum to Missionary Kids. Holding a Swedish passport, she grew up in the Congo, and has worked for a decade in Thailand.

Postscript

DC Collard:
On a Mission[76]

David has very kindly given us permission to reproduce the entire text of his debut album DC Collard On a Mission, *together with this introduction in his own words.*

I WAS BORN IN MALAYSIA and grew up there with my younger sister and English parents. My father, ex-army and an ordained minister, and my mother, a nurse in the Red Cross, met for the first time in Far East Asia, having both joined the OMF as missionaries.

We lived in several villages on those tropical plains; and later, when I turned four, moved up into the cooler air of the mountains to a mission school called Chefoo. We were surrounded by jungle, the oldest rainforest in the world – and that's where Part One of my album, *On A Mission*, begins...

As kids, we often looked up in the morning to see mist creeping down from the mountains and would cry out, "Look, the White Witch, the White Witch is coming!"

Life in a jungle school was intense and exciting, but – especially at night – also lonely and scary for young children. Aged five to twelve, and away from parents for four months at a time, most children as adults now look back on their time at Chefoo School with fear and love in equal measure.

I lived at the school year-round, as my parents administered the property until I was eight, at which time they relocated to a town called Tapah. At age nine, I was sent away to a foreign country called England, to attend Monkton Combe School, a boarding school near Bath, UK – a culture shock of biblical proportions.

Many years later, I'm riding my motorcycle from Chicago to Kansas City when my mind drifts back in time, inadvertently starting the process that becomes this album. It's a journey that will reconnect me with my past, some once very young old friends, and also my deeply suppressed emotions, numbed and buried since childhood. To quote my song A Silent Scream:

To facilitate this need in me
I must return to where I'm from
And there unearth the buried truth
That I've ignored for far too long

Have you ever yearned (have you ever yearned for)
Have you ever cried (have you ever cried out)
Can I forgive? Can I forget?
Can I accept? Or just deflect
This smouldering flame year after year
This numbing pain I hold so dear
A silent scream crawls up my throat ...

... as I return to the country of my birth and prepare to face the consequences!

It's taken me fifty-nine years on this planet to commit to my own album – commitment being one of the many issues missionary kids struggle with throughout their adult lives. This album attempts to deal with a number of these, including fear, faith, love, childhood separation, grief and anger; and that great survival technique, numbed emotions. I was born in Malaysia, and lived the first ten years of my life there – I wouldn't change that for the world, except for what came next...

Part Two of the album, *On A Mission*, focuses on my experience revisiting Malaysia after forty years, that sense of coming home, feeling truly alive again, but also the fear of some potential aftermath –
I hope this brief history gives you some insight, and helps connect you to the words and music, as you take your own trip with me – allowing for a little artistic license here and there – across the ever-changing emotional landscape of this record.

Lyrics: PART ONE

Careless Children Theme (The Arrival)

Negligent, remiss, irresponsible
Reckless, foolhardy, devil-may-care
Negligent, remiss, irresponsible
Reckless, foolhardy, devil-may-care
Negligent, remiss, irresponsible
Reckless, foolhardy, devil-may-care
Careless children, care-less children, care less children ...

The White Witch Jungle Stomp

From mountain tops her fingers creep
Down through the trees as children sleep
She hears their longing, thoughts forlorn
As dreams are stolen by the dawn
Their eyes all share both fear and love
Her tendrils snake down from above
They cry, We see the White Witch now
There's pain and joy across their brow

The sun has come to take her place
Of the White Witch there is no trace
She's crawled back up the mountainside
Into the clouds where she'll reside

Until another night rolls in
Until another dawn begins
Enjoy this day, dear children all
For what awaits we dare not call

The White Witch Jungle Stomp
The White Witch Jungle Stomp
All you kids from six to ninety-three
Do the White Witch Jungle Stomp with me

Come one come all it's time to play
A brand new game for this fine day
In darkness we will make you see
The path to light comes with a fee

Beneath the desks and curtain scrim
Blindfolded child on hand and limb
Do you remember Halloween?
The touch of things that made you scream

The White Witch Jungle Stomp
The White Witch Jungle Stomp
All you kids from six to ninety-three
Do the White Witch Jungle Stomp with me

The White Witch Jungle Stomp
The White Witch Jungle Stomp
All you kids from six to ninety-three
Do the White Witch Jungle Stomp

The moral of this tale's unclear
Emotions mixed with love and fear
The White Witch will be ever there
Her breath a fragrance of cool air
She'll catch your soul and leave you bare
Defenceless to her harm or care
You can decide which hand's for you
The dance is yours, now take it to ...

The White Witch Jungle Stomp
The White Witch Jungle Stomp
All you kids from six to ninety-three
Do the White Witch Jungle Stomp with me

Dance on, dance on
Come on everyone
Dance on, dance on
Down from Chefoo to Brinchang

(in the White Witch Jungle ... Stomp)

Dance on, dance on
In your jungle home
Dance on, dance on
Are you ever alone
Ever alone, ever alone?

(in the White Witch Jungle ...
Do the White Witch Jungle Stomp)

Like a Child Crucified

Like a child crucified, I buckle in my seat
On a plane to foreign lands
On a journey of deceit
Like a child crucified, I focus on the pain
Then numb myself to everything
So nothing hurts again

How am I supposed to live
In this foreign land? (England)
How am I supposed to give
With nothing in my hand?
How will I count the ways
That say I am still loved? (no love)
All alone

So far away from home (so far away)
Like a child crucified, I buckled in my seat
On a plane to foreign lands
On a journey of deceit
Like a child crucified, I focused on the pain
Then numbed myself to everything
So nothing hurt again

Mother, how I miss you
Father, where are you now?
Mother, how I love you
Father, can you feel me now?

(Malaysia is my home)
Father, how I miss you
Mother, where are you now?
(Malaysia is my home)
Father, how I love you
Mother, can you feel me now?
(Malaysia is my home
Yeah, yeah, yeah ...
Yeah, yeah, yeah)

I no longer ask these questions
I no longer look for love (no love)
I just keep rolling forward
Like a robot in a crowd
My mind ever empty
My heart hard as rock (cold heart)
Tears are dry, the streaks a crust
There's nothing left to shock (nothing left for ...)

A mindless boy-machine
Moving through this life
Give me something I can feel
Something that is real
Yeah, something I can feel that's real

Like a child crucified, I buckle in my seat
On a plane to foreign lands
On a journey of deceit
Like a child crucified, I focus on the pain
Then numb myself to everything
So nothing hurts again

Like a child crucified,
(Mother, behold your son) I buckled in my seat
On a plane to foreign lands
On a journey of deceit
Like a child crucified,
(Father, why have you forsaken me?) I focused on the pain
Then numbed myself to everything
So nothing hurt again
(It is finished!)

Dirge Time

... and yet life carries on ...
Time passing by without rhyme
Or reason

Kansas City Blue

It's early mornin' and I'm on the road
Haulin' hard south with a heavy load
It ain't a weight measured by the pound
That ton of trouble buried way under ground

Down down down under ground
Down down down under ground
Kansas City Blue

I'm clawin' on up through rock and through dirt
Gotta breathe in clean air to breathe out the hurt

Now feelin' the sun wash over my face
Though some memories I just can't erase, from

Down down down under ground
Down down down under ground
Down down Kansas City Blue

I've rolled in some filth, lain on freshly-cut grass
I wallow in the truth of my checkered past
But now it's time for me to rise
Yes, it is time for me to rise
Kansas City here I come
Kansas City here I come

You know it's where the Count spent some years
He rose above those heartaches and fears
Hate broke his fingers but never never
Never broke his soul

Kansas City here I come
Kansas City here I come
Kansas City here I come
Kansas City here I come

So look up now and you will see
He's smilin' down on you and me
He's smilin' down on you and me
He's smilin' down on Kansas City (Blue)

Down down down under ground
Down down down under ground
Down down down under ground
Down down
Down down Kansas City Blue

A Silent Scream!

(Have you ever yearned for) something you have lost?
(Have you ever cried out) I just can't count the cost!
Maybe I should try to walk that path again
The one I trod so long before without fear or shame

I know this place, I see its face
I hear the sounds and feel its power
Like water falls in deafening roar
A tiger stalks the jungle floor
I hold its gaze and say its name
Into the dream's dissolving shower
Find me there alone and free
Take my hand and walk with me

A silent scream crawls up my throat
I force it back before I choke
I'm longing for that dream to be
The answer in reality
A silent scream!

A silent ... scream

To facilitate this need in me
I must return to where I'm from
And there unearth the buried truth
That I've ignored for far too long

Have you ever yearned (have you ever yearned for)
Have you ever cried (have you ever cried out)
Can I forgive? Can I forget?
Can I accept? Or just deflect
This smouldering flame year after year
This numbing pain I hold so dear

A silent scream crawls up my throat
I force it back before I choke

I'm longing for that dream to be
The answer in reality

(Can I forgive? Can I forget?
Can I accept? Or just deflect
This smouldering flame year after year
This numbing pain I hold so dear)

A silent scream crawls up my throat
I force it back before I choke
I'm longing for my dream to be
The answer in reality
A silent scream
A silent scream
A silent scream!

PART TWO
(Do not adjust your device)

Back from the Dead
Been away a long time now
In mind and heart, body and soul
My brain just ran a flat line through
All the things I once knew

Zipping through the streets of life
A no-emotion automaton
In vain hopes of avoiding a crash
I never found that overpass!

Now
Back from the dead
Blood pounding in my head
I'm burning up, baby
Can't remember, can't forget

Back from the dead
I feel a beat in my heart
A rhythm spark to light a path
Before I fall apart ... again
Back from the dead

Three things I knew for sure
The silent beat, no music to near death
Running away from the clawing past
And facing fears of something that will last

Now
Back from the dead
Blood pounding in my head
I'm burning up, baby
Can't remember, can't forget
Back from the dead
I'm moving on ahead
Living in the present now
And living easy on the edge
Living easy on the edge
Back from the dead
Back from the dead

Back ... From ... The dead
Back ... From ... The dead
Back ... From ... The dead
Back ... From ... The dead

Living easy on the edge
Back from the dead
Back from the dead

Beware: Mission Statement

Your mission statement is all out of date, mate
So time to review, write a new set of rules
You're punch-drunk and you're sprawled out on the pavement
Ha! Bloodied and bruised from us world-weary fools

It's time to give you a run for your money
It's time to quit cutting you so much slack
I'm not really sure what you believe in any more
But sure as hell it ain't the way to give back!

Negligent, remiss, irresponsible
Reckless, foolhardy, devil-may-care
How can words like these ever be appropriate
When there are children at large in the jungle mountain air!

Your mission statement is all out of date, mate
So time to review, write a new set of rules
You're punch-drunk and you're sprawled out on the pavement
Ha! Bloodied and bruised from us world-weary fools

We're pounding our fists on the jungle floor
Then digging a hole in the ground
We'll either bury ourselves or bury you there
'Cause something's gotta give in this one-tiger town

It's time to pick yourselves up, stagger home from the pub
Make amends to the wife, even beg for your life
Then you remember she's been long gone, and you're in the wrong
Your children once again have been left alone all night
(Left alone all right, left alone all night) left alone
Day and night for years and years and years ...

Your mission statement is all out of date, mate
So time to review, write a new set of rules
You're punch-drunk and you're sprawled out on the pavement
Ha! Bloodied and bruised from us world-weary fools

Your mission statement is all out of date, mate
So time to review, write a new set of rules
You're punch-drunk and you're sprawled out on the pavement
Ha! Bloodied and bruised from us world-weary fools

Bloodied and bruised are we, world-weary fools
Bloodied and bruised are we, world-weary fools
Beware!

Vision 2022

Butterflies with tiger eyes
In a dream or nightmare
Only we can decide
Where the snakes are spirits
Yellow, green or blue
In a rainforest paradise made for me and you

Monkey cups filled to their brims
Watch the White Witch coming
See how she skims
Over jungle-tops as we taste her dew
It's the garden of Eden 2022

I don't know what's going on
In this world anymore
Can we fix the stuff that's wrong?
I only know one thing for sure
I want to be 2022

Take me back to where I'm from
Lay me down in the tropical sun
Shoot me up with a blowpipe dart
I'll hallucinate my life from the start
Then I will face the shadows of the past
And make my peace with you at last
In the garden of Eden 2022

I'll give my life back to you
In my Vision 2022

I don't know what's going on
In this world anymore
Can we fix the stuff that's wrong?
I only know one thing for sure
I want to be 2022
Yes, I want to be …

Vision 2022
In my Vision 2022
Vision 2022

I don't know what's going on
In this world anymore
Can we fix the stuff that's wrong?
I only know one thing for sure
I don't know what's going on (I want to be)
In this world anymore (for sure)
Can we fix the stuff that's wrong? (I want to be)
I only know one thing for sure (for sure)
I want to be 2022
Yes, I want to be 2022 (2022)

Vision 2022
In my Vision 2022
Vision 2022

Vision 2022
In my Vision 2022
Vision 2022

End of the Tunnel

Is there light at the end of the tunnel?
Are there any straight roads up ahead?
Will I find you in this life or another?
Will you hold me in your arms again?

In your house, is there good all about you?
Is evil knocking at your front door?
Will I find my way home through the crisscross of streets
And circles that keep turning me around?

Is there light at the end of the tunnel?
Are there any straight roads up ahead?
Will I find you in this life or another?
Will you hold me in your arms once again?

I want to believe there is something more
I'm living the best way I know how
I just long for a place where I can be safe
And never be left to the wind (and the rain)
When I'm there at the end of the tunnel
And looking into your brilliant eyes
I'll finally see this journey has been
A way through the pain and love of this world

To the light at the end of the tunnel
To that clear straightaway ahead
I'll find you in this life or another for sure
And hold you in my arms again
Hold you in my arms
Hold you in my arms
I will hold you in my arms once again

Reprisal?

Negligent, remiss, irresponsible
Reckless, foolhardy, devil-may-care
Negligent, remiss, irresponsible
Reckless, foolhardy, devil-may-care
Negligent, remiss, irresponsible
Reckless, foolhardy, devil-may-care
Careless Children
Crucified Kansas City
Blue as a Silent Scream:
Back from the Dead, Beware
Mission Tunnel Vision
The White Witch Jungle
Could Stomp on you!

Careless Children Theme (The Return)

The White Witch Jungle
(The White Witch Jungle)
Could Stomp on you...

Printed Works Cited

Barclay, William (1975), *A Spiritual Autobiography*, Grand Rapids, MI: William B. Eerdmans Publishing Co.

Brown, Brené (2017), *Braving the Wilderness*, New York, NY: Random House Publishing.

Curtis, Brent & Eldredge, John (1997), *The Sacred Romance*, Nashville, TN: Thomas Nelson, 1997.

Dahl, Roald (1984), *Boy: Tales of Childhood*, London, Jonathan Cape

Duffell, Nick (2001), *The Making of Them*, London: Lone Arrow Press.

Ernvik, Ulrika (2019), *Third Culture Kids: A Gift to Care For.* Mariestad, Sweden: familjegladje.

Frost, Jack (2002), *Experiencing Father's Embrace*, Shippensbury, PA: Destiny Image Publishers.

Hogben, M. M. (1978). Effects of Separating School Age Children from their Parents. A Statistical Survey. *Social Psychiatry*, 13, 187-192.

Instone-Brewer, D. (2002) *Divorce and Remarriage in the Bible: The Social and Literary Context*, Grand Rapids, MI: William B. Eerdmans Publishing Co.

Jersak, Bradley (2015), *A More Christlike God*, Pasadena, CA: Plain Truth Ministries.

Keller, Tim (2009), *The Prodigal God*, London: Hodder & Stoughton

Levine, Peter (2010), *In an Unspoken Voice*, Berkeley, CA: North Atlantic Books

Lewis, CS, (2017, first published 1955), *Surprised by Joy*, San Francisco, CA: HarperOne

Mackenzie, Rebecca (2016), *In a Land of Paper Gods*, London, UK: Tinder Press

McManus, Erwin (2019), *The Way of the Warrior*, New York, NY: Random House Publishing.

Miller, Sheila (1981), *Pigtails, Petticoats and the Old School Tie*, Sevenoaks, UK: OMF Books

Nouwen Henri (1992/2002), *Life of the Beloved*, New York, NY: Crossroad Publishing.

Pearce, Joseph Chilton (2004), *The Biology of Transcendence*, New York, NY: Simon & Schuster.

Pollock, D.C., & Van Reken, R.E. (2017 3rd edition). *Third culture Kids – Growing Up Among Worlds*. Boston, MA: Nicholas Brealey Publishing.

Pridmore, John (2017), *Playing with Icons*, London, UK: All Saints Church.

Thompson, Curt (2010), *Anatomy of the Soul*, Carol Stream, IL: Tyndale House Publishers.

Van Reken, R.E. (1988), *Letters Never Sent*, Colorado Springs, CO: David C. Cook

Weatherhead, Leslie (1987, first published 1944), *The Will of God*, Nashville, TN: Abingdon Press

White, John (1991), *Changing on the Inside*, Ann Arbor, MI: Servant Publications.

Young, W. P. (2007). *The Shack*. Newbury Park, CA: Windblown Media.

Made in the USA
Monee, IL
25 October 2020